Alan Palmer was Head of the History Department of Highgate School from 1953 to 1969. His books include *A Dictionary of Modern History, 1789–1945* (1962), *Metternich* (1972), *The Life and Times of George IV* (1972), *Russia in War and Peace* (1972), *Alexander I* (1974), *Bismarck* (1976), *The Kaiser* (1978), *The Penguin Dictionary of Twentieth-Century History, 1900–1978* (1979) and *Princes of Wales* (1979), *The Chancelleries of Europe* (1983) and *An Encyclopaedia of Napoleon's Europe* (1984), *The German Connection* (1985).

Veronica Palmer is an Oxford MA with a specialist interest in the classical and medieval periods. She has worked with her husband Alan Palmer on the research and writing of earlier books, as well as teaching classics. Jointly Alan and Veronica Palmer are also authors of *Who's Who in Shakespeare's England* (1981) and *Royal England: A Historical Gazetteer* (1983).

D1642884

ALAN AND VERONICA PALMER

A Dictionary of
Historical Quotations

Granada Publishing

Paladin Books
Granada Publishing Ltd
8 Grafton Street, London W1X 3LA

This revised and expanded edition published by Paladin
Books 1985

First published in Great Britain by
Harvester Press 1976
under the title *Quotations in History*

Copyright © Alan and Veronica Palmer 1976, 1985

ISBN 0-586-08507-6

Printed and bound in Great Britain by
Collins, Glasgow

Set in Ehrhardt

Contents

Preface

This book is an enlarged and updated version of our *Quotations in History*, which first appeared in 1976. Published collections of quotations traditionally fulfil three functions. They enable us to verify the form of half-remembered phrases; they give us the opportunity to enrich our spoken or written words from 'the wisdom of the wise and the experience of ages'; and they provide us with the delights of author browsing without even having to reach for another volume, so that we may turn the pages of a single book and – with Montaigne – contentedly scent 'a nosegay of other people's flowers'. Each of these functions was in our minds as we were compiling *Quotations in History*. We hope that the book will be a source both of reference and pleasure to those who dip into it.

There must necessarily be differences in content and character between dictionaries of predominantly literary quotations and a book which is primarily historical in emphasis. This collection does not, for example, 'pervert the Prophets and purloin the Psalms', nor does it include a single quotation from Shakespeare. Although we have concentrated on the famous names of political history, we also cite travellers, diarists, letter-writers, poets and novelists. At the same time we have quoted theorists who anticipated politics in action, or (more frequently) retrospectively justified what had already taken place – Hobbes, Locke, Marx, Mill, Mao, and others. We have also selected passages on the nature of historical craftsmanship from masters of their trade. Political songs, slogans and verses help preserve the form of popular reaction to past events; and we have chosen a few extracts from the Press in the nineteenth and twentieth centuries just as we have chosen extracts from chronicles in the middle ages. Not all our entries are concerned with the State and the Church, war and revolution; we have tried to find some which reflect society in peace and at leisure. The index includes 'dancing', 'dandies', 'football' and 'gaiety', even though most keywords ring with a sterner and more sober tone.

History is a continuous movement through time and not a succession of static set-pieces. It was therefore difficult to decide on a starting-point. Since most entries come from the Europeanized World, and from English-speaking countries in particular, it seemed appropriate to begin with the revival of political institutions and intellectual life in the West after invasion had destroyed the unity imposed by classical civilization. On the European mainland this revival springs from the reign of Charlemagne. The earliest of our quotations comes accordingly from his spiritual counsellor, Alcuin, who has a good claim to be reckoned the first truly literate Yorkshireman. Our terminal date – the autumn of 1984 – is necessarily arbitrary. So, too, in a slightly different sense, are the quotations chosen from the last two decades. It is probable that at the close of this century people will still remember the phrases of Kennedy and Macmillan, but who can say what speeches and sayings of their successors will endure? Much that has excited comment during recent years seems likely, in the end, to have been writ in water.

At an early stage in compiling *Quotations in History* we were faced by the problem of time-honoured phrases of dubious authenticity. A king seeking rid of a turbulent priest; a prince left to win his spurs; cake for a hungry mob; delinquent tree-felling in colonial Virginia. In the end we decided to include all these legendary episodes, and others too. We have, however, tried to discover their origins, and where this has been possible, we have inserted a note in the text. Every quotation of questionable authenticity is marked with an asterisk.

Briefly, we considered arranging the quotations under subject-headings or in some form of chronological order. We decided, however, to follow the usual practice with dictionaries of quotations published in England and to have the entries set out under the name of their author or originator. The reader may thus see for himself the full span of a Jefferson, a Disraeli, a Gladstone or a Churchill. At the same time we have inserted numbered cross-references to entries where the person is mentioned elsewhere in the book. So far as possible, we have given the precise date of a quotation; with passages from books we have tried to indicate when they were written as well as when they were published. Unfortunately, there remain several quotations which cannot be dated precisely, and not all of these come from the earlier period in time. If some of our readers are able to amplify details or to correct us, we hope they will do so.

Even the more familiar phrases of recent history cause trouble. Mr Macmillan did not tell the British public 'You have never had it so good' in 1957 and Mr Callaghan did not ask 'Crisis? What crisis?' on his return from Guadeloupe in 1979. It is not clear which particular week first seemed 'a long time in politics' to Lord Wilson nor what criticism first rung a Tina response ('There is no alternative') from Mrs Thatcher. And if the origins of this anodyne acronym are obscure, so too is the use of the term 'wet' to describe a liberal group of British Conservatives. The phrase appears to have originated within the right-wing Monday Club before the 1979 General Election. The media had taken it up by the end of that year; a letter to *The Times* from Lord Alport in February 1980 showed concern that 'the Tory Democrat section of the party . . . are now denounced as wet'. But in this Dictionary, 'wet' appears only once, as a phrase contributing in a very different sense 'to the political atmosphere' of America in the twenties. So do the simplest monosyllables change significance within a brief passage of time.

Inevitably there must be users of this book who will look for particular quotations and be surprised to find them omitted. No doubt, too, there will be some who are puzzled by what seems to them the trivia we have added to the famous phrases and passages no one could have left out. Ultimately the selection must depend upon our own judgement, and it is this process of inclusion and rejection which gives to any dictionary of quotations some of the characteristics of an anthology. We have chosen several lesser-known sayings or statements of interest which we think have historical significance or contemporary relevance. At the same time we have tended to include rather longer passages than is customary in collections of quotations, for we found that some well-known remarks had become distorted in popular historical usage by over-abbreviated presentation with little reference to their context. This is especially true of extracts from political speeches: misrepresentation of Lord Salisbury's phrase 'splendid isolation' is a characteristic example, and we hope our entries make it clear he neither originated the concept nor believed it to be a condition for self-congratulation.

The index is arranged alphabetically both for keywords and for the brief phrases entered under them. Only the initial letter of the keyword is given under individual entries. Where quotations appear in their original form in a foreign language as well as in translation, they will be found in a small, separate index. Although the main index is constructed on the principle of keyword identification, it includes proper nouns. We therefore hope it may serve in part as a subject index. All references are to entry numbers and not to page numbers.

Alan Palmer
Veronica Palmer

Woodstock, Oxford
12 November 1984

Abbreviations

H of C: House of Commons
H of L: House of Lords

QUOTATIONS

(Quotations of highly doubtful authenticity are marked with an asterisk)

Dean Gooderham ACHESON (1893–1971): former US Secretary of State

1 Great Britain has lost an empire and not yet found a role.

(Speech, West Point, 5 December 1962)

J. E. E. Dalberg (Lord) ACTON (1834–1902): British historian

2 Power tends to corrupt, and absolute power corrupts absolutely. Great men are almost always bad men, even when they exercise influence and not authority. There is no worse heresy than that the office sanctifies the holder of it.

(Letter to Bishop Mandell Creighton, 3 April 1887)

John ADAMS (1735–1826): second President of USA

3 The repeal [of the Stamp Act] has composed every wave of popular disorder into a smooth and peaceful calm.

(Letter, March 1766)

4 Every post and every day rolls in upon us independence like a torrent.

(On effects of publishing Paine's *Common Sense*, January 1776)

5 The second day of July 1776 will be the most memorable epoch in the history of America. It ought to be commemorated as the day of deliverance, by solemn acts of devotion to God Almighty. It ought to be solemnized with pomp and parade, with shows, games, sports, guns, bells, bonfires and illuminations from one end of this continent to the other, from this time forward, for ever more.

(Letter to Mrs Adams on the significance of the day when the

Continental Congress voted for independence: 3 July 1776)

(First Message to Congress, 1825)

John Quincy ADAMS (1767–1848): sixth President of the USA

6 Think of your forefathers! Think of your posterity!

(Speech, Plymouth, Massachusetts, seeking adoption as Senatorial candidate, 22 December 1802)

7 I take it for granted that the present question is a mere preamble – a title-page to a great tragic volume.

(Diary entry concerning the Missouri Compromise of March 1820)

8 It would be more candid as well as more dignified, to avow our principles explicitly to Russia and to France than to come in as a cock-boat in the wake of the British man-of-war.

(Comment, as Secretary of State, to President Monroe's cabinet criticizing a British proposal for Anglo-American collaboration against foreign intervention in Latin America, 7 November 1823)

9 The great object of the institution of civil government is the improvement of those who are parties to the social compact.

Samuel ADAMS (1722–1803): 'Founding Father' of the USA

10 Driven from every corner of the earth, freedom of thought and the right of private judgment in matters of conscience direct their [i.e. refugees'] steps to this happy country as their last asylum.

(Speech, Philadelphia, Pa., 1 August 1776)

11 A Nation of shopkeepers are very seldom so disinterested.

(The phrase appears only in an English printed version, 1776, of his speech at Philadelphia on 1 August of that year)

Konrad ADENAUER (1876–1967): West German Chancellor

12 We must free ourselves from thinking in terms of nation states ... The countries of western Europe are no longer in a position to protect themselves individually; not one of them is any longer in a position to salvage Europe's culture.

(Speech, May 1953)

13 I do not know what will become of Germany when I am no longer on hand unless we can still manage to create Europe in time.

(To M. Spaak, conversation in London, September 1954)

Victor ADLER (1852–1918): Austrian socialist

14 The Austrian Government ... is a system of despotism tempered by casualness [*Schlamperei*].

(Speech, International Socialist Congress, Paris, 17 July 1889)

ADMIRALTY, Board of

15 Winston's back.

(Radio message to all ships of the Royal Navy on reappointment of Churchill as First Lord, 3 September 1939)

Cornelis AERSSENS (1543–1627): Flemish official

16 Throughout all the town [of Delft] there is such deep mourning that the little children are weeping in the streets.

(Report to the States-General of Brussels on the day following the assassination of William the Silent, 11 July 1584)

St AGOBARD (?779–840): Spanish-born Archbishop of Lyons

17 There is neither Gentile nor Jew, barbarian nor Scythian, Aquitanian nor Lombard, Burgundian nor Alaman, slave nor free. All are one in Christ and Christ is all ... For it often happens that five men walk or sit together, and no one of them has a law in common with another, as far as external and earthly things are concerned, while in everlasting things they are bound by the one law of Christ.

(Letter to Emperor Louis I about the Holy Roman Empire, *c.* 817)

ALCUIN (?735–804): Saxon priest and scholar

18 I ... endeavour to minister to some the honey of the Scriptures, to intoxicate others with the pure wine of ancient wisdom; others I begin to nourish with the fruits of grammar, and to enlighten many by the order of the stars. But above all things I strive to train them to be useful to the Holy Church of God and for the glory of your kingdom.

(Letter to Charlemagne on his school at Tours, 796, ?797)

19 If many people follow your enthusiastic endeavours, perhaps a new Athens might be created in the land of the Franks, or rather a much better one.

(Letter to Charlemagne, March 799)

20 Happy is the people for whom divine mercy has provided so good and wise a ruler.

(Letter to Charlemagne while he was in Italy after his coronation in Rome, September/October 801)

Jean d'ALEMBERT (1717–83): French philosopher and mathematician

21 If, free from bias, one looks at the present state of our know-ledge it is impossible to deny that philosophy has shown progress among us. Day by day natural science accumulates new riches . . . The true system of the World has been recognized, developed and perfected . . . Everything has been discussed and analyzed, or at least mentioned.

(Survey of the achievement of the Encyclopedists in *Elements of Philosophy*, 1759)

ALEXANDER I (1777–1825): Tsar of Russia
[see also 957]

22 I shall never forget the tokens of friendship afforded me by the Emperor Napoleon. The more I think of them, the more happy I am to have known him. What an extraordinary man!

(To the French ambassador, July 1807, after Tilsit)

23 Napoleon thinks I am a fool, but he who laughs last laughs longest.

(Letter to his sister, Catherine, 8 October 1808, after meeting Napoleon at Erfurt)

24 [of Napoleon] All this devilish political business is going from bad to worse and that infernal creature who is the curse of all the human race becomes every day more and more abominable.

(Letter to his sister, Catherine, 5 January 1812)

25 It is enough for people to know that the Emperor of Russia and his army have crossed over the bridge.

(To French officials who asked him, when the Allies occupied Paris, if he wished the name of the Pont d'Austerlitz changed to something less humiliating, April 1814)

ALEXANDER II (1818–81): Tsar of Russia
[see also 1329]

26 It is better to begin to abolish serfdom from above than to wait for it to abolish itself from below.

(Speech to the Moscow nobility, 30 March 1856)

27 A [Polish] constitution or national army is totally out of the question. I will allow neither the one nor the other in any form. To accept these ideas would be to abdicate from Poland and concede independence, with the most terrible consequences for Russia, that is to say the loss of everything conquered in times past by Poland, which the Poland patriots still regard as their possessions.

(Letter to Grand Duke Constantine, Viceroy of Poland, June 1862)

28 Thank God, Sebastopol is now avenged.

(Comment on hearing of the surrender of Napoleon III to the Prussians, September 1870)

ALEXANDRA FEODOR-OVNA (1872–1918): Empress-Consort of Russia

29 I am no longer the slightest bit shy or affraid [*sic*] of the ministers and speak like a waterfall in Russian. And they kindly don't laugh at my faults. They see I am energetic & tell all to you I hear & see & that I am yr. wall in the rear wh. is a very firm one.

(Letter in English to her husband, Nicholas II, 5 October 1916)

30 To follow our Friend's [Rasputin's] councils, lovy – I assure is right – He prays *so* hard day and night for you, only one must listen trust & ask advice – not think He does not know. God opens everything to Him ... He will be less mistaken in people than we are – experience in life blessed by God.

(Letter in English to Nicholas II, 18 December 1916)

31 Be the Emperor, be Peter the Great, John the Terrible, the Emperor Paul – crush them all under you – Now don't you laugh, naughty one – but I long to see you so with those men who try to govern *you* and it must be the contrary.

(Letter in English to Nicholas II, 27 December 1916)

ALFRED, the Great (849–901): King of West Saxons
[see also 42, 62]

32 Therefore it seems better to me ... for us also to translate some books which are most needful for men to know into the language which we can all understand; and ... that all the youth now in England of free men, who are rich enough to be able to devote themselves to it, be set to learn as long as they are not fit for any other occupation, until they are able to read English writing well.

(Preface to translation of Pope Gregory's *Cura Pastoralis*, 894)

33 This I can now truly say, that so long as I have lived I have striven to live worthily, and after my death to leave my memory to my descendants in good works.

(Translation of Boethius, *Consolation of Philosophy*, II, ?897)

34 . . . a king's raw materials and instruments of rule are a well-peopled land, and he must have men of prayer, men of war, and men of work.

(Ibid.)

John   Peter   ALTGELD (1847–1902): Governor of Illinois

35 No community can be said to possess local self-government if the executive can, at his pleasure, send military forces to patrol its streets under pretense of enforcing some law. The kind of local self-government that could exist under these circumstances can be found in any of the monarchies of Europe, and it is not in harmony with the spirit of our institutions.

(Letter to President Grover Cleveland protesting at the use of Federal troops in the Chicago Pullman Strike, 6 July 1894)

Ferdinand Alvarez de Toledo, Duke   of   ALVA (1508–82): Spanish General

36 I have tamed men of iron and why, then, shall I not be able to tame these men of butter?

(*Alleged reply to Philip II of Spain on his appointment as Governor-General of the Netherlands, 1567)

H. Julian AMERY (b. 1919): English Conservative politician

37 We have suffered the inevitable consequences of a combination of unpreparedness and feeble counsel.

(Speech in debate on Argentina's seizure of the Falkland Islands, H of C, 3 April 1982)

L. S. AMERY (1873–1955): English Conservative politician

38 Speak for England!

(Interjection in debate when Labour spokesman, Arthur Greenwood, rose to follow Neville Chamberlain after the invasion of Poland, H of C, 2 September 1939)

39 Somehow or other we must get into the Government men who can match our enemies in fighting spirit, in daring, in resolution and in thirst for victory . . . I will quote certain other words. I do it with great reluctance, because I am speaking of those who are old friends and associates of mine, but they are words which, I think, are applicable to the present situation. This is what Cromwell said to the Long Parliament when he thought it was no longer fit to conduct the affairs of the nation; 'You have sat too long for any good you have been doing. Depart, I say, and let us have done with you. In the name of God, go!'

(Speech attacking Chamberlain Government, H of C, 7 May 1940 (cf. 476))

Yuri Vladimirovitch ANDRO-POV (1914–83): Soviet President

40 Let no one expect us to disarm unilaterally. We are not a naive people.

(Speech to Central Committee of Soviet Communist Party, 22 November 1982)

ANGLO-SAXON Chronicle (1042–1154)

41 And in the same year after Easter, about the Rogations (May 29th) or earlier, appeared the star which in Book-Latin is called '*cometa*'. Some men say in English, that it is a long-haired star, because there stands a long ray from it, sometimes on one side, sometimes on each side. (892)

42 Then King Alfred commanded long ships to be built against them [the Danes], which were full nigh twice as long as the others; some had sixty oars, some more; they were both swifter and steadier, and also higher than the others. (897)

43 Then the force went home; and when they [the Danes] were east, then was the force held west; and when they were south, then was our force north ... though something was then resolved, it stood not even for a month.

(Of campaign of Ethelred against Danes, 1010)

44 In this king's time there was nothing but disturbance and wickedness and robbery, for forthwith the powerful men who were traitors rose against him ... I have neither the ability nor the power to tell all the torments they inflicted upon wretched people in this country ... The land was all ruined by such doings, and they said openly that Christ and his saints were sleeping.

(Description of the reign of Stephen in England, 1135–54)

ANNE (1665–1714): Queen of England
[see also 97]

45 My dear sister can't imagine the concern and vexation I have been in that I should be so unfortunate to be out of town when the Queen was brought to bed, for I shall never now be satisfied whether the child be true or false. It may be it is our brother but God only knows . . .

(Letter to her sister, Mary, commenting on the birth of a son to Mary of Modena, June 1688)

46 As I know my heart to be entirely English, I can very sincerely assure you that there is not one thing you can expect or desire of me which I shall not be ready to do for the happiness or prosperity of England.

(First speech to Parliament, 11 March 1702)

47 I have changed my ministers, but I have not changed my measures; I am still for moderation and will govern by it.

(To Harley, St John and other members of the new Tory government, January 1711)

St **ANSELM** (1033–1109): Archbishop of Canterbury [see also 1926]

48 Do you realize what you are trying to do? You are arranging to yoke together in the plough the untamed bull and a poor old feeble sheep. What good will come of that?

(1093, on being forced to become Archbishop; the 'bull' is King William II)

Susan   B.   **ANTHONY** (1820–1906): American women's suffrage leader

49 The true Republic: men, their rights and nothing more; women, their rights and nothing less.

(Caption printed on the front page of her newspaper, *Revolution*, from 1868 onwards)

ANTONY (?–1390): Patriarch of Constantinople

50 It is not a good thing, my son, for you to say 'We have a Church, but no Emperor'. It is not possible for Christians to have a Church without an Emperor, for the imperial sovereignty and the Church form a single entity . . . if by God's decree the infidel has encircled the realm of the Emperor, he still . . . is consecrated Emperor and Autocrator of the Romans, that is, of all Christians.

(Letter to Basil I, Grand Duke of Russia, *c.* 1395)

St   **Thomas   AQUINAS** (1225–74):   Italian   scholastic theologian

51 Human law is law only by virtue of its accordance with right reason, and by this means it is clear that it flows from Eternal law. In so far as it deviates from right reason it is called an Unjust law; and in such a case, it is no law at all, but rather an assertion of violence.

(*Summa Theologiae*, 1a–2a, Q XCIII, *c.* 1260)

Lewis ARMISTEAD (1817–63): Confederate General

52 Give them the cold steel, boys!

(Battle of Gettysburg, 3 July 1863)

Archie ARMSTRONG (?–1672): court jester

53 Great praise be given to God, and little *laud* to the Devil!

(Reported grace before dinner, as part of attack on Archbishop Laud [a small man] which led to Armstrong's dismissal in 1637)

Neil ARMSTRONG (b. 1930): American astronaut

54 That's one small step for a man, one giant leap for mankind.

(On stepping down on the moon's surface, 20 July 1969)

Matthew ARNOLD (1822–88): English poet and critic

55 The great apostle of the Philistines, Lord Macaulay.

(*Essays in Criticism*, 1st series: 'Joubert', 1865)

56 Our society distributes itself into Barbarians, Philistines and Populace; and America is just ourselves, with the Barbarians quite left out, and the Populace nearly.

(Preface to *Culture and Anarchy*, 1869)

Thomas ARNOLD (1795–1842): Headmaster of Rugby School

57 It is not necessary that this should be a school for three hundred, or even one hundred, boys, but it is necessary that it should be a school of Christian gentlemen.

(Address at Rugby, 1828)

Chester ARTHUR (1830–86): Twenty-first President of the USA

58 We have to deal with the appalling fact that though thousands of lives have been sacrificed and hundreds of millions of dollars expended in the attempt to solve the Indian problem, it has until within the past few years seemed scarcely nearer a solution than it was half a century ago.

(Message to Congress, November 1881)

Herbert Henry ASQUITH (1852–1928): British Liberal Prime Minister

59 We had better wait and see.

(Reply to a question by a Unionist MP over government intentions if the Lords rejected the Parliament Bill: H of C, 3 March 1910)

60 We shall never sheathe the sword which we have not lightly drawn until Belgium receives in full measure all and more than all that she has sacrificed, until France is adequately secured against the menace of aggression, until the rights of the smaller nationalities of Europe are placed upon an unassailable foundation, and until the military domination of Prussia is wholly and finally destroyed.

(Speech at Guildhall, London, 9 November 1914)

61 It is fitting that we should have buried the Unknown Prime Minister by the side of the Unknown Soldier.

(Alleged remark on leaving Westminster Abbey after the funeral of Bonar Law, whom ill-health had forced to give up the premiership after only 29 weeks in office, 5 November 1923)

ASSER (?–908/10): Saxon priest and biographer

62 He [Alfred] was enthusiastic and generous in almsgiving to fellow-countrymen and foreigners, extremely affable and pleasant to all men, and a skilful inquirer into the unknown. Many Franks, Gauls, Pagans, Britons, Scots, and Armoricans, nobles and poor men alike, submitted voluntarily to his dominion; all of whom he ruled, loved, honoured and enriched as if they were his own people.

(*Life of Alfred*, Ch. 76, *c*. 900–1)

Sir Jacob ASTLEY (1579–1652): English Royalist soldier

63 O Lord, thou knowest how busy I must be this day; if I forget thee, do not thou forget me.

(Prayer before Battle of Edgehill, 23 October 1642)

64 You have now done your work, and you may go play, unless you will fall out amongst yourselves.

(To his Parliamentary captors, Stow-on-the-Wold, after the last fight of English Civil War, March 1646)

Kemal ATATURK (1880–1938): founder of the Turkish Republic

65 Gentlemen, it was necessary to abolish the fez, which sat on the heads of our nation as an emblem of ignorance, negligence, fanaticism and hatred of progress and civilization, to accept in its place the hat, the headgear worn by the whole civilized world.

('Six Day' Speech to the Turkish Assembly, October 1927)

Clement ATTLEE (1883–1967): British Labour politician and Prime Minister

66 I think this House in this country ought to say that we will not countenance for a moment the yielding to Hitler and force what was denied to Stresemann and reason.

(Speech, H of C, 13 April 1933)

67 We believe in a League system in which the whole world should be ranged against an aggressor ... We do not think that you can deal with national armaments by piling up national armaments in other countries.

(Speech, H of C, 11 March 1935)

68 You cannot divide peace in Europe. You must have one peace running right through. I think we ought to give up altogether the old traditional doctrine of the balance of power, that balance of armed strength which we used to support for so many years ... That is obsolete now. The way to get peace is not through the balance of power but through the League.

(Speech, H of C, 26 March 1936)

69 We have seen today a gallant, civilized and democratic people betrayed and handed over to a ruthless despotism.

(Speech, H of C, 3 October 1938, the 'Munich' debate)

70 I count our progress ... [in the Labour Party] by the extent to which what we cried in the wilderness five and thirty years ago has now become part of the assumptions of the ordinary man and woman ... It is, I suggest, better to argue from what has been done to what may be done rather than to suggest that very little has been accomplished.

(Letter to H. J. Laski, 1 May 1944)

71 Russian communism is the illegitimate child of Karl Marx and Catherine the Great.

(Speech, 11 April 1956)

Thomas ATTWOOD (1783–1856): English radical

72 All that these honest men said was that the Members of that House of Commons by birth, parentage, habits of life, wealth and education, had not shown that anxiety to relieve the sufferings and redress the wrongs of the working classes, which they believed to be their rights, as enjoying the privileges of British subjects. Therefore they had adopted the extreme course of entering upon their separate path, with the view of endeavouring to recover those ancient privileges which they believed to form the original and constitutional right of the Commons of England.

(Speech presenting Chartist Petition, H of C, 14 June 1839)

John AUBREY (1625–97): English biographer

73 How these curiosities would be quite forgot, did not such idle fellows as I am put them down.

(On Lady Venetia Digby, *Brief Lives*, 1680ff)

74 The day of Hobbes's birth was April the fifth, Anno Domini 1588, on a Friday morning, which that year was Good Friday. His mother fell in labour with him upon the fright of the Invasion of the Spaniards.

(On Thomas Hobbes, ibid.)

Henri d'Orleans, Duke of AUMALE (1822–97): French General and historian

75 There was still France [*Il y avait la France*].

(Comment, as President of the Court-Martial of Marshal

Bazaine, on the defendant's claim that at Metz in 1870 there was no authority to whom he owed obedience except his own conscience: Grand Trianon, Versailles, October 1873)

Jane AUSTEN (1775–1817): English novelist

76 I suppose all the World is sitting in Judgement upon the Princess of Wales's Letter. Poor woman, I shall support her as long as I can, because she *is* a Woman, and because I hate her Husband . . . If I must give up the Princess, I am resolved at least always to think that she would have been respectable, if the Prince had behaved only tolerably by her at first.

(Letter to her friend, Martha Lloyd, 16 February 1813 [A letter from the estranged Princess Caroline of Wales to her husband, the Prince Regent, was returned unopened, and duly published in the *Morning Chronicle* on 10 February; it sought to defend her reputation])

77 . . . with regard to an American war I mean; they consider it as certain, and as what is to ruin us. The [Americans] cannot be conquered, and we shall only be teaching them the skill in War which they now want . . . I place my hope of better things on a claim to the protection of Heaven as a Religious Nation, a Nation in spite of much Evil improving in Religion, which I cannot beleive [*sic*] the Americans to possess.

(Letter to Martha Lloyd, 2 September 1814) [Great Britain and the USA had already been at war for two years and the reference would appear to be concerned with a projected major invasion of the United States]

Alfred AUSTIN (1835–1913): English poet

78 Flash'd from his bed, the
    electric tidings came,
     'He is no better, he is much
      the same.'

(On the illness of the then Prince of Wales, later Edward VII, 1871)

79 Let lawyers and statesmen
    addle
    Their pates over points of
    law:
    If sound be our sword, and
    saddle,
    And gun-gear, who cares one
    straw? . . .

(From *Jameson's Ride*, his first published ode as Poet Laureate, printed in *The Times*, 11 January 1896, a fortnight after the abortive Jameson Raid on Johannesburg)

François-Emile BABEUF (1760–97): primitive French socialist

80 The French Revolution is merely the herald of a far greater and much more solemn revolution, which will be the last . . . To the cry of 'Equality', let the forces of justice and happiness organize themselves. The hour has come for founding the Republic of Equals, that great refuge open to every man.

(*Conjuration des Egaux*, 1796)

Francis BACON (1561–1626): Lord Chancellor of England, philosopher and writer
[see also 822]

81 I have as vast contemplative ends, as I have moderate civil ends; for I have taken all knowledge to be my province.

(Letter to Lord Burghley, asking for an appointment, 1592)

82 Though I confess I love some things much better than I love your lordship, as the Queen's service, her quiet and contentment, her honour, her favour, the good of my country, and the like, yet I love few persons better than yourself . . . I was ever sorry that your Lordship should fly with waxen wings, doubting Icarus's fortune.

(Letter to the Earl of Essex, 20 July 1600)

83 It is as hard and severe a thing to be a true politician as to be truly moral.

(*Advancement of Learning*, Book 2, 1605)

84 It is the true office of history to represent the events themselves, together with the counsels, and to leave the observations and conclusions thereupon to the liberty and faculty of every man's judgement.

(Ibid.)

85 I remember Drake, in the vaunting style of a soldier would call the Enterprise 'the singeing of the King of Spain's beard'.

(Of the raid on Cadiz, 1587. *Considerations touching a war with Spain*, ?1607)

86 If we do not maintain Justice, Justice will not maintain us.

(Speech for prosecution, as Attorney General, in Overbury murder case, November 1615)

Roger BACON (1210/15–92/4): English monk and scientist

87 All science requires mathematics ... the knowledge of mathematical things is almost innate in us ... this is the easiest of sciences. A fact which is obvious in that no one's brain rejects it. For laymen and people who are utterly illiterate know how to count and reckon.

(*Opus Maius*, Part IV, I, 1267)

88 Argument is conclusive ... but ... it does not remove doubt, so that the mind may rest in the sure knowledge of the truth, unless it finds it by the method of experiment ... For if any man who never saw fire proved by satisfactory arguments that fire burns ... his hearer's mind would never be satisfied, nor would he avoid the fire until he put his hand in it ... that he might learn by experiment what argument taught.

(Ibid.)

George BAER (1842–1914): American railroad chief

89 The rights and interests of the laboring man will be protected and cared for, not by the labor agitators, but by the Christian men to whom God in His infinite wisdom has given control of the property interests of the country.

(Open letter to the Press during Pennsylvania miners' strike, October 1902)

Walter BAGEHOT (1826–77): British political writer

90 The Crown is, according to the saying, the 'fountain of honour'; but the Treasury is the spring of business.

(*The English Constitution*, Ch. 1. 1867)

91 The best reason why Monarchy is a strong government is, that it is an intelligible government. The mass of mankind understand it, and they hardly anywhere in the world understand any other.

(Ibid, Ch. 2.)

92 A family on the throne is an interesting idea. It brings down the pride of sovereignty to the level of petty life.

(Ibid.)

93 A princely marriage is the brilliant edition of a universal fact, and, as such, it rivets mankind.

(Ibid.)

94 Throughout the greater part of his life George III was a kind of consecrated obstruction.

(Ibid.)

95 The Sovereign has, under a constitutional monarchy such as ours, three rights – the right to be consulted, the right to encourage, the right to warn. And a king of great sagacity would want no others.

(Ibid.)

96 It has been said, not truly, but with a possible approximation of truth, 'that in 1802 every hereditary monarch was insane'.

(Ibid, Ch. 6.)

97 Queen Anne was one of the smallest people ever set in a great place.

(Ibid.)

98 In every particular state of the world, those nations which are strongest tend to prevail over the others; and in certain marked peculiarities the strongest tend to be the best.

(*Physics and Politics*, 1876)

Robert BAILLIE (1599–1662): Scottish Presbyterian leader

99 The Parliament of England cannot have on earth so strong pillars and pregnant supporters of all their privileges as free protestant assemblies established by law and kept in their full freedom from the lowest to the highest, from the congregational eldership to the general synod of the nation.

(*A Disuasive from the Errors of the Time*, 1646)

Stanley BALDWIN (1867–1947): British Conservative Prime Minister
[see also 118, 119, 325]

100 I met Curzon in Downing Street, from whom I got the sort of greeting a corpse would give to an undertaker.

(Remark in late May 1923 soon after becoming Prime Minister, a post for which Curzon had himself hoped)

101 Constitutional Government is being attacked . . . The general strike is a challenge to Parliament, and is the road to anarchy and ruin.

(*The British Gazette*, 6 May 1926)

102 [of the Press magnates, Lords Beaverbrook and Rothermere] What the proprietorship of these papers is aiming at is power, and power without responsibility – the prerogative of the harlot throughout the ages.

(Speech, Westminster, 17 March 1931)

103 When you think about the defence of England you no longer think of the chalk cliffs of Dover. You think of the Rhine. That is where our frontier lies today.

(Speech, H of C, 30 July 1934)

104 There is a wind of nationalism and freedom blowing round the world, and blowing as strongly in Asia as elsewhere.

(Speech, London, 4 December 1934)

Arthur **BALFOUR** (1848–1930): British Conservative Prime Minister
[see also 733]

105 I look forward to a time when Irish patriotism will as easily combine with British patriotism as Scottish patriotism combines now.

(Speech, Glasgow, December 1889)

106 Science is the great instrument of social change . . . the most vital of all revolutions which have marked the development of modern civilization.

(Address, London, 1908)

107 His Majesty's Government views with favour the establishment in Palestine of a national home for the Jewish people . . .

(Letter to Lord Rothschild, 2 November 1917, 'The Balfour Declaration')

John **BALL** (?–1381): English priest and rebel leader
[see also 1494]

108 From the beginning all were created equal by nature, slavery was introduced through the injust oppression of worthless men, against the will of God; for, if God had wanted to create slaves, he would surely have decided at the beginning of the world who was to be slave and who master.

(Sermon at Blackheath, spring
1381)

John BANKES (1589–1644):
Attorney-General to Charles I

109 Let us obey the King's command by his writ, and not dispute.
He is the first mover among these
orbs of ours; and he is the circle
of this circumference; and he is
the centre of us all, wherein we
all, as the lines, should meet; he is
the soul of this body, whose
proper act is to command.

(Speaking for the Crown in
Hampden's Case, 1637)

Joseph BANKS (1744–1820):
member of Cook's expedition to
Australasia

110 Upon the whole New Holland, tho' in every respect the
most barren country I have seen,
is not so bad that between the
products of sea and land, a company of people who should have
the misfortune of being ship-
wrecked upon it might support
themselves.

(Journal entry on leaving the
future New South Wales, August
1770)

**Guillaume-Prosper, Baron de
BARANTE**   (1782–1866):
French diplomat

111 Napoleon never wished to
be justified. He killed his enemy

according to Corsican traditions
(*le droit corse*) and if he sometimes
regretted his mistake, he never
understood that it had been a
crime.

(Of the execution of the Duc
d'Enghien, 1804, *Souvenirs*, Vol.
VII, written about 1865)

George BARRINGTON (1755–
1804): transported Irish-born
London pickpocket and pioneer
Australian historian

112 True patriots we; for be it
         understood
     We left our country for our
         country's good.

(Prologue to celebrate the
opening of the first Playhouse,
Sydney, New South Wales, 16
January 1796)

Bernard BARUCH (1870–
1965): American millionaire and
adviser to US Presidents

113 Let us not be deceived – we
are today in the midst of a cold
war.

(Speech, South Carolina
Legislature, Columbia, S.C., 16
April 1947)

Richard BAXTER (1615–91):
English Puritan divine

114 Be wholly taken up in dili-
gent business of your lawful call-

ings when you are not exercised in the immediate service of God.

(*Call to the Unconverted*, 1657)

[Earl of Beaconsfield, *see* Benjamin DISRAELI]

David BEATTY (1871–1936): British Admiral

115 Chatfield, there seems to be something wrong with our bloody ships today. Turn two points to port [i.e. closer to the German battle-cruisers].

(Remark to his Flag-Captain at the Battle of Jutland, 31 May 1916)

116 The German flag is to be lowered at 3.57 today (Thursday) and is not to be hoisted again without permission.

(Order requiring the surrender of the German High Seas Fleet, North Sea, 21 November 1918)

Max Aitken, Lord BEAVERBROOK (1879–1964): Canadian-born English newspaper magnate, Conservative politician and member of the wartime coalition government
[see also 102]

117 [of Northcliffe] The greatest figure who ever strode down Fleet Street.

(*Politicians and the War*, I, 1928)

118 His [Baldwin's] successive attempts to find a policy remind me of the chorus of a third-rate revue. His evasions reappear in different scenes and in new dresses, and every time they dance with renewed and despairing vigour. But it is the same old jig.

(Attack on Baldwin for opposing 'Empire Free Trade', October 1930)

119 Baldwin talks a lot about pigs but he really means pig-iron.

(Letter to Lord Melchett, 11 November 1930)

120 The people have lost confidence in themselves, and they turn to the Government, looking for a restoration of that confidence. It is the task of the Government to supply it.

(Letter to Churchill after the fall of Singapore, 17 February 1942)

121 I remember once a terrible scene with him [Churchill] ... Churchill on top of the wave has in him the stuff of which tyrants are made.

(*Politicians and the War*, 1959 edn)

St Thomas BECKET (?1117/18–70): Archbishop of Canterbury
[see also 840, 841]

122 No one shall set the sea between me and my Church. I

did not come here to run away: anyone who wants me may find me.

(To the four knights who had come to murder him, Canterbury, 29 December 1170)

Barnard BEE (1823–61): Confederate General

123 [of General T. J. Jackson] Let us determine to die here, and we will conquer. There is Jackson standing like a stone wall. Rally behind the Virginians.

(At the Battle of First Bull Run (Manassas), 21 July 1861)

Ludwig van BEETHOVEN (1770–1827): composer

124 He [Napoleon] is an ordinary human being after all! Now he will trample underfoot the Rights of Man, being a slave to his own ambition; now he will put himself above everyone else and become a tyrant.

(To his pupil, Ferdinand Ries, on hearing that Napoleon Bonaparte, to whom Beethoven intended to dedicate the new 'Eroica' Symphony, had declared himself Emperor, 1804)

Julien BENDA (1867–1956): French novelist and critic of society

125 Our age is the age of the nationalisation of intellect in political hatreds.

(*La Trahison des Clercs*, 1927)

Anthony Wedgwood BENN (b. 1925): British Labour politician.

126 The House of Lords is the British Outer Mongolia for retired politicians.

(Comment, 10 February 1962, during his campaign to disclaim the hereditary peerage he had inherited as eldest son of Viscount Stansgate)

127 Britain today is suffering from galloping obsolescence.

(Comment, *c.* 31 January 1963)

128 We are not just here to manage capitalism but to change society and to define its finer values.

(Speech, Labour Party Conference, Blackpool, 1 October 1975)

Jeremy BENTHAM (1748–1832): British jurist

129 The said truth is that it is the greatest happiness of the greatest number that is the measure of right and wrong.

(*Fragment of Government*, 1776, repeated with minor variants in later writings, cf. 913)

130 When security and equality are in conflict, it will not do to hesitate a moment. Equality must yield.

(*Principles of Legislation*, written 1780, published 1789)

131 It is with government as with medicine, its only business is the choice of evils. Every law is an evil, for every law is an infraction of liberty.

(Ibid.)

132 The schoolmaster is abroad! And I trust to him armed with his primer against the soldier in full military array.

(Speech on educational reform, H of C, 29 January 1828)

Jean Baptiste BERNADOTTE (1763–1844): French General, subsequently King of Sweden (Charles XIV John)

133 A Republican by principle and devotion, I will, until my death, oppose all Royalists ... and all enemies of my Government and the Republic.

(Letter to the French Directory, September 1797)

134 If it is necessary to proclaim Bonaparte an outlaw you will have at your side a General and a large body of troops.

(To Generals Augereau and Jourdan, 10 November 1799, '19 Brumaire')

135 Napoleon has not been conquered by men. He was greater than any of us. God punished him because he relied solely on his own intelligence until that incredible instrument was so strained that it broke.

(Public announcement, as King of Sweden, on hearing of Napoleon's death, 1821)

St BERNARD of Clairvaux (1090–1153): monastic innovator

136 The earth trembled and quaked, when the Lord suffered His own Land to be lost ... Servants of the Cross, to whom is wanting neither bodily strength nor worldly means; why do you delay? Why do you hesitate? Take upon you the sign of the Cross.

(Letter to all faithful Christians, preaching the Second Crusade, 1147)

137 [of Henry II] From the Devil he came and to the Devil he shall return.

(Comment on the King's behaviour as a boy at the Angevin Court in the 1140s)

Theobald von BETHMANN HOLLWEG (1856–1921): German Chancellor

138 Just for a word – 'neutrality', a word which in wartime has so often been discarded, just for a scrap of paper – Great Britain is going to make war.

(To Sir Edward Goschen, British Ambassador, 4 August 1914)

Aneurin BEVAN (1897–1960): British Labour politician

139 [of Neville Chamberlain] The worst thing I can say about democracy is that it has tolerated the Right Honourable Gentleman for four and a half years.

(Speech, H of C, 23 July 1929)

140 This island is almost made of coal and surrounded by fish. Only an organizing genius could produce a shortage of coal and fish in Great Britain at the same time.

(Speech, Blackpool, 18 May 1945)

141 We have been the dreamers, we have been the sufferers, now we are the builders ... We want the complete political extinction of the Tory Party and twenty-five years of Labour Government. We cannot do in five years what requires to be done.

(Speech, Blackpool, 18 May 1945)

142 Our hospital organization has grown up with no plan, with no system; it is unevenly distributed over the country ... I would rather be kept alive in the efficient if cold altruism of a large hospital than expire in a gush of warm sympathy in a small one.

(Speech, introducing the second reading of the National Health Service Bill, H of C, 30 April 1946)

143 No amount of cajolery can eradicate from my heart a deep burning hatred for the Tory Party that inflicted those experiences on me. So far as I am concerned they are lower than vermin.

(Speech at Manchester, recalling the inter-war Depression, 4 July 1948)

144 Winston Churchill ... does not like the language of the twentieth century; he talks the language of the eighteenth century. He is still fighting Blenheim all over again. His only answer to a difficult diplomatic situation is to send a gunboat.

(Speech, Labour Party Conference, Scarborough, 2 October 1951)

145 It is not possible to create peace in the Middle East by jeopardizing the peace of the World.

(Speech, anti-Suez demonstration, Trafalgar Square, 4 November 1956)

146 [on allegations of Anglo-French collusion before their joint intervention in the Suez Crisis of 1956] Did Marianne take John Bull to a secret rendezvous? Did Marianne say to John Bull there was a forest fire going to start and did John Bull then say 'we ought to put it out' but Marianne then said, 'No, let us warm our hands by it, it is a nice fire'? Did Marianne deceive John Bull or seduce him?

(Speech, H of C, 5 December 1956. Marianne has been a familiar name for the French Republic since 1848; John Bull has been generically applied to Englishmen since Queen Anne's reign)

147 If you carry this resolution and follow out all its implications and do not run away from it you will send a Foreign Secretary, whoever he may be, naked into the conference chamber.

(Speech opposing unilateral nuclear disarmament, Labour Party Conference, Brighton, 2 October 1957)

Sir William (later, Lord) BEVERIDGE (1879–1963): British economist

148 Ignorance is an evil weed, which dictators may cultivate among their dupes, but which no democracy can afford among its citizens.

(*Full Employment in a Full Society*, Part IV, 1944)

Ernest BEVIN (1881–1951): British Labour politician, Minister of Labour, and (later) Foreign Secretary

149 The most conservative man in the world is the British Trade Unionist when you want to change him.

(Speech, Trade Union Congress, Edinburgh, 8 September 1927)

150 There is not a single state in Europe where a vast population can live by themselves. The old Austro-Hungarian Empire was economically perhaps the soundest thing that existed in Europe, even if politically wrong.

(Speech, Labour Party Conference, Bournemouth, 5 October 1937)

151 I deny Hitler's right, I deny any State's right, to put a limitation on the progress of the human mind.

(Speech, Swansea, 1 November 1941)

152 You cannot settle the problems of Europe by long-distance telephone calls and telegrams. Round the table we must get, but do not present us with *faits accomplis* when we get there.

(Speech, Labour Party Conference, Blackpool, 19 May 1945)

153 Left understands Left, but the Right does not.

(Speech, Labour Party Conference, Blackpool, 19 May 1945 [context shows reference is to Anglo–French relations, not Anglo–Soviet])

Otto von BISMARCK (1815–98): Prussian Prime Minister and German Chancellor

154 Nobody, not even the most malevolently sceptical of democrats, would believe what charlatanry and pomposity there is in this diplomacy.

(Letter to his wife, 18 May 1851)

155 The great questions of the day will not be settled by means of speeches and majority decisions – that was the great mistake of 1848 and 1849 – but by iron and blood.

(Speech to Prussian Budget Commission, Berlin, 29 September 1862)

156 In Prussia it is only the kings who make revolution.

(In conversation with Napoleon III, 1862)

157 Gentlemen, let us work speedily! Let us put Germany, so

to speak, in the saddle. You will see, well enough, that she can ride.

(Speech to the constituent parliamentary assembly of the North German Confederation, Berlin, 11 March 1867)

158 Anyone who has ever looked into the glazed eyes of a soldier dying on the battlefield will think hard before starting a war.

(Speech, Berlin, August 1867)

159 I always hear the word 'Europe' on the lips of politicians who seek from other Powers what they dare not demand in their own name.

(Marginal comment, 9 January 1871)

160 Do not fear: we shall not go to Canossa either in body or in spirit.

(Speech, Reichstag, 14 May 1872 [refers to the conflict of Church and State in Germany])

161 Whoever speaks of Europe is wrong: it is a geographical concept. (*Qui parle Europe a tort: notion géographique.*)

(Marginal comment on a letter from the Russian Chancellor, Gorchakov, November 1876)

162 I am supposed to have said that in the whole of the Orient there is no interest worth the revenues of a single Pomeranian manor. That is incorrect ... What I said was that I will not advise the active participation of Germany in these things so long as I see no interest in it which ... would be worth the healthy bones of a single Pomeranian musketeer.

(Speech, Reichstag, 5 December 1876)

163 If we are to negotiate peace ... I imagine an essentially modest role ... that of an honest broker, who really intends to do business.

(Speech on the Eastern Crisis, Reichstag, 19 February 1878)

164 This policy cannot succeed through speeches and shooting competitions and songs; it can succeed only through blood and iron.

(Speech to Prussian Lower House, on the social question, Berlin, 28 January 1886)

165 I repeat everything I said earlier when I used that phrase – so much misquoted and ridden to death since then – about the bones of a Pomeranian Grenadier: in the whole of the Eastern Question there remains no question of a war for us.

(Speech, Reichstag, 11 January 1887, cf. 162)

166 We Germans fear God and nothing else on earth; and it is the fear of God, and nothing else, that makes us love and cherish peace.

(Speech, Reichstag, 6 February 1888)

Sir William BLACKSTONE (1723–80): jurist and legal writer

167 The Royal Navy of England has ever been its greatest defence and ornament; it is its ancient and natural strength, the floating bulwark of the island.

(*Commentaries*, Bk 1, Ch. 13, 1765)

Robert BLAKE (1599–1657): English Admiral

168 [Blake said] England had done so [i.e. become a republic] already; France was following in her wake; and as the natural gravity of the Spaniards rendered them somewhat slower in their operations, he gave them ten years for the revolution in this country.

(Remarks in Cadiz, Spain, February 1651 [as reported by the Venetian ambassador to the Doge])

Marc BLOCH (1886–1944): French historian and hero of the Resistance

169 The reactionaries of 1815 hid their faces at the very name of revolution: those of 1940 used it to camouflage their seizure of power.

(*Apologie pour l'Histoire, ou Métier d'Historien*, written 1941, published 1949)

Gebhard BLÜCHER (1742–1819): Prussian Field-Marshal [see also 1898]

170 What a place to plunder!

(*Alleged remark on visiting London 1814)

171 Me a Doctor? Then they should at least make Gneisenau an apothecary, for he has provided the pills.

(On learning that Oxford University wished to award him an honorary Doctorate, June 1814)

172 What I promised I have performed. On the 16th I was forced to fall back a short distance; the 18th – in conjunction with my friend Wellington – completed Napoleon's ruin.

(Letter to his wife after Waterloo, night of 18/19 June 1815)

Nicolas BOILEAU-Despreaux (1636–1711): French writer

173 Sire, as your Historians Royal, we beg you not to finish our history so soon.

(To Louis XIV, in company with Racine, on hearing that the King had narrowly avoided being hit by a cannon ball, October 1677)

Anne BOLEYN (1504–36): English Queen-Consort [see also 456, 849, 850]

174 Never had a prince a more dutiful wife than you have in Anne Boleyn; with which name and place I could willingly have contented myself, if God and your Grace's pleasure had so been pleased.

(*Alleged last letter to Henry VIII from the Tower of London, 6 May 1536)

Henry St John, Viscount BOLINGBROKE (1678–1751): English Tory politician and writer

175 Faction is to party what the superlative is to the positive: party is a political evil and faction is the worst of all parties.

(*The Patriot King*, written 1738, published 1749)

176 Nations, like men, have their infancy.

(*On the Study of History*, published 1752)

Letizia BONAPARTE (?1749/50–1836): 'Madame Mère', the mother of Napoleon I

177 If only it lasts [*Pourvou que cela doure*].

(Comment overheard on several occasions between 1805 and 1811)

Lucien BONAPARTE (1775–1840): brother of Napoleon I

178 To tell the truth, Napoleone is a dangerous man in a free country. He seems to me to have the makings of a tyrant and I believe that were he a king he would be fully capable of playing such a part and his name would become an object of detestation to posterity and every rightminded patriot.

(Letter to his brother Joseph, 1790)

Lady Violet BONHAM CARTER (1887–1968): British political hostess

179 [of Harold Macmillan] He held his party together by not allowing his left wing to see what his right wing was doing.

(Comment, March 1964)

BONIFACE VIII (1235–1303): Pope

180 Unless there is discord between the Kings and Princes of the world, the Pope in Rome cannot be Pope indeed . . . unless there is discord between the great

men of Rome, the Pope in Rome cannot be Pope indeed, or dominate the city or the lands of the Church.

(Words of Boniface alleged at his posthumous trial in 1310)

William BOOTH (1829–1912): General, and founder, of the Salvation Army

181 A population sodden with drink, steeped in vice, eaten up by every social and physical malady, these are the denizens of Darkest England amidst whom my life has been spent.

(*In Darkest England, and the Way Out*, 1880)

William Edgar BORAH (1865–1940): US Senator

182 A democracy must remain at home in all matters which affect the nature of her institutions. They are of a nature to call for the undivided energy and devotion of the entire nation. We do not want the racial antipathies or national antagonisms of the Old World translated to this continent, as they will should we become a part of European politics. The people of this country are overwhelmingly for a policy of neutrality.

(Broadcast address on isolationism, 22 February 1936)

BORIS Godunov (?1550–1604): Tsar of Russia

183 May God be my witness that there will not be a poor man in my Tsardom! And even to my last shirt I will share with all.

(At his Coronation, Moscow, 1 September 1598)

Pierre BOSQUET (1810–61): French General, later Marshal

184 *C'est magnifique, mais ce n'est pas la guerre* [It is magnificent, but not war].

(Remark on observing Charge of Light Brigade, Balaklava, 25 October 1854)

Jacques-Benigne BOSSUET (1627–1704): French theologian and bishop

185 Kings and Princes are by the law of God not subject to any ecclesiastical power nor to the Keys of the Church in respect to their temporal government.

(Draft of the First Article of the Gallican *Déclaration des Quatre Articles*, 1682)

Robert BOYLE (1627–91): British scientist

186 It is my intent to beget a good understanding between the chymists and the mechanical philosophers who have hitherto been too little acquainted with one another's learning.

(*The Sceptical Chymist*, 1661)

William BRADFORD (1590–1657): Pilgrim Father

187 So they left the goodly and pleasant city, which had been their resting-place near twelve years; they knew they were pilgrims, and looked not much on those things, but lift up their eyes to the heavens, their dearest country, and quieted their spirits.

(*Of Plymouth Plantation*, Ch. VII, 1620, the departure from Leyden)

188 ... after long beating at sea they fell with that land which is called Cape Cod; the which being made and certainly known to be it, they were not a little joyful.

(Ibid., Ch. X, 1620, the arrival)

189 May not and ought not the children of these fathers rightly say: 'Our fathers were Englishmen which came over this great ocean, and were ready to perish in this wilderness.'

(Ibid., Ch. X, 1620, after the arrival)

Omar Nelson BRADLEY (b. 1893): US General

190 The wrong war, at the wrong place, at the wrong time, and with the wrong enemy.

(To Senate inquiry into General
MacArthur's proposal to carry
the Korean conflict into China,
May 1951)

Wernher von BRAUN (1912–
77): German-born pioneer of
ballistic missiles

191 Don't tell me that man
doesn't belong out there. Man
belongs wherever he wants to go;
and he'll do plenty well when he
gets there.

(Of space flights: 17 February
1958)

Leonid Ilyich BREZHNEV
(1906–82): Soviet President

192 Whatever may divide us,
Europe is our common home; a
common fate has linked us
through the centuries, and it continues to link us today.

(Speech while visiting Bonn,
Federal Republic of Germany, 23
November 1981)

Aristide BRIAND (1862–
1932): French Prime Minister
[see also 416]

193 Draw back the rifles, draw
back the machine-guns, draw
back the cannons – trust in conciliation, in arbitration, in peace!
... A country grows in history not
only because of the heroism of its
troops on the field of battle, it
grows also when it turns to justice

and to right for the conservation
of its interests.

(Speech welcoming Germany to
the League of Nations, Geneva,
10 September 1926)

**BRIDLINGTON, Chronicle of
Canon of** (1307–?77)

194 How extraordinary and contrary to reason is this ordinance
for man to legislate about buying
and selling or fix a definite price;
for it is quite sure that the fertility
or barrenness of the earth and all
living things, yes, of everything
that multiplies, rests in the power
of God alone.

(Of Ordinances of 1315, which
fixed food prices)

John BRIGHT (1811–99): English radical

195 If our forefathers two hundred years ago ... refused to be
the bondmen of a king, shall we
be the born thralls of an aristocracy like ours? Shall we, who
struck the lion down, shall we pay
the wolf homage?

(Speech at anti-Corn Law
demonstration, Opera House,
Covent Garden, 19 December
1845)

196 If this phrase of the 'balance
of power' is to be always an argument for war, the pretext for war
will never be wanting, and peace

can be never secure ... This whole notion of the 'balance of power' is a mischievous delusion which has come down to us from past times; we ought to drive it from our minds, and to consider the solemn question of peace and war in more clear, more definite, and on far higher principles than any that are involved in the phrase.

(Speech, H of C, 31 March 1854)

197 Let it not be said that I am alone in my condemnation of this [Crimean] war, and of this incapable and guilty Administration. And, even if I were alone, if mine were a solitary voice, raised amid the din of arms and the clamours of a venal press, I should have the consolation I have tonight ... the priceless consolation that no word of mine has tended to promote the squandering of my country's treasure or the spilling of one drop of my country's blood.

(Speech, H of C, 22 December 1854)

198 The angel of death has been abroad throughout the land; you may almost hear the beating of his wings.

(Speech, H of C, appealing for armistice in the Crimean War, 23 February 1855)

199 This regard for the liberties of Europe, this care at one time

for the Protestant interest, this excessive love for the balance of power, is neither more nor less than a gigantic system of outdoor relief for the aristocracy of Great Britain.

(Speech, Birmingham, 29 October 1858)

200 I am for 'Peace, retrenchment, and reform', the watchword of the great Liberal party thirty years ago.

(Speech, Birmingham, 28 April 1859)

201 England is the mother of Parliaments.

(Speech, Birmingham, 18 January 1865)

202 The right hon. Gentleman [Robert Lowe] ... has retired into what may be called his political Cave of Adullam – and he has called about him every one that was in distress and every one that was discontented.

(Speech, H of C, 13 March 1866)

203 No nation, I believe, has been in disposition more friendly to this nation than Russia. There is no nation on the Continent of Europe that is less able to do harm to England, and there is no nation on the Continent of Europe to whom we are less able to do harm than we are to Russia. We are so separated that it seems

impossible that the two nations, by the use of reason or common sense at all, could possibly be brought into conflict with each other.

(Speech, Birmingham, 13 January 1878)

Thomas BRINTON (*c.* 1320–89): Bishop of Rochester

204 There was a time when God was wont to be English, and our princes . . . gained manly victories over their enemies.

(Sermon, St Paul's Cathedral, 13 May 1375)

205 It is neither fitting nor safe that all the keys should hang from the belt of one woman.

(Sermon, Westminster Abbey, 18 May 1376, criticizing the influence of Alice Perrers over the ageing Edward III,

Charlotte BRONTË (1816–55): English novelist

206 As to the sufferers whose sole inheritance was labour, and who had lost that inheritance . . . they were left to suffer on, perhaps inevitably left . . . Misery generates hate; these sufferers hated the machines which they believed took their bread from them; they hated the buildings which contained these machines;

they hated the manufacturers who owned those buildings.

(On the effect of the introduction of knitting frames into the mills of northern England, about 1813: *Shirley*, Ch. 2, 1849)

John BROWN (1800–59): American slave abolitionist [see also 617]

207 I am as content to die for God's eternal truth on the scaffold as in any other way.

(Letter to his children on eve of his execution, 2 December 1859)

Sir Frederick BROWNING (1896–1965): Lieutenant-General: British airborne army commander

208 But, sir, I think we might be going a bridge too far.

(To F.M. Montgomery, about Arnhem when considering projected assault on the Lower Rhine bridges: 10 September 1944)

George Bryan BRUMMEL (1778–1840): English dandy

209 Who's your fat friend?

(To Lord Alvanley [of the Prince Regent], London, July 1813)

William Jennings BRYAN (1860–1925): American politician and lawyer

210 You shall not press down upon the brow of labor this crown of thorns, you shall not crucify mankind upon a cross of gold.

(Speech at Democratic National Convention, Chicago, 8 July 1896)

211 The burning issue of imperialism growing out of the Spanish War involves the very existence of the Republic and the destruction of our free institutions.

(Speech, Democratic National Convention, 5 July 1900)

James (Viscount) BRYCE (1838–1922): British historian, politician and diplomat

212 There is a hearty Puritanism in the view of human nature which pervades the instrument of 1787 [the US Constitution]. It is the work of men who believed in original sin, and were determined to leave open for transgressors no door which they could possibly shut.

(*The American Commonwealth*, 1888)

Sir George BUCK, or Buc (1562/3–1622): historian

213 (The king's friends) . . . had provided ready at the door of the general's tent a fair and a very swift and strong horse. And they offered and presented this horse to the king, and they desired and pray him earnestly to mount that good horse and be gone with all speed . . . but . . . he scorned very much to fly.

(*The History of Richard III*, 1646)

214 Jack of Norfolk, be not too bold
   For Dickon thy master is bought and sold.

(Ibid.; message sent to Duke of Norfolk on eve of Bosworth (1485) to persuade him to leave King Richard's side)

Samuel Dickinson BURCHARD (1812–91): American politician

215 We are Republicans and don't propose to leave our party and identify ourselves with the party whose antecedents are rum, Romanism, and rebellion.

(Speech, New York City, 29 October 1884)

William Cecil, Lord BURGHLEY (1520–98): English statesman, Lord High Treasurer to Queen Elizabeth I
[see also 599]

216 That realm cannot be rich whose coin is poor or base.

(?1599, at time of Elizabeth's reform of coinage)

217 I cannot find such care in the heads of houses there to supply my lack, as I hoped for, to the ruling of inordinate youth ... For I see (if the wiser sort that have authority, will not join earnestly together, to overrule the licentious parts of youth in breaking orders) ... I shall shortly hear no good, comfortable report from thence.

(To the University of Cambridge [one of his reasons for resigning as Chancellor], June 1562)

218 I advise thee not to affect, or neglect, popularity too much. Seek not to be Essex; shun to be Raleigh.

(Advice to his son Robert, some time between 1570 and 1580)

219 Bring thy children up in learning and obedience, yet without outward austerity. Praise them openly, reprehend them secretly ... Marry thy daughters in time, lest they marry themselves. And suffer not thy sons to pass the Alps. For they shall learn nothing there, but pride, blasphemy, and atheism.

(Ibid.)

220 Neither borrow money of a neighbour or a friend, but of a stranger; where paying for it, thou shalt hear no more of it.

(Ibid.)

221 Towards thy superiors be humble, yet generous. With thine equals, familiar, yet respective. Towards thine inferiors shew much humanity, and some familiarity ... The first prepares thy way to advancement. The second makes thee known for a man well bred. The third gains a good report.

(Ibid.)

222 Where her majesty hath pronounced her gracious sentence of me, as of her '*spirit*', and hath commanded you, as you write, to give me a million of thanks; I am most glad of her favourable censure. But, for her million of thanks, you may as merrily say from me, that she may be noted somewhat over liberal, for to give a million of thanks, where she oweth none.

(Letter to his son Robert, 1595)

223 As long as I may be allowed to give advice, I will not change my opinion by affirming the contrary ... But, as a servant, I will obey her majesty's commandment ... Presuming that she, being God's chief minister, it shall be God's will to have her commandments obeyed ...

You see I am in a mixture of divinity and policy.

(Letter to his son Robert, 13 March 1596)

224 [of Essex's expedition to Ireland] By the lord deputy's letters in Ireland, I see no towardliness of any good end there, but a perpetual charge here to the realm in levying still new men . . . I lament it, to see the great waste of people of the English, and of armour and munition, and of the country's charge in levying to be so great as it is.

(Letter to his son Robert, 2 October 1597)

225 I pray you diligently and effectually let her majesty understand, how her singular kindness doth overcome my power to acquit it; who, though she will not be a mother, yet she sheweth herself, by feeding me with her own princely hand, as a careful nurse.

(Letter to his son Robert, 10 July 1598. Burghley's last letter in his own hand)

Sir John BURGOYNE (1722–92): British General

226 After a fatal procrastination, not only of vigorous measures but of preparations for such, we took a step as decisive as the passage of the Rubicon, and now find ourselves plunged at once in a most serious war without a single requisition, gunpowder excepted, for carrying it on.

(Letter from Boston, April 1775, after the Battle of Lexington)

Edmund BURKE (1729–97): British political philosopher and orator
[see also 999, 1400, 1404]

227 Parliament is a deliberative assembly of *one* nation, with *one* interest, that of the whole . . . You choose a member indeed; but when you have chosen him, he is not a member of Bristol, but he is a member of *parliament*.

(Speech to the Electors at Bristol, 3 November 1774)

228 A nation is not conquered which is perpetually to be conquered.

(Speech on Conciliation with America, 22 March 1775)

229 An Englishman is the unfittest person on earth to argue another into Slavery.

(Ibid.)

230 Magnanimity in politics is not seldom the truest wisdom; and a great empire and little minds go ill together.

(Ibid.)

231 I do not know a method of drawing up an indictment against a whole people.

(Ibid.)

232 I know many have been taught to think that moderation, in a case like this, is a sort of treason.

(Letter to the Sheriffs of Bristol, defending his sympathy for the Americans, 1777)

233 Among a people generally corrupt, liberty cannot long exist.

(Ibid.)

234 Individuals pass like shadows; but the commonwealth is fixed and stable.

(Speech on Economical Reform, H of C, February 1780)

235 The people are the masters.

(Ibid.)

236 [of William Pitt, the Younger] Not merely a chip off the old block, but the old block itself.

(On Pitt's first speech, 1781)

237 [of C. J. Fox] He has put to hazard his ease, his security, his interest, his power, even his darling popularity, for the benefit of a people whom he has never seen.

(Speech on Fox's East India Bill, 1783)

238 Whenever our neighbour's house is on fire, it cannot be amiss for the engines to play a little on our own.

(*Reflections on the Revolution in France*, 1790)

239 [of Marie Antoinette] I thought 10,000 swords must have

leaped from their scabbards to avenge a look that threatened her with insult. But the age of chivalry is gone.

(Ibid.)

240 A state without the means of some change is without the means of its conservation.

(Ibid.)

241 Kings will be tyrants from policy when subjects are rebels from principle.

(Ibid.)

242 Nobility is a graceful ornament to the civil order. It is the Corinthian capital of polished society.

(Ibid.)

243 An event has happened upon which it is difficult to speak and impossible to be silent.

(Speech, the Impeachment of Warren Hastings, Westminster Hall, 5 May 1789)

244 There is but one law for all, namely that law which governs all law, the law of our Creator, the law of humanity, justice, equity – the law of nature and of nations.

(Ibid., 28 May 1794)

245 To innovate is not to reform.

(*Letter to a Noble Lord on the attacks made upon him and his pension in the House of Lords by the Duke of Bedford and the Earl of Lauderdale*, 1796)

246 The king and his faithful subjects, the lords and commons of this realm – the triple cord which no man can break.

(Ibid.)

Gilbert BURNET (1643–1715): royal chaplain and Bishop of Salisbury

247 [of Charles II and James, Duke of York (James II)] The Duke of Buckingham gave me once a short but severe character of the two brothers. It was the more severe, because it was true: the King (he said) could see things if he would, and the Duke would see things if he could.

(*History of my own Times, c.* 1702–3)

248 [of Charles II] He said once to myself that he was no atheist but he could not think God would make a man miserable only for taking a little pleasure out of the way.

(Ibid.: Conversation probably in 1674)

249 [Lauderdale] told me the King spoke to him to let that [Presbytery] go, for it was not a religion for gentlemen.

(Ibid.)

250 Halifax said he had known many kicked down stairs, but he never knew any kicked up stairs before.

(On promotion of the Earl of Rochester from First Lord of the Treasury to the (powerless) Presidency of the Council, October 1684; ibid.)

251 [on the downfall of James II, 1688] One of the strangest catastrophes that is in any history. A great king, with strong armies and mighty fleets, a great treasure and powerful allies, fell all at once, and his whole strength, like a spider's web, was ... irrecoverably broken at a touch.

(Ibid.)

252 I thought a little more seriousness had done as well, when she came into her father's Palace, and was to be sat on his throne the next day.

(On Mary II's arrival in London, 21 February 1689)

(Ibid.: cf. Evelyn, no. 630)

253 What reason have we all to rejoice in God who has now saved us by a train of wonders. We were, God knows, upon the point of at least confusions, if not of utter ruin, and are now delivered and rendered as safe as any human constitution can be.

(Private letter, late September 1714, welcoming the arrival of George I in London)

Fanny BURNEY (1752–1840): diarist, novelist, Keeper of the Robes to Queen Charlotte

254 The Vice-Chancellor and Professors begged for the honour of kissing the King's hand ... The sight, at times, was very ridiculous. Some of the worthy collegiates, unused to such ceremonies and unaccustomed to such a presence, the moment they had kissed the King's hand, turned their backs to him and walked away as in any common room; ... others ... plumped down on their knees, and could hardly get up again; and many, in their confusion arose by pulling his Majesty's hand to raise them.

(Diary: George III's visit to the Sheldonian Theatre, Oxford, 13 August 1786)

255 The King bathes, and with great success; a machine follows the Royal one into the sea, filled with fiddlers, who play *God Save the King* as his Majesty takes his plunge.

(Diary: George III at Weymouth, 8 July 1789)

George Gordon, Lord BYRON (1788–1824): English poet

256 Never under the most despotic of infidel governments did I behold such squalid wretchedness as I have seen since my return in the very heart of a Christian country. And what are your remedies? After months of inaction, and months of action worse than inactivity, at length comes forth the grand specific, the never failing nostrum of all state physicians, from the days of Draco to the present time ... Death ... Is there not blood enough upon your penal code, that more must be poured forth to ascend to Heaven and testify against you?

(Maiden speech, against death penalty for machine wrecking, H of L, 27 February 1812)

257 I am sure my bones would not rest in an English grave, or my clay mix with the earth of that country.

(Letter to Murray, 4 June 1817)

258 Nought's permanent among
        the human race
    Except the Whigs *not* getting
        into place.

(*Don Juan*, Canto xi, written in 1820)

259 [of Wellington]
    Call'd 'Saviour of the Nations'
        – not yet saved,
    And 'Europe's Liberator' – still
        enslaved.

(Ibid.)

260 [Of the landlords during the Napoleonic wars]
Safe in their barns, these
    Sabine tillers sent
Their brethren out to battle.
    Why? For rent!
Year after year they voted cent
    for cent,
Blood, sweat, and tear-wrung
    millions – Why? For rent!
They roar'd, they dined, they
    swore they meant
To die for England – why then
    live? For rent!

(*The Age of Bronze*, 1823)

261 The Sword, the Banner and
    the Field,
    Glory and Greece around
    me see!

(Verses written 22 January 1824)

Etienne CABET (1785–1856): French social reformer

262 The democrat become communist in spite of himself.

(Title of article in the Parisian *Le Communautaire*, Vol. 1, no. 1, 1840 [apparently first use of the word communist in print])

Sebastian CABOT (1474–1557): Italian-born seaman and explorer

263 When news were brought that Don Christoph Colonus Genoese [Christopher Colum-

bus] had discovered the coasts of India ... insomuch that all men with great admiration affirmed it to be a thing more divine than human, to sail by the West into the East where spices grow, by a way that was never known before, by this fame and report there increased in my heart a great flame of desire to attempt some notable thing ...

(In conversation with Galeacius Butrigarius, Papal Legate in Spain, as reported by Hakluyt, *Voyages*, III)

264 Every nation is to be considered advisedly and not to provoke them by any disdain, laughing, contempt, or suchlike, but to use them with prudent circumspection, with all gentleness, and courtesy.

(Instructions for the expedition of Chancellor and Willoughby to Cathay, which actually reached Moscow, 9 May 1553)

John Caldwell CALHOUN (1782–1850): American Senator, lawyer and Vice-President

265 The Government of the absolute majority instead of the Government of the people is but the Government of the strongest interests; and when not efficiently checked, it is the most tyrannical and oppressive that can be devised.

(Speech, US Senate, 15 February 1833)

266 We are not a Nation, but a Union, a confederacy of equal and sovereign States.

(Letter to Oliver Dyer, 1 January 1849)

267 I have, Senators, believed from the first that the agitation of the subject of slavery would, if not prevented by some timely and effective measure, end in disunion.

(Speech, US Senate, 4 March 1850, read for Calhoun by Senator James M. Mason)

L. James CALLAGHAN (b. 1912): British Labour Prime Minister

268 I don't think that other people in the world would share the view that there is mounting chaos.

(Comment when interviewed for television at London Airport, 10 January 1979, on returning from conference at Guadeloupe; refers to industrial dislocation caused by a lorry drivers' strike. Generally misquoted as: – 'Crisis? What crisis?')

269 For God's sake stop arguing; the public is crying out for unity.

(Address as Leader of the Opposition, Labour Party Conference, Blackpool, 30 September 1980)

John CALVIN (1509–64): French-born Protestant religious reformer

270 It is the purpose of temporal rule . . . to foster and support the external worship of God, to defend pure doctrine and the standing of the Church, to confirm our lives to human society, to mould our conduct to civil justice, to harmonize us with each other, and to preserve the common peace and tranquillity.

(*Institutes of the Christian Religion*, 1536)

271 In conformity to the clear teaching of scripture we assert that by an eternal and immutable counsel God has once for all determined both whom he would admit to salvation and whom he would condemn to destruction. We affirm that this counsel, as far as concerned the Elect, is founded on his gratuitous mercy, totally irrespective of human merit; but that to those whom he devotes to condemnation the gate of life is closed by a just and irreprehensible but incomprehensible judgment.

(*Institutes of the Christian Religion*, Book III, originally written in 1536 and revised in 1539)

Charles Pratt, Earl CAMDEN (1714–94): Lord Chancellor of Great Britain

272 The British parliament has no right to tax the Americans ... Taxation and representation are inseparably united. God hath joined them: no British parliament can put them asunder. To endeavour to do so is to stab our very vitals.

(Speech, H of L, on proposed taxing of American colonies, December 1765)

Sir Henry CAMPBELL-BANNERMAN (1836–1908): British Liberal politician and (later) Prime Minister

273 An infraction of good feeling, good taste and good manners.

(Criticism in speech on 5 June 1899, of Kitchener's orders for the destruction of the Mahdi's tomb at Omdurman in the previous autumn)

274 When was a war not a war? When it was carried on by methods of barbarism.

([A criticism of the Boer War] Speech, National Reform Union Dinner, 14 June 1901)

275 The Duma is dead: long live the Duma [*La Douma est morte; vive la Douma*].

(Speech, in French, to the Inter-Parliamentary Union Conference in London, 23 July 1906, the day on which news was received that Tsar Nicholas II had suspended his parliament, the Duma, some of whose members were present)

George CANNING (1770–1827): British Foreign Secretary and Prime Minister

276 And O! if again the rude
    whirlwind should rise,
  The dawning of peace
    should fresh darkness
    deform,
  The regrets of the good and
    the fears of the wise
  Shall turn to the pilot that
    weathered the storm.

(Verses written, under a *nom-de-plume*, to celebrate Pitt's forty-third birthday; declaimed at a public banquet, Merchant Taylors Hall, London, 28 May 1802)

277 Away with the cant of 'Measures, not men!' – the idle supposition that it is the harness and not the horses that draw the chariot along. No, Sir, if the comparison must be made, if the distinction must be taken, men are everything, measures comparatively nothing.

(Speech attacking the Addington Ministry, H of C, 9 December 1802)

278 For 'Alliance' read 'England'; and you have the clue to my policy.

(Private letter to his friend, J. H. Frere, 7 August 1823)

279 I am compelled to confess that, in the conduct of public affairs, the grand object of my contemplation is the interest of England ... Intimately connected as we are with the system of Europe, it does not follow that we are therefore called upon to mix ourselves on every occasion, with a restless and meddling activity, in the concerns of the nations which surround us.

(Speech, Plymouth, 28 October 1823)

280 In matters of commerce the
        fault of the Dutch
    Is offering too little and
        asking too much.
    The French are with equal
        advantage content,
    So we clap on Dutch bot-
        toms just 20 per cent.

(Despatch from the Foreign Secretary to the British ambassador at The Hague concerning duties on Dutch shipping, 31 January 1826)

281 If France occupied Spain, it was necessary ... to avoid the consequences of that occupation ... I sought materials for compensation in another hemisphere. Contemplating Spain as our ancestors had known her, I resolved that if France had Spain, it should not be Spain with the

Indies. I called the New World into existence to redress the balance of the old.

(Speech, H of C, seeking to justify his foreign policy in face of French intervention to suppress Spanish liberal revolts, 12 December 1826)

Sir Robert CAREY (?1560–1639): 1st Earl of Monmouth

282 [On the death of Elizabeth I] (The queen) took me by the hand ... and said 'No, Robin, I am not well' ... she remained upon her cushions four days and nights at least. All about her could not persuade her either to take any sustenance or go to bed ... On Wednesday morning, the twenty-third of March, she grew speechless ... by putting her hand to her head, when the King of Scots was named to succeed her, they all knew he was the man she desired should reign after her.

(*Memoirs*, ?1626)

283 [On Charles I, aged four] There were many great ladies suitors for the keeping of the Duke; but when they did see how weak a child he was, and not likely to live, their hearts were down and none of them was desirous to take charge of him ... he was not able to go, nor scant stand alone, he was so weak in his joints. The king was desirous that the string under his tongue should be cut, for he was so long beginning to speak ... he would have him put in iron boots ... my wife protested so much against them both, as she got the victory.

(Ibid. Lady Carey had charge of the Prince until he was eleven)

Thomas CARLYLE (1795–1881): British historian

284 France was long a despotism tempered by epigrams.

(*The French Revolution*, 1837)

285 A whiff of grapeshot.

(Description of Bonaparte's dispersal of the Paris mob, 5 October 1795. Ibid.)

286 [of Robespierre, June 1791] 'A Republic?', said the Seagreen, with one of his dry husky unsportful laughs, 'What is that?'. O seagreen Incorruptible, thou shalt see!

(Ibid.)

287 A feeling very generally exists that the condition and disposition of the Working Classes is a rather ominous matter at present; that something ought to be said, something ought to be done, in regard to it.

(*Chartism*, 1839)

288 A man willing to work, and unable to find work, is perhaps

the saddest sight that fortune's inequality exhibits under the sun.

(Ibid.)

289 Burke said there were Three Estates in Parliament; but, in the Reporters' Gallery yonder, there sat a *Fourth Estate* more important far than they all.

(*Heroes and Hero-Worship*, 1841)

290 There are already Factory Inspectors ... Perhaps there might be Mine-Inspectors too: might there not be Furrowfield Inspectors withal, and ascertain for us how on seven and sixpence a week a human family does live?

(*Past and Present*, 1843)

291 Happy the people whose annals are blank in history-books!

(*Frederick the Great*, written mid-1850s)

Lazare CARNOT (1753–1823): organizer of victory for the French Revolutionary armies

292 The General Order is always to manoeuvre in a body and on the attack; to maintain strict but not pettifogging discipline; to keep the troops constantly at the ready; to employ the utmost vigilance on sentry go; to use the bayonet on every possible occasion; and to follow up the enemy remorselessly until he is utterly destroyed.

(First Order of the Day to army
commanders, 2 February 1794)

CAROLINE of Anspach
(1683–1737): Queen-Consort of
George II
[see also 706]

293 Look there he goes! That
wretch! That villain! I wish the
ground would open this moment
and suck the monster to the lowest
hole in Hell.

(On seeing her son, Frederick,
Prince of Wales, from the window
of St James's Palace on the day
that his parliamentarian
supporters sought an increase in
his revenue at the expense of his
father's, February 1737: from
Sedgwick, Hervey's Memoirs, III)

CAROLINE of Brunswick
(1768–1821): consort of the
Prince-Regent (George IV)
[see also 76, 718, 720]

294 Since the English deny
giving me the great honour of
being a *Princesse de Galles* [Wales],
I will be Caroline, a happy merry
soul.

(On her voluntary departure from
England to live on the Continent,
August 1814)

295 The King's party and mine
are like two rival Inns on the road,
the George and the Angel.

(Alleged remark noted by Lady
Cowper, 15 June 1821, during
Caroline's final attempts to be
accepted as Queen-Consort)

Robert CARR, Earl of Somerset (1585/7–1645): favourite of
James I

296 Remember your Majesty,
that I am the workmanship of
your hands, and bear your stamp
deeply imprinted in all the characters of favour; that I was the
first plant ingrafted by your
Majesty's hand in this place,
therefore not to be uprooted by
the same hand, lest it should taint
all the same kind, with the touch
of that fatalness.

(Letter to James I after
Somerset's condemnation for the
murder of Overbury, 1616)

James Earl CARTER (born
1924): thirty-eighth President of
the USA
[see also 1559, 1560]

297 Show me a good loser and
I'll show you a loser.

(After losing election to
Governorship of Georgia, 1966)

298 My name's Jimmy Carter
and I'm running for President.

(As comparatively unknown
candidate for Presidential
election, 1976)

299 We have been shaken by a tragic war abroad and by scandals and broken promises at home. Our people are searching for new voices and new ideas and new leaders.

(Acceptance speech after Presidential nomination by the Democratic Party Convention, New York, 14 July 1976)

300 Our nation has been aroused and unified as never before in peacetime. Our position is clear. We shall never yield to blackmail.

(State of Union Message, 23 January 1980; refers to the holding of US embassy staff as hostages by the Khomeini administration in Tehran).

Fidel CASTRO (b. 1927): Prime Minister of Cuba

301 A person who does not believe in human beings is not a revolutionary.

(Speech, San Andres de Caiguanabo, 29 January 1967)

CATHERINE II (1729–96): Empress of Russia
[see also 1076, 1855]

302 I must rule after my own fashion.

(To the Russian Senate soon after her accession, June 1762)

303 The sovereign is absolute; for, in a state whose expanse is so vast, there can be no other appropriate authority except that which is concentrated in him ... It is better to obey the laws of one master than to seek to please several ... The intention of autocracy is the glory of the citizen, the state and the sovereign.

(From the *Nakaz* of 1767, draft instructions for a legal code)

304 I am but a crow strutting about in peacock feathers. If I were Pope I would certainly canonise Montesquieu, and that without listening to a devil's advocate.

(To Frederick II of Prussia after publication of the *Nakaz*, 1767; cf. *supra*)

305 In all your plans of reform you forgot the difference between our positions. All your work is done on paper, which does not mind how you treat it ... But I, poor Empress, must work upon human skin, which is much more ticklish and irritable.

(Alleged letter to Diderot, *c.* 1770, cited in the *Souvenirs et Anecdotes* of Ségur)

306 The month of May has been for me ill-fated: I lost two men whom I have never seen, who loved me and whom I honoured – Voltaire and the Earl of Chatham; not for a long time, if ever at all, will men of equal stature be found to replace them ... Upon my return to Petersburg in the autumn I shall collect the letters that great man [Voltaire] wrote to me and send them to you ... If possible please purchase his library and whatever is left of his papers ... I shall for my part willingly pay a high price to his heirs, who probably have no idea of their value.

(Letter to Melchior Grimm, 21 June 1778)

Edith CAVELL (1865–1915): English nurse

307 I realize that patriotism is not enough. I must have no hatred or bitterness towards anyone.

(Shortly before her execution by the Germans as an alleged spy, in Brussels, 13 October 1915)

Camillo CAVOUR (1810–61): first Prime Minister of a unified Italy

308 If we were to do for ourselves what we have done for our country, we should indeed be very great rogues.

(To d'Azeglio, September 1860)

309 Rome must be the capital of Italy because without Rome Italy cannot be constituted.

(Speech, Turin, 25 March 1861)

310 Throughout Italy we are ready to proclaim the great principle of a free Church in a free State.

(Speech, Turin, 27 March 1861)

Robert CECIL (later, Earl of Salisbury) (1563–1612): Secretary of State under Queen Elizabeth I, and chief minister to James I
[see also 610]

311 We went to your brother's shop, where your brother desired me to write to my wife, in any wise not to let anybody know that she paid under £3–10s a yard for her cloth of silver. I marvel she is so simple as to tell anybody what she pays for everything.

(Private letter to Michael Hicks, secretary to his father, Burghley, no date, probably early 1590s)

312 I have been, though unworthy, a member of this House in six or seven Parliaments, yet never did I see the House in so great confusion ... This is more fit for a grammar school than a Court of Parliament.

(Speech in debate on monopolies, H of C, 24 November 1601)

313 [On escaped Gunpowder plotters] Some martial man should presently repair down to those counties where those Robin Hoods are assembled ... this faggot will be burnt to ashes before he shall be twenty miles on his way.

(Letter to Sir Charles Cornwallis, ambassador in Madrid, 9 November 1605)

314 As long as any matter of what weight soever is handled only between the Prince and the Secretary, those counsels are compared to the mutual affections of two lovers, undiscovered to their friends.

(*The State and Dignity of a Secretary of State's Place*, printed 1642)

[Robert Cecil (1830–1903), *see* Marquis of SALISBURY]

[William Cecil (1520–98), *see* Lord BURGHLEY]

Conrad CELTES (1459–1508): German scholar

315 O free, strong people, O noble, brave race, clearly worthy of the Roman Empire; the Pole and the Dane hold our famous harbour and the gateway to our sea! On the east our most powerful peoples are enslaved, Bohemians, Moravians, Slovaks and Silesians; they live like limbs cut off from the body of our Germany.

(Inaugural address at University of Ingolstadt, 1492)

Edwin CHADWICK (1800–90): English lawyer and social reformer

316 By the workhouse system is meant having all relief through the workhouse, making this workhouse an uninviting place of wholesome restraint.

(*Report of Royal Commission on the Poor Laws*, recommending all assistance to be administered through the workhouse, 1834)

317 Sir, it was said of Augustus that he found Rome brick and left it marble. May it be said of you that you found Paris stinking and left it sweet.

(To Napoleon III, on being asked for his opinion on the improvements in the French capital, *c.* 1856)

Sir Austen CHAMBERLAIN (1863–1937): British Conservative Foreign Secretary

318 I yield to no one in my devotion to this great League of Nations, but not even for this

League of Nations will I destroy that smaller but older league of which my own country was the birthplace, and of which it remains the centre . . . Beware how you so draw tight the bonds, how you so pile obligation on obligation and sanction on sanction, lest at last you find you are not living nations but dead States.

(Speech to the Assembly of the League of Nations, Geneva, 9 September 1927)

Joseph   CHAMBERLAIN (1836–1914): British politician, originally Radical but later Liberal Unionist

319 Lord Salisbury constitutes himself the spokesman of a class, of the class to which he himself belongs, who 'toil not neither do they spin'; whose fortunes, as in his case, have originated by grants made in times gone by for the services which courtiers rendered kings, and have since grown and increased, while they have slept, by levying an increased share on all that other men have done by toil and labour to add to the general wealth and prosperity of the country.

(Speech, Birmingham, 30 March 1883)

320 True democracy does not consist in the dismemberment and disintegration of the empire, but rather in the knitting together of kindred races for similar objects.

(Speech, Toronto, 30 December 1887)

321 Since the Crimean War, nearly fifty years ago, the policy of this country has been a policy of strict isolation. We have had no allies – I am afraid we have had no friends . . . A new situation has arisen, and it is right the people of this country should have it under their consideration. All the powerful States of Europe have made alliances, and as long as we keep outside those alliances . . . we are liable to be confronted at any moment with a combination of Great Powers so powerful that not even the most extreme, the most hotheaded politician, would be able to contemplate it without a sense of uneasiness.

(Speech, Birmingham, 13 May 1898)

322 Provided that the City of London remains as it is at present, the clearing-house of the world.

(Speech, Guildhall, London, 19 January 1904)

323 Learn to think Imperially.

(Ibid.)

324 We are not downhearted. The only trouble is, we cannot understand what is happening to our neighbours.

(Speech, Smethwick, 18 January 1906)

Neville   CHAMBERLAIN
(1869–1940): British Conservative Prime Minister
[see also 139, 1796]

325 I always gave him [Baldwin] the impression, he said, when I spoke in the House of Commons, that I looked on the Labour party as dirt.

(Diary entry, when Minister of Health, 19 June 1927)

326 How horrible, fantastic, incredible it is that we should be digging trenches and trying on gas-masks here because of a quarrel in a far-away country between people of whom we know nothing.

(Radio speech, 27 September 1938, with reference to Czechoslovakia)

327 This is the second time in our history that there has come back from Germany to Downing Street Peace with Honour: I believe it is peace for our time.

(Speech to jubilant crowd outside No. 10 Downing Street after his return from the Munich Conference, 30 September 1938: cf. 560, 561)

328 We should seek by all means in our power to avoid war, by analysing possible causes, by trying to remove them, by discussion in a spirit of collaboration and good will. I cannot believe that such a programme would be rejected by the people of this country, even if it does mean the establishment of personal contact with the dictators.

(Speech, H of C, 6 October 1938)

329 I have to inform the House that . . . in the event of any action which clearly threatened Polish independence and which the Polish Government accordingly considered it vital to resist with their national forces, His Majesty's Government would feel themselves bound at once to lend the Polish Government all support in their power.

(Speech, H of C, 31 March 1939)

330 This is a sad day for all of us, and to none is it sadder than to me. Everything that I have worked for, everything that I have hoped for, everything that I have believed in during my public life, has crashed into ruins.

(Speech, H of C, 3 September 1939, after announcing the outbreak of war with Germany)

331 Whatever may be the reason – whether it was that Hitler thought he might get away with what he had got without fighting for it, or whether it was that after all the preparations were not sufficiently complete – however, one thing is certain: he missed the bus.

(Speech to Conservative Association, London, 4 April 1940)

Richard   CHANCELLOR (?–1556): English seaman and explorer

332 Moscow itself is great; I take the whole town to be greater than London with the suburbs; but it is very rude and standeth without all order. Their houses are all of timber very dangerous for fire. There is a fair Castle, the walls whereof are of brick and very high; they say they are eighteen foot thick, but . . . I do not certainly know it, for no stranger may come to view it.

(Account of the first Englishman's visit to Russia in 1553)

CHARLEMAGNE (742–814): Holy Roman Emperor [see also 18, 19, 20]

333 Our task is, with the aid of divine piety, to defend the holy Church of Christ with arms . . . Your task, most holy father, is to lift up your hands to God, like Moses, so as to aid our troops.

(Letter to Pope Leo III, 796)

334 I should never have entered the church on that day, though it was an important feast, could I have known the Pope's intention in advance.

(Of his coronation as Emperor on 25 December 800)

CHARLES I (1600–49): King of England [see also 283, 1194, 1974, 1975]

335 Assure all my servants that I am constant to the discipline and doctrine of the Church of England established by Queen Elizabeth and my father, and that I resolve, by the Grace of God, to die in the maintenance of it.

(Message from Edinburgh to the Lords at Westminster, October 1641)

336 Well, since I see all the birds are flown, I do expect from you that you shall send them unto me as soon as they return hither.

(Unsuccessful attempt to arrest the five members of parliament, H of C, 4 January 1642: cf. 1068, 1642)

337 The nature of Presbyterian government is to steal or force the Crown from the King's head.

(Letter to Queen Henrietta Maria, 3 March 1646)

338 A Subject and a Sovereign are clean different things . . . If I

would have given way to an arbitrary way, for to have all Laws chang'd according to the Power of the Sword, I needed not to have come here; and therefore I tell you ... that I am the Martyr of the People.

(Speech on scaffold, 30 January 1649)

CHARLES II (1630–85): King of England
[see also 247, 248, 249, 627, 1435, 1437, 1441, 1601, 1602]

339 I am so weary that I am scarce able to speak but I desire that you should know ... that whatsoever many concern the good of this people I shall be as ready to grant as you shall be to ask.

(To Speaker of the Commons, 29 May 1660, on his return from exile to London)

340 You will have heard of our taking of New Amsterdam, which lies just by New England. 'Tis a place of great importance to trade. It did belong to England heretofore, but the Dutch by degrees drove our people out and built a very good town, but we have got the better of it, and 'tis now called New York.

(Letter to his sister, Henrietta, 24 October 1664)

341 It is upon the navy under the Providence of God that the safety, honour and welfare of this realm do chiefly attend.

(Preamble to the *Articles of War*, issued in the King's name, 1666)

342 The thing which is nearest the heart of this nation is trade and all that belongs to it.

(To his sister, Henrietta, 14 September 1668)

343 This is very true; for my words are my own and my actions are my ministers.

(Comment on Lord Rochester's mock epitaph) (see 1601)

344 Nobody will kill me to make James king.

(*Alleged remark *c.* 1673, when urged not to risk his life by strolling casually in St James's Park)

345 You had better have one King than five hundred.

(28 March 1681, after dissolving Parliament)

346 I am weary of travelling, I am resolved to go abroad no more: But when I am dead and gone, I know not what my Brother will do: I am much afraid, that when he comes to the Crown, he will be obliged to travel again.

(To Sir Richard Bulstrode, 1683(?4) [often quoted as addressed to James, Duke of York])

347 He had been, he said, an unconscionable time dying; but he hoped that they would excuse it.

(Alleged words on his deathbed, Macaulay, *History of England* (1848))

348 Let not poor Nelly starve.

(On his deathbed, to his brother James, 5 February 1685)

CHARLES V (1500–58): Holy Roman Emperor and King of Spain
[see also 1070, 1226]

349 A single friar who goes counter to all Christianity for a thousand years must be wrong.

(In answer to Martin Luther, at the Diet of Worms, 19 April 1521)

350 My Lord Ambassador, we understand that the king your master hath put his faithful servant and grave wise councillor, Sir Thomas More, to death ... This will we say, that if we had been master of such a servant, of whose doings ourselves have had these many years no small experience, we would rather have lost the best city of our dominions, than have lost such a worthy councillor.

(To Sir Thomas Eliott, Henry VIII's envoy, on hearing of More's execution, July 1535)

351 Name me an Emperor who was ever struck by a cannonball.

(*Alleged remark to his military commanders when urged not to risk his life recklessly at the Battle of Mühlberg, 23 April 1547)

352 I came, I saw, God conquered.

(After beating Protestant princes at Battle of Mühlberg, 23 April 1547)

353 Depend on none but yourself.

(Maxim left in his papers for his son, Philip II of Spain (*c.* 1558))

CHARLES ALBERT (1798–1849): King of Piedmont

354 Italy will do it alone [*Italia farà da sè*].

(Proclamation calling for a war to liberate and unify Italy, March 1848)

Salmon Portland CHASE (1808–73): American Senator

355 No more slave States: no slave Territories.

(Platform of Free Soil National Convention, 1848)

François-René, Vicomte de CHATEAUBRIAND (1768–1848): French writer and diplomat

356 Silently there enters Vice leaning on the arm of Crime: M. de Talleyrand supported by M. Fouché. Slowly this hellish vision passes before me, makes its way into the King's closet and disappears.

(Account of Fouché's appointment as a Minister to Louis XVIII, July 1815, *Mémoires d' Outre Tombe*, IV, 1849–50)

357 One must not be more royalist than the King.

(A phrase said by Chateaubriand to be current in Paris about 1819, *La Monarchie selon la Charte*)

[Lord Chatham, *see* **William PITT**

Philip Dormer Stanhope CHESTERFIELD, 4th Earl of (1694–1773): statesman and letter writer

358 [Of George I] His views and affections were singly confined to the narrow compass of the Electorate; England was too big for him.

(*Letters*)

Rufus CHOATE (1799–1859): Massachusetts lawyer

359 Its [i.e. Republican Party's] constitution the glittering and sounding generalities of natural rights which make up the Declaration of Independence.

(Public letter giving support to Whig Democrats in Maine, 9 August 1856)

David CHRISTY (1802–?59): American writer

360 His majesty, King Cotton, is forced to continue the employment of his slaves; and, by their toil, is riding on, conquering and to conquer.

(*Cotton is King: or Slavery in the Light of Political Economy*, 1855)

Lord Randolph CHURCHILL (1849–94): British Conservative politician

361 The expression 'Tory Democracy' has excited the wonder of some, the alarm of others, and great and bitter ridicule from the Radical party. But the Tory Democracy may yet exist; the elements for its composition only require to be collected and the labour may some day possibly be effected by the man, whoever he may be, upon whom the mantle of Elijah has descended.

(Article in *Fortnightly Review*, May 1883)

362 Ulster will not be a consenting party; Ulster at the proper moment will resort to the supreme arbitrament of force; Ulster will fight and Ulster will be right.

(Public letter to a Liberal-Unionist, 7 May 1886)

363 This monstrous mixture of imbecility, extravagance and political hysterias, better known as 'the Bill for the future Government of Ireland' ... this farrago of superlative nonsense ... is to be put in motion ... for this reason and no other: to gratify the ambition of an old man in a hurry.

(Attack on Gladstone's Home Rule Bill in printed address circulated to the electors of South Paddington, June 1886)

364 All great men make mistakes: Napoleon forgot Blücher; I forgot Goschen.

(Remark on finding his resignation as Chancellor of the Exchequer accepted by Lord Salisbury, who appointed G. J. Goschen to succeed him, December 1886)

Winston   CHURCHILL (1874–1965): British statesman and Prime Minister [see also 15, 121, 144]

365 I have frequently been astonished since I have been in this House to hear with what composure and how glibly Members, and even Ministers, talk of a European war ... A European war can only end in the ruin of the vanquished and the scarcely less fatal commercial dislocation and exhaustion of the conquerors.

(Speech, H of C, 13 May 1901)

366 It cannot in the opinion of His Majesty's Government be classified as slavery in the extreme acceptance of the word without some risk of terminological inexactitude.

(Speech, soon after taking office as a Liberal Under-Secretary for the Colonies, on the position of indented Chinese labourers working on the Rand mines in the Transvaal, H of C, 22 February 1906)

367 I like things to happen, and if they don't happen I like to make them happen.

(Remark in conversation with Arthur Ponsonby, when they were both Liberal Members of Parliament: date not known, probably about 1909)

368 The British Navy is to us a necessity and, from some points of view, the German Navy is to them more in the nature of a luxury. Our naval power involves British existence. It is existence to us; it is expansion to them.

(Speech, Glasgow, 9 February 1912)

369 If Ulster is to become a tool in party calculations; if the civil and parliamentary systems under which we have dwelt so long, and our fathers before us, are to be brought to the rude challenge of force; if the Government and the Parliament of this great country and greater Empire are to be exposed to menace and brutality; if all the loose, wanton and reckless chatter we have been forced to listen to, these many months, is in the end to disclose a sinister and revolutionary purpose; then I can only say to you, 'Let us go forward together and put these grave matters to the proof'.

(Speech, during the Irish Crisis, Bradford, 14 March 1914)

370 Sure I am of this, that you have only to endure to conquer. You have only to persevere to save yourselves.

(His first wartime speech, Guildhall, London, 4 September 1914)

371 Beyond those few miles of ridge and scrub on which our soldiers, our French comrades, our gallant Australians and our New Zealand fellow-subjects are now battling, lie the downfall of a hostile empire, the destruction of an enemy's fleet and army, the fall of a world-famous capital, and probably the accession of powerful allies ... Through the narrows of the Dardanelles and across the ridges of the Gallipoli Peninsula lie some of the shortest paths to a triumphant peace.

(Speech, Dundee, 5 June 1915)

372 Of all tyrannies in history the Bolshevik tyranny is the worst, the most destructive, the most degrading ... Every British and French soldier killed last year was really done to death by Lenin and Trotsky, not in fair war, but by the treacherous desertion of an ally without parallel in the history of the world.

(Speech, Connaught Rooms, London, 11 April 1919)

373 The day must come when the nation's whole scale of living must be reduced. If that day comes, Parliament must lay the burden equally on all classes ... I am not invested with dictatorial powers. If I were, I should be quite ready to dictate.

(Speech, as Chancellor of the Exchequer, H of C, 7 August 1925)

374 I decline utterly to be impartial as between the Fire Brigade and the fire.

(Retort to complaints that, as editor of the *British Gazette* during the General Strike of 1926, he had shown bias against the demands of the workers)

375 It is a good thing for an uneducated man to read books of quotations ... The quotations, when engraved upon the memory, give you good thoughts. They also make you anxious to read the authors and look for more.

(*My Early Life*, Ch. 9, written in 1929–30 although the passage refers to 1897)

376 The [First World] War was decided in the first twenty days of fighting, and all that happened afterwards consisted in battles which, however formidable and devastating, were but desperate and vain appeals against the decision of Fate.

(Preface to E. L. Spears, *Liaison 1914*, 1930)

377 The loss of India would mark and consummate the downfall of the British Empire. That great organism would pass at a stroke out of life into history. From such a catastrophe there could be no recovery.

(Speech to Indian Empire Society, London, 12 December 1930)

378 It is ... alarming and also nauseating to see Mr Gandhi, a seditious Middle Temple lawyer, now posing as a fakir of a type well known in the East, striding half-naked up the steps of the Viceregal Palace, while he is still organizing and conducting a defiant campaign of civil disobedience, to parley on equal terms with the representative of the King-Emperor.

(Speech to the West Essex Unionist Association, Epping, 23 February 1931; Gandhi had been released from prison in India to discuss political devolution with the Viceroy)

379 Dictators ride to and fro upon tigers which they dare not dismount. And the tigers are getting hungry.

(*While England Slept*, 1936)

380 I will begin by saying what everybody would like to ignore or forget but which must nevertheless be stated, namely, that we have sustained a total and unmitigated defeat and that France has suffered even more than we have ... All is over. Silent, mournful, abandoned, broken, Czechoslovakia recedes into the darkness ... We have sustained a defeat without a war.

(Speech on Munich Agreement, H of C, 5 October 1938)

381 This is not a question of fighting for Danzig or fighting for Poland. We are fighting to save the whole world from the pestilence of Nazi tyranny and in defence of all that is most sacred to men. This is no war for domination or imperial aggrandisement or material gain ... It is a war ... to establish, on impregnable rocks, the rights of the individual and it is a war to establish and revive the stature of man.

(Speech, H of C, 3 September 1939)

382 I cannot forecast to you the action of Russia. It is a riddle wrapped in a mystery inside an enigma; but perhaps there is a key. That key is Russian national interest.

(Broadcast talk, 1 October 1939)

383 Come, then, let us to the task, to the battle, to the toil – each to our part, each to our station. Fill the armies, rule the air, pour out the munitions, strangle the U-boats, sweep the mines, plough the land, build the ships, guard the streets, succour the wounded, uplift the downcast, and honour the brave. Let us go forward together in all parts of the Empire, in all parts of the Island. There is not a week, nor a day, nor an hour to lose.

(Speech, as First Lord of the Admiralty, Free Trade Hall, Manchester, 27 January 1940)

384 I have nothing to offer but blood, toil, tears and sweat.

(Speech, H of C, 13 May 1940)

385 You ask, What is our policy? I will say: It is to wage war by sea, land and air, with all our might and with all the strength that God can give us; to wage war against a monstrous tyranny, never surpassed in the dark, lamentable catalogue of human crime. That is our policy. You ask, What is our aim? I can answer in one word: Victory – victory at all costs, victory in spite of all terror; victory, however long and hard the road may be; for without victory there is no survival.

(Speech, H of C, 13 May 1940)

386 We shall not flag or fail ... we shall fight on the beaches, we shall fight on the landing grounds, we shall fight in the fields and in the streets, we shall fight in the hills; we shall never surrender.

(Speech, H of C, 4 June 1940)

387 Let us therefore brace ourselves to our duty and so bear ourselves that if the British Commonwealth and Empire last for a thousand years men will still say 'This was their finest hour'.

(Speech, H of C, 18 June 1940)

388 Never in the field of human conflict was so much owed by so many to so few.

(Speech, H of C, 20 August 1940)

389 We shall not fail or falter; we shall not weaken or tire. Neither the sudden shock of battle nor the long-drawn trials of vigilance and exertion will wear us down. Give us the tools and we will finish the job.

(Broadcast address, 9 February 1941: this passage was addressed specifically to President Roosevelt)

390 No one has been a more consistent opponent of Communism than I have for the last twenty-five years. I will unsay no word that I have spoken about it. But all this fades away before the spectacle which is now unfolding. The past, with its crimes, its follies, and its tragedies, flashes away. I see the Russian soldiers standing on the threshold of their native land, guarding the fields which their fathers have tilled from time immemorial ... Any man or state who fights on against Nazidom will have our aid. Any man or state who marches with Hitler is our foe.

(Broadcast on German invasion of USSR, 22 June 1941)

391 I feel greatly honoured that you should have invited me to ... address the representatives of both branches of Congress ... I cannot help reflecting that if my father had been American and my mother British, instead of the other way round, I might have got here on my own.

(Speech to US Congress, 26 December 1941)

392 What kind of people do they [Japanese] think we are?

(Speech, US Congress, 26 December 1941)

393 When I warned them [French Government] that Britain would fight on alone whatever they did, their Generals told their P.M. and his divided Cabinet: 'In three weeks England will have her neck wrung like a chicken.' Some chicken! Some neck!

(Speech, Canadian Parliament, 30 December 1941)

394 This is not the end. It is not even the beginning of the end. But it is, perhaps, the end of the beginning.

(Speech, Mansion House, London, 10 November 1942)

395 I have not become the King's First Minister in order to preside over the liquidation of the British Empire.

(Ibid.)

396 The paramount task before us is, first, to conquer the African

shores of the Mediterranean ...
and, secondly, using the bases on
the African shore to strike at the
under-belly of the Axis in effective strength and in the shortest
time.

(Memorandum, 25 November
1942)

397 What is to happen about
Russia? ... An iron curtain is
drawn down upon their front. We
do not know what is going on
behind ... It is vital now to come
to an understanding with Russia,
or see where we are with her,
before we weaken our armies
mortally or retire to the zones of
occupation.

(Telegram to President Truman,
12 May 1945)

398 I believe in the instinctive
wisdom of our well-tried democracy.

(Eve of election broadcast, 4 July
1945)

399 From Stettin in the Baltic to
Trieste in the Adriatic an iron
curtain has descended across the
Continent.

(Speech, Fulton, Missouri, 5
March 1946)

400 In War: Resolution.
In Defeat: Defiance.
In Victory: Magnanimity.
In Peace: Goodwill.

('Moral of the Work', *The Second
World War*, 1948)

**Edward Hyde, Earl of
CLARENDON** (1609–74):
English historian and chief min-
ister to King Charles II

401 [of Hampden] Without
question, when he first drew the
sword, he threw away the scab-
bard.

(*History of the Rebellion*, written
1647)

402 [Lord Falkland] would passionately profess 'that the very
agony of war ... took his sleep
from him ...' This made some
think, or pretend to think, 'that
he was so much enamoured on
peace, that he would have been
glad the king should have bought
it at any price', which was a most
unreasonable calumny.

(Ibid., referring to the early
months of 1643)

403 [of Charles I] He was
always an immoderate lover of
the Scottish nation, having not
only been born there but educated by that people and besieged by them always, having
few English about him till he was
King.

(*History of the Great Rebellion*,
written 1672)

404 [of Cromwell] He will be looked upon by posterity as a brave bad man.

(Ibid.: last line)

George Villiers, Earl of CLARENDON (1800–70): British diplomat and Foreign Secretary

405 Spanish dynasties go and come; Spanish Kings go and come; and Spanish ministers go and come; but there is one thing in Spain that is always the same – they never answer letters.

(*Alleged remark, 1846)

Abraham CLARK (1726–94): New Jersey member of the American Continental Congress

406 We set out to oppose Tyranny in all its Strides, and I hope we shall persevere.

(Letter to John Hart, 8 February 1777)

James Beauchamp CLARK (1850–1921): Speaker of US House of Representatives

407 I hope to see the day when the American flag will float over every square foot of the British North American possessions clear to the North Pole.

(In debate on Canadian reciprocity trade bill, June 1911)

Karl von CLAUSEWITZ (1780–1831): Prussian general and military theorist

408 War is the continuation of politics by other means.

(*On War*, 1832)

409 War belongs, not to the Arts and Sciences, but to the province of social life.

(Ibid.)

410 It is politics which beget war. Politics represents the intelligence, war merely its instrument, not the other way around. The only possible course in war is to subordinate the military viewpoint to the political.

(Ibid.)

Henry CLAY (1777–1852): American Congressman and Senator

411 It was in the provinces that were laid the seeds of the ambitious projects that overturned the liberties of Rome.

(In US Senate, on seeing popular acclaim for Andrew Jackson's forward policy in eastern Florida, May 1818)

412 I had rather be right than be President.

(To Senator William Preston, 1839)

413 I am the most unfortunate man in the history of parties: always run by my friends when sure to be defeated, and now betrayed for a nomination when I, or any one, would be sure of an election.

(On failing to get the Whig nomination for the 1840 Presidential election)

Georges   CLEMENCEAU (1841–1929):   French   Prime Minister
[see also 1019]

414 My home policy? I wage war. My foreign policy? I wage war. Always, everywhere, I wage war . . . And I shall continue to wage war until the last quarter of an hour.

(Speech as Prime Minister of France, Chamber of Deputies, 8 March 1918)

415 It is thanks to the armies of the Republic that France, yesterday the soldier of God and today the soldier of Humanity, will be for ever the soldier of the Ideal.

(Speech, Chamber of Deputies, 11 November 1918)

416 This   devil   of   a   man [Raymond Poincaré] is the opposite of Briand: the latter knows nothing and understands everything; the other one knows everything and understands nothing.

(In conversation, ?1917)

417 The good Lord needed but Ten Commandments.

(*Alleged comment on reading President Woodrow Wilson's Fourteen Points, 1918)

418 It is far easier to make war than to make peace.

(Speech, Verdun, 14 July 1919)

Stephen Grover CLEVELAND (1837–1908):   twenty-second President of the USA

419 I have considered the pension list of the republic a roll of honour.

(Veto of Dependent Pension Bill, 5 July 1888)

420 There is no calamity which a great nation can invite which equals that which follows a supine submission to wrong and injustice and   the   consequent   loss   of national self-respect and honour, beneath which are shielded and defended a people's safety and greatness.

(Message to Congress, warning Britain of interference in Venezuelan affairs, 17 December 1895)

Robert   (Lord)   CLIVE (1725–74): English soldier and Governor of Bengal
[see also 1146]

421 It appears I am destined for something; I will live.

(*Alleged comment on finding that, on two occasions, the pistol with which he wished to kill himself would not fire, Madras, 1744)

422 By God, Mr Chairman, at this moment I stand astonished at my own moderation!

(Reply to accusations of rapacity in India by select committee of House of Commons, March 1773)

CNUT (995–1035): King of the English, Danes and Norwegians

423 We give warning that a festival must be observed on Sunday and honoured with full intent from noon on Saturday until dawn on Monday, and that no person shall presume either to practise trade or attend any meeting on this Holy Day; and all men, poor and rich, shall go to their church and offer supplication for their sins and observe zealously every appointed fast and honour readily those saints whose feasts shall be commended by the priests.

(Letter to the Archbishops and people of England sent from Denmark, ?December 1019/January 1020)

William COBBETT (1762–1835): English radical writer and politician

424 By machines mankind are able to do that which their own bodily powers would never effect to the same extent. Machines are the produce of the mind of man; and their existence distinguishes the civilized man from the savage.

(*Letter to the Luddites of Nottingham*, 1816)

425 [of London] What is to be the fate of the great wen of all? The monster, called by the silly coxcombs of the press, 'the metropolis of the empire'! ... The dispersion of the wen is the only real difficulty that I see in settling the affairs of the nation and restoring it to a happy state.

(*Rural Rides*, 4 December 1821)

426 While spewy sands and gravel near London are enclosed and built on, good lands in other parts are neglected. These enclosures are a waste; they are means misapplied; they are a proof of national decline and not of prosperity.

(Ibid., 8 January 1822)

427 I have come through the counties of corn and meat and iron and coal, and from the banks of the Humber to those of the Severn I find all the people who do not share in the taxes, in a state of distress, greater or less.

([At Worcester] Ibid., 18 May 1830)

Richard COBDEN (1804–65): English radical politician

428 Poland . . . upon which has been lavished more false sentiment, deluded sympathy, and amiable ignorance, than on any subject of the present age.

(Pamphlet, *Russia*, 1836, *Political Writings*, I)

429 The progress of freedom depends more upon the maintenance of peace, the spread of commerce, and the diffusion of education, than upon the labours of cabinets and foreign offices.

(Speech in the 'Don Pacifico' debate, H of C, 26 June 1850)

430 I believe it has been said that one copy of *The Times* contains more useful information than the whole of the historical works of Thucydides.

(Speech, Manchester, 27 December 1850)

431 I have travelled much . . . and I confess I have arrived at the conclusion that there is no country where so much is required to be done before the mass of the people become what it is pretended they are, what they ought

to be, and what I trust they will yet be as in England . . . It is to this spirit of interference with other countries, the wars to which it has led, and the subsequent diversion of men's minds from home grievances, that we must attribute the unsatisfactory state of the mass of our people.

(Open letter, III, January 1853, *Political Writings*, II)

432 What are the grounds on which we are to continue this war [Crimean War]? . . . Is it that war is a luxury? Is it that we are fighting – to use a cant phrase of Mr Pitt's time – to secure indemnity for the past and security for the future? Are we to be the Don Quixotes of Europe, to go about fighting for every cause where we find that someone has been wronged?

(Speech, H of C, 22 December 1854)

Frederick Donald COGGAN (b. 1910): Archbishop of York (later Canterbury)

433 [The Church] can always be a gadfly in the conscience of those who make the economic order, and I think that is its main function.

(Interviewed on Independent Television, 11 June 1961)

Sir Edward COKE (1552–1634): Chief Justice of England

434 The law of the realm cannot be changed but by Parliament.

(Dictum in the case *Articuli Cleri*, 1605)

435 We have a maxim in the House of Commons . . . that old ways are the safest and surest ways.

(Speech, London, 8 May 1628)

436 Prerogative is part of the law, but 'sovereign power' is no parliamentary word. In my opinion it weakens Magna Charta and all our statutes, for they are absolute, without any saving of 'Sovereign power'; and we shall now add to it, we shall weaken the foundation of law, and then the building must needs fall. Take heed what we yield to: Magna Charta is such a fellow that he will have no 'sovereign'.

(In opposing Lords' amendment to Petition of Right, 17 May 1628)

Jean-Baptiste COLBERT (1619–83): French statesman, chief minister to Louis XIV
[see also 1230]

437 Oh what a pity were the greatest and most virtuous of kings, of that real virtue which makes the greatest of princes, to be measured by the yardstick of Versailles!

(Letter to Louis XIV, 28 September 1665)

Christopher COLUMBUS (?1451–1506): Italian-born seaman, explorer
[see also 263, 1050]

438 Your Highnesses commanded I should not go eastward by land in the usual manner but by the western way which no one about whom we have definite information has ever followed. And thus having expelled all the Jews from all your realms and dominions in the same month of January Your Highnesses did command me that, with a sufficient fleet, I should sail to the said parts of India; and for that purpose Your Highnesses did grant me great honours and ennobled me so that henceforth I should be styled Don and should be Grand Admiral of the Ocean Sea and Viceroy and Governor-General in perpetuity of the Islands and mainland.

(From Columbus's log-book, addressed to Ferdinand and Isabella, refers to January 1492)

439 When I reached Cuba, I followed its north coast westwards, and found it so extensive that I thought this must be the mainland, the province of Cathay.

(Letter written off the Canary Islands on his return, 15 February 1493)

440 I believe that the earthly Paradise lies here, which no one can enter except by God's leave. I believe that this land which your Highnesses have commanded me to discover is very great, and that there are many other lands in the south of which there have never been reports.

(Narrative of his third voyage, on which he discovered S. America, 1500 [cf. also 1050])

James CONNOLLY (1870–1916): Irish syndicalist and Republican leader

441 It is an axiom enforced by all the experience of the ages, that they who rule industrially will rule politically.

(*Socialism made Easy*, 1905)

Benjamin CONSTANT (1767–1830): French author and political polemicist

442 The flames of Moscow were the aurora of the liberty of the world.

(Preface to an anti-Napoleonic pamphlet, *De l'Esprit de Conquête et de l'Usurpation*, 1813)

James COOK (1728–79): British seaman and explorer

443 At daylight in the morning we discovered a bay, which appeared to be tolerably well sheltered from all winds, into which I resolved to go with the ship.

(Discovery of Botany Bay, NSW, Journal, 28 April 1770)

444 From what I have said of the natives of New Holland [i.e. Australia] they may appear to some to be the most wretched people upon earth; but in reality they are far happier than we Europeans, being wholly unacquainted not only with the superfluous, but with the necessary conveniences so much sought after in Europe; they are happy in not knowing the use of them.

(Journal, August 1770)

445 Altho' the discoveries made in this Voyage are not great, yet I flatter myself they are such as may merit the Attention of their Lordships; and altho' I have failed in discovering the so much talked of Southern Continent (which perhaps do not exist) and which I myself had much at heart ... but as it is, I presume this Voyage will be found as compleat as any before made to the so. seas on the same account.

(Letter to the Admiralty reporting on his first voyage, in which he discovered New South Wales, 25 October 1770)

446 After such a long continuance at sea, in a high southern
latitude, it is but reasonable to
think that many of my people
must be ill of the scurvy. The
contrary, however, happened . . .
we had only one man on board
that could be called very ill of this
disease.

(Journal, 26 March 1773, off
New Zealand on second voyage)

Calvin COOLIDGE (1872–
1933): thirtieth President of the
USA
[see also 1510]

447 There is no right to strike
against the public safety by anybody, anywhere, anytime.

(Telegram sent, when Governor
of Massachusetts, to the
President of the American
Federation of Labor when
confronted by a police strike in
Boston, 14 September 1919)

448 Colonel, never go out to
meet trouble. If you will just sit
still, nine cases out of ten someone will intercept it before it
reaches you.

(In conversation with Theodore
Roosevelt Jnr soon after winning
the Presidential Election,
November 1924)

449 The business of America is
business.

(Speech to newspaper editors, 17
January 1925)

450 Prosperity is only an instrument to be used, not a deity to be
worshipped.

(Speech, Boston, Massachusetts,
11 June 1928)

451 Perhaps one of the most important accomplishments of my
administration has been minding
my own business.

(To newspaper reporters,
Washington DC, 1 March 1929)

452 When a great many people
are unable to find work, unemployment results.

(*Alleged remark in a syndicated
newspaper article, 1930)

Sir Charles CORNWALLIS
(?1580–1629): British ambassador in Madrid

453 [On Spanish reaction to
Gunpowder Plot] (The Spaniards) in general sorrow that so
monstrous a wickedness should
be found harboured within the
breast of any of their religion . . .
whatsoever they were in their
outside, in their entrails they were
Atheists and Devils.

(Letter to Robert Cecil, Earl of
Salisbury, November 1605)

Ferdinand CORTES (1485–1547): Spanish explorer

454 I have had much information that [the mainland towards Darien] is very rich and many pilots believe that there is a strait between that bay and the other sea, and this is the one thing in the world which I most desire to discover, because of the great service which I am certain Your Caesarean Majesties would receive thereby.

(Letter to Charles I (V) of Spain and Queen Joanna from Temixtitan, New Spain, 15 October 1524)

Thomas (Baron) COVENTRY (1578–1640): English politician

455 Our wooden walls are the strength and safety of our kingdom, and bring our Riches and Wealth.

(Speech in Star Chamber to judges, 17 June 1635)

Thomas CRANMER (1489–1556): Archbishop of Canterbury [see also 851, 1193]

456 [She came] sitting in her hair upon a horse litter richly apparelled ... you may not imagine that this coronation was before her marriage; for she was married much about St Paul's day last, as the condition thereof doth well appear, by reason she is now somewhat big with child. Notwithstanding it hath been reported throughout a great part of the realm that I married her; which was plainly false, for I myself knew not thereof a fortnight after it was done.

(Letter to the Archdeacon of Ely about Anne Boleyn's coronation, 17 June 1533)

457 We should easily convert even the Turks to the obedience of our gospel, if only we would agree among ourselves and unite in some holy confederacy.

(Letter to the Swiss scholar, Joachim Vadian, 1537)

458 This is the hand that wrote it and therefore shall it suffer first punishment.

(21 March 1556, repudiating his recantation just before his execution)

Thomas CREEVEY (1768–1838): British Whig politician and diarist

459 Friday morning, ½ past two – The girls just returned from a ball at the Duke of Richmond's ... Our troops are all moving from this place at present. Lord Wellington was at the ball tonight as composed as ever.

(*Journal*, Brussels, 16 June 1815)

460 So poor Prinney is really
dead – on a Saturday too.

(Letter to Elizabeth Ord, 26 June
1830, the day of George IV's
death)

461 A letter from Lady Cowley
today with an account of her
dinner at *Viccy's* one day this week
... The Queen, she said, was
excessively civil to everyone, had
excellent manners, but was *Royal*
(and quite right, little Vic, too, I
say again): ... in the evening ...
nothing could be more amiable
and agreeable than she was. Can
you wish for a better account of a
little tit of 18 made all at once into
a Queen?

(Letter to Elizabeth Ord, 5
August 1837)

Sir Ranulph CREW (1558–
1646): Chief Justice of the King's
Bench

462 Where is Bohun? Where's
Mowbray? Where's Mortimer?
... Nay, which is more, and most
of all, where is Plantagenet? They
are intombed in the urns and
sepulchres of mortality.

(Speech, concerned with decline
of noble families, in case of the
Earl of Oxford, 1625)

Sir Stafford CRIPPS
(1889–1952): British Labour
politician

463 When the Labour Party
comes to power we must act rapidly, and it will be necessary to
deal with the House of Lords and
the influence of the City of
London. There is no doubt that
we shall have to overcome opposition from Buckingham Palace
and from other places as well.

(Speech to a Labour Party rally,
Nottingham, 6 January 1934)

464 What we are lacking today in
our productive effort in this country is a Christian approach – a
Christian background ... A
merely materialistic, self-centred
outlook on our work cannot give
us a high morale ... Inducements
of a material kind can never replace the spiritual urge which can
only come from our sense of devotion to a cause which transcends
our own personal interests.

(Address in a Birmingham
church, 11 May 1947)

465 There is only a certain sized
cake to be divided up, and if a lot
of people want a larger slice they
can only take it from others who
would, in terms of real income,
have a smaller one.

(Speech, as Chancellor of the
Exchequer, to the Trade Union
Congress, Margate, 7 September
1948)

466 [of Mohandas Karamchand
Gandhi] I know of no other man

in our time, or indeed in recent history, who so convincingly demonstrated the power of the spirit over material things.

(Speech, Commonwealth prime ministers' conference, London, 1 October 1948)

John Wilson CROKER (1780–1857): British Tory politician

467 We now are, as we always have been, decidedly and conscientiously attached to what is called the Tory, and which might with more propriety be called the Conservative, party.

(*Quarterly Review*, January 1830)

Oliver CROMWELL (1599–1658): Parliamentarian general, and Lord Protector of England [see also 404, 652, 1726]

468 I had rather have a plain russet-coated captain that knows what he fights for, and loves what he knows, than that which you call a gentleman and is nothing else. I honour a gentleman that is so indeed.

(Letter to Sir William Spring, September 1643)

469 Sir, the State, in choosing men to serve them, takes no notice of their opinions.

(Letter to Major-General Cauford, March 1644)

470 Truly England and the Church of God hath had a great favour from the Lord, in this great victory given to us, such as the like never was since this war began ... We never charged but we routed the enemy ... God made them as stubble to our swords ... Sir, God hath taken away your eldest son by a cannonshot ... There is your precious child full of glory, to know no sin nor sorrow any more ... God give you his comfort.

(To his brother-in-law, Valentine Wauton, after the Battle of Marston Moor; 5 July 1644)

471 [of Charles I] We will cut off his head with the crown upon it.

(Comment to Algernon Sidney, January 1649)

472 We come (by the assistance of God) to hold forth and maintain the lustre and glory of English liberty in a nation where we have the undoubted right to do it ... [the Irish] may equally participate in all benefits, to use liberty and fortune equally with Englishmen if they keep out of arms.

(Declaration as Lord Lieutenant of Ireland, spring of 1650)

473 I beseech you in the bowels of Christ think it possible you may be mistaken.

(To the General Assembly of the Scottish Kirk, 3 August 1650)

474 The dimensions of this mercy are above my thoughts. It is, for aught I know, a crowning mercy.

(To Speaker Lenthall, after Battle of Worcester, 4 September 1651)

475 If I were ten years younger, there is not a king in Europe I would not make to tremble.

(*Attributed remark, *c.* 1652/3)

476 It is not fit that you should sit here any longer! . . . you shall now give place to better men.

(Speech, Rump Parliament, 20 April 1653)

477 What are we to do with this bauble? Take it away.

(To a musketeer with reference to the Speaker's mace when expelling the Rump Parliament, 20 April 1653)

478 Were I as young as you, I should not doubt, ere I died, to knock at the gates of Rome.

(*Alleged remark to General Lambert, *c.* 1653/4)

479 Necessity hath no law.

(Speech, Parliament, 12 September 1654)

480 We are Englishmen: that is one good fact.

(Speech, Parliament, 17 September 1656)

481 Mr Lely, I desire you would use all your skill to paint my picture truly like me and not flatter me at all; but remark all these roughnesses, pimples, warts and everything as you see me, otherwise I will never pay a farthing for it.

(To Sir Peter Lely, ?1657)

482 Your poor army, these poor contemptible men, came up hither.

(Speech to Committee of Parliament, 21 April 1657)

483 You have accounted yourselves happy on being environed with a great ditch from all the world beside.

(Speech, Parliament, 25 January 1658)

484 A man never mounts higher than when he knows not whither he is going.

(*Attributed remark)

Thomas   CROMWELL (?1485–1540): chief minister to King Henry VIII

485 Pity it is that the folly of one brainsick Pole – or, to say better, of one witless fool – should be the ruin of so great a family.

(Letter to Pole's confidant, Michael Throgmorton [on the denunciation of Reginald Pole (the King's cousin) for siding with the Pope in the disputes of the English Reformation], September 1537)

486 The Abbot of Reading to be sent down to be tried and executed at Reading.

(Memorandum, September 1539)

487 I must now beseech your Grace of pardon . . . God is good and knoweth both towards your Majesty and your Realm how dear your person was, is, and ever hath [been to me] . . . It much grieves me that I should be noted a traitor when I always had your laws on my breast, and that I should be a sacramentary. God he knoweth the truth, and that I am of the one and the other guiltless.

(Letter to Henry VIII from the Tower of London after being condemned to death for treason and heresy, 30 June 1540)

Richard   CROSSMAN
(1907–74): British Labour politician

488 I say to myself that I mustn't let myself be cut off in there, and yet the moment I enter my bag is taken out of my hand, I'm pushed in, shepherded, nursed and above

all cut off, alone. Whitehall envelops me.

(Diary entry after his first week in the Cabinet, 22 October 1964)

John   Philpot   CURRAN
(1750–1817): Irish judge

489 The condition upon which God hath given liberty to men is eternal vigilance.

(Speech upon Election Rights, Dublin, 10 July 1790)

George Nathaniel CURZON
(1859–1925): British Conservative Foreign Secretary and Viceroy of India
[see also 100]

490 It is only when you get to see and realize what India is – that she is the strength and the greatness of England – it is only then that you feel that every nerve a man may strain, every energy he may put forward, cannot be devoted to a nobler purpose than keeping tight the cords that hold India to ourselves.

(Speech, Southport, 15 March 1893)

491 To those who believe that the British Empire is under Providence the greatest instrument for good that the world has seen, and who hold, with the writer, that its work in the Far East is not yet accomplished.

(Dedication of his book *Problems of the Far East*, 1894)

492 I am almost astounded at the coolness, I might even say the effrontery, with which the British Government is in the habit of parcelling out the territory of Powers whose independence and integrity it assures them at the same time it has no other intention than to preserve, and only informs the Power concerned of the arrangement that has been made after the agreement has been concluded.

(Speech, H of L, 6 February 1908)

493 The British flag has never flown over a more powerful or a more united empire ... Never did our voice count for more in the councils of nations; or in determining the future destinies of mankind.

(Speech, H of L, 18 November 1918)

494 The inkpot used by Secretaries of State ... should be of crystal and silver, not glass and brass. It must be replaced immediately.

(On taking up his appointment as Foreign Secretary, 6 January 1919)

DAILY EXPRESS

495 The *Daily Express* declares

that Britain will not be involved in a European war this year, or next year either.

(Caption at the top of the front page, 30 September 1938)

Edouard   DALADIER (1884–1970):   French   Prime Minister

496 It is a phoney war. [Contemporary translation of *C'est une drôle de guerre.*]

(Speech, Chamber of Deputies, Paris, 22 December 1939)

St Peter DAMIAN (1007–72): Bishop of Ostia

497 As these two, the kingdom and the priesthood, are brought together by divine mystery, so are their two heads, by the force of mutual loves; the King may be found in the Roman pontiff, and the Roman pontiff be found in the King.

(*Disceptatio synodalis*, written just after the enthronement of Pope Alexander II, October 1062)

Georges DANTON (1759–94): French Revolutionary leader

498 The tocsin you hear today is not an alarm but an alert: it sounds the charge against our enemies. To conquer them we must dare, and dare again, and dare for ever; and thus will

France be saved [*Pour les vaincre il nous faut de l'audace, encore de l'audace, toujours de l'audace, et la France est sauvée*].

(Speech to rally support against the foreign invaders, Paris, 2 September 1792)

499 My address will soon be Annihilation. As for my name you will find it in the Pantheon of History.

(Reply to formal questions at his trial before the Revolutionary Tribunal, Paris, 2 April 1794)

Jefferson DAVIS (1808–89): Confederate President
[see also 751]

500 All we ask is to be let alone.

(Inaugural address, 18 February 1861)

John DAVIS (?1550–1605): English seaman and explorer

501 The 17 of this month, being in the latitude of 63′ 8″, we fell upon a most mighty and strange quantity of ice, in one entire mass, so big as that we knew not the limits thereof, and being withal so very high, in form of a land, with bays and capes.

(Description of an iceberg, Journal, 17 July 1586)

502 This land is very high and mountainous, having before it on the west side a mighty company of isles full of fair sounds and harbours ... [the people] eat all their meat raw, they live most upon fish, they drink salt water, and eat grass and ice with delight: they are never out of the water.

(Report on 2nd voyage to Greenland and Eskimoes, 14 October 1586)

Sir Humphry DAVY (1778–1829): English scientist

503 The wealth of our island may be diminished, but the strength of mind of the people cannot easily pass away ... The dignity of our nature depends little upon external relations. When we had fewer colonies than Genoa we had Bacons and Shakespeares. The wealth and prosperity of the country are only the comeliness of the body, the fullness of the flesh and fat; but the spirit is independent of them; it requires only muscle, bone and nerve for the true exercise of its functions. We cannot lose our liberty, because we cannot cease to think.

(Letter to Thomas Poole, 28 August 1807)

Eugene V. DEBS (1855–1926): pioneer American socialist

504 When great changes occur in history, when great principles are involved, as a rule the majority are wrong.

(Speech, defending himself against a charge of sedition, in court at Cleveland, Ohio, 12 September 1918)

Stephen DECATUR (1779–1820): American naval commander

505 Our country! In her intercourse with foreign nations, may she always be in the right; but our country, right or wrong.

(Toast proposed at a banquet to celebrate his victories over the 'barbary pirates' of Algeria, December 1815)

DECLARATION OF INDEPENDENCE

506 We hold these truths to be self-evident, that all men are created equal, that they are endowed by their Creator with certain unalterable rights, that among these are life, liberty, and the pursuit of happiness. That to secure these rights, Governments are instituted among Men, deriving their just powers from the consent of the governed . . .

(4 July 1776)

DECLARATION OF THE RIGHTS OF MAN

507 The representatives of the French people, constituted as a National Assembly, believing that ignorance, forgetfulness, or contempt of the rights of man are the only causes of public misfortunes and of the corruption of governments, have resolved to set forth in a solemn declaration the natural, inalienable and sacred rights of Man . . . (1) Men are born free and equal in rights . . . (2) The aim of every political association is the preservation of the natural and imprescriptible rights of man. These rights are liberty, property, security and resistance to oppression. (3) The principle of all sovereignty resides essentially in the nation . . .

(Drafted and discussed August 1789, formally published September 1791)

John DEE (1527–1608): Welsh astrologer

508 [It would be wise] to make England both abroad and at home to be Lord and ruler of the Exchange.

(*Chart to Make This Kingdom Flourishing, Triumphant, Famous and Blessed*, 1570)

509 . . . being (as it becommeth me, a Suibject) carefull for the Godly prosperity of this British Impire, under our most Peaceable Queen Elizabeth.

(*General & Rare Memorials
pertaining to the Perfect Arte of
Navigation*, 1577: first use of
phrase 'British Empire')

510 Most excellent Royall
Majesty, of our *Elizabeth* (sitting
at the *Helm* of this Imperial Monarchy: or rather, at the Helm of
the Imperiall Ship).

(Ibid.)

511 [King Arthur] not only Conquered Iseland, Groenland, and
all the Northern Iles cumpassing
unto Russia, But even unto the
North Pole (in manner) did
extend his jurisdiction.

(On back of map of America,
intended for Elizabeth I, 1580)

Charles DE GAULLE
(1890–1970): French General
and President of the Fifth Republic

512 I, General de Gaulle, now in
London, call on all French
officers and men who are at present on British soil, or who may be
in the future . . . to get in touch
with me. Whatever happens the
flame of French resistance must
not and shall not be extinguished.

(Broadcast from London, 18 June
1940)

513 To all Frenchmen: France
has lost a battle but France has
not lost the war.

(Proclamation circulated in Great
Britain, late June 1940)

514 A revolutionary France
would always rather win a war
with General Hoche than lose it
with Marshal Soubise.

(Speech, London, 1 April 1942)

515 That our allies of yesterday
should convene yet again in our
absence . . . could only cause us
renewed agitation. Yet at heart we
considered it as well for us not to
be brought into discussions which
could, in the future, be nothing
but superogatory . . . What could
I have done at Potsdam?

(*War Memoirs*, Vol. III, of the
Potsdam Conference in 1945,
completed 1959)

516 [In 1945] I intended to
safeguard the primacy of France
in western Europe by preventing
the rise of a new Reich which
might again threaten its safety; to
cooperate with East and West . . .
to transform the French Union
into a free association to avoid
dangers of upheaval not yet per-
ceived; to persuade the states
along the Rhine, the Alps and the
Pyrenees to form a political,
economic and strategic bloc; and
to establish this association as one
of the three world powers, acting
if necessary as arbiter between
the Soviet and Anglo-American
camps. Since 1940 every word
and every act of mine was dedi-

cated to bringing about this possibility.

(Ibid.)

517 In the tumult of great events, solitude was what I hoped for. Now it is what I love. How is it possible to be contented with anything else when one has come face to face with History?

(Ibid.: end)

518 Foch, Clemenceau, De Gaulle – it is the same thing; and it is important the French people have no doubts on that score.

(To his political staff, Mont-Valerian, 18 June 1946)

519 From her very beginning the vocation of France, the purpose of France has been a calling to serve humanity . . . She remains faithful to this purpose when she offers you loyal and friendly collaboration in the creation, establishment and progress of your State.

(Speech to the people of Mali, on eve of their independence, Dakar, 13 December 1959)

520 I have never personally, in any of my statements, spoken of a Europe of Nations (*Europe des patries*) although it is always being claimed that I have done so . . . I have already said, and I repeat, that at the present time there cannot be any other Europe than a Europe of States, apart of course from myths, stories and parades.

(Press Conference, 15 May 1962)

521 For all of us Frenchmen, the guiding rule of our epoch is to be faithful to France.

(Speech, Lyons, 28 September 1963)

Edward Stanley, Earl of DERBY (1799–1869): British Conservative Prime Minister [see also 537]

522 When I first came into Parliament, Mr Tierney, a great Whig authority, used always to say that the duty of an Opposition was very simple – it was, to oppose everything, and propose nothing.

(Speech, H of C, 4 June 1841)

523 The foreign policy of the noble Earl . . . may be summed up in two truly expressive words: 'meddle' and 'muddle'.

(Speech, H of L, February 1864 (referring to Earl Russell's policy in the American Civil War)

524 We have dished the Whigs.

(Of Second Parliamentary Reform Act, 1867)

Camille   DESMOULINS (1760–94): French Revolutionary leader

525 Citizens to arms! ... Let us take as our emblem green cockades, green the colour of hope!

(Extempore speech to a crowd outside Palais Royal, Paris, 14 July 1789, as recalled by Desmoulins in *Le Vieux Cordelier* for 5 January 1794)

526 Clemency is also a revolutionary measure.

(Ibid., 24 December 1793)

527 My age is that of the *bon Sansculotte Jésus*; an age fatal to Revolutionists.

(Answer at trial, Paris, 2 April 1784)

John   DICKINSON (1732–1808): American revolutionary

528 Our cause is just. Our union is perfect.

(Declaration on Taking up Arms, 1775)

Sir Dudley DIGGES (1583–1639): MP, colonialist

529 A glorious state and renowned Great Britain would be, had the same discovered the North Pole and passage into the South Sea unto the rich countries of China, Cataya and Japon.

(Pamphlets(?), 1611, urging expedition to discover North-West passage)

530 The Indians in Virginia continually assure our people that 12 days' journey westward from the Falls they have a sea ... whereby see but how great a part of the back of America is clean wiped away?

(Ibid.)

Benjamin DISRAELI (Earl of Beaconsfield) (1804–81): British Conservative Prime Minister

531 A man may speak very well in the House of Commons, and fail very completely in the House of Lords. There are two distinct styles requisite: I intend, in the course of my career, if I have time, to give a specimen of both.

(*The Young Duke*, written 1829)

532 Read no history, nothing but biography, for that is life without theory.

(*Contarini Fleming*, written 1831, published May 1832)

533 Though I sit down now, the time will come when you will hear me.

(Maiden speech, H of C, 7 December 1837)

534 The Continent will not

suffer England to be the workshop of the world.

(Speech, H of C, 15 March 1838)

535 'A sound Conservative government', said Taper, musingly. 'I understand: Tory men and Whig measures.'

(*Coningsby*, written in the winter of 1843–4)

536 Consider Ireland ... You have a starving population, an absentee aristocracy, and an alien Church, and in addition the weakest executive in the world. That is the Irish Question.

(Speech, H of C, 16 February 1844)

537 The noble lord [Lord Stanley, later 14th Earl of Derby] is the Prince Rupert of parliamentary discussion; his charge is resistless; but when he returns from pursuit he always finds his camp in the possession of the enemy.

(Speech, H of C, 24 April 1844)

538 Two nations between whom there is no intercourse and no sympathy; who are as ignorant of each other's habits, thoughts and feelings, as if they were dwellers in different zones or inhabitants of different planets ... The rich and the poor.

(*Sybil*, Book 2, Ch. 5, written winter of 1844–5)

539 The right hon. Gentleman [Peel] caught the Whigs bathing, and walked away with their clothes.

(Speech, H of C, 28 February 1845)

540 Protection is not a principle but an expedient.

(Speech, H of C, 17 March 1845)

541 Dissolve if you please the Parliament you have betrayed and appeal to the people who, I believe, mistrust you. For me there remains this at least – the opportunity of expressing thus publicly my belief that a Conservative Government is an Organized Hypocrisy.

(Addressing Peel; Ibid.)

542 [of Peel] He is so vain that he wants to figure in history as the settler of all the great questions; but a Parliamentary constitution is not favourable to such ambitions: things must be done by parties, not by persons using parties as tools.

(Letter to Lord John Manners, 17 December 1846)

543 London is a modern Babylon.

(*Tancred*, written 1846)

544 Nationality is the miracle of

political independence: race is the principle of physical analogy.

(Speech, H of C, 9 August 1848)

545 I read this morning an awful, though monotonous, manifesto in the great organ of public opinion, which always makes me tremble. Olympian bolts; and yet I could not help fancying amid their rumbling terrors I heard the plaintive treble of the Treasury Bench.

(Speech, H of C, 13 February 1851)

546 [of the Crystal Palace] That enchanted pile which the sagacious taste and the prescient philanthropy of an accomplished and enlightened Prince have raised for the glory of England and the delight of two hemispheres.

(1851)

547 Let us not be deluded by forms of government. The word may be republic in France, constitutional monarchy in Prussia, absolute monarchy in Austria, but the thing is the same. Wherever there is a vast standing army, the government is the government of the sword ... [Some] irresistible law ... dooms Europe to the alternate sway of disciplined armies or secret societies; the camp or the convention.

(*Lord George Bentinck: a Political Biography*, written 1851)

548 The movement of the middle class for the abolition of slavery was virtuous, but it was not wise. It was an ignorant movement. The history of the abolition of slavery by the English and its consequences would be a narrative of ignorance, injustice, blundering, waste, and havoc, not easily paralleled in the history of mankind.

(Ibid.)

549 These wretched Colonies will all be independent, too, in a few years and are a millstone round our necks.

(Letter to Lord Malmesbury, 13 August 1852)

550 Coalitions though successful have always found this, that their triumph has been brief. This too I know, that England does not love coalitions.

(Speech, H of C, 16 December 1852)

551 Is man an ape or an angel? My Lord, I am on the side of the angels.

(Speech, under the chairmanship of the Bishop of Oxford, Samuel Wilberforce, Sheldonian Theatre, Oxford, 25 November 1864)

552 Yes, I have climbed to the top of the greasy pole.

(Comment to his friends when first appointed Prime Minister, 27 February 1868)

553 There is in his [the Bishop of London's] idiosyncrasy a strange fund of enthusiasm, a quality which ought never to be possessed by an Archbishop of Canterbury or a Prime Minister. The Bishop of London sympathizes with everything that is earnest; but what is earnest is not always true; on the contrary, error is often more earnest than truth.

(To Queen Victoria, 4 November 1868, concerning the appointment of Bishop Tait of London as Archbishop of Canterbury)

554 As I sat opposite the Treasury Bench the ministers reminded me of one of those marine landscapes not very unusual on the coasts of South America. You behold a range of exhausted volcanoes. Not a flame flickers on a single pallid crest.

(Speech, Manchester, 3 April 1872)

555 In my opinion no Minister in this country will do his duty who neglects any opportunity of reconstructing as much as possible our Colonial Empire, and of responding to those distant sympathies which may become the source of incalculable strength and happiness to this land.

(Speech, Crystal Palace, 24 June 1872)

556 King Louis Philippe once said to me that he attributed the great success of the British nation in political life to their talking politics after dinner.

(Speech, at installation as Lord Rector of Glasgow University, 19 November 1873)

557 [of Lord Salisbury] Not a man who measures his words . . . [but] . . . a great master of gibes and flouts and jeers.

(Speech, H of C, 5 August 1874)

558 Permissive legislation is the characteristic of a free people.

(Speech, H of C, 18 June 1875)

559 Gladstone, like Richelieu, can't write. Nothing can be more unmusical, more involved or more uncouth than all his scribblement.

(Private letter, 3 October 1877)

560 Gentlemen, we bring you peace; and I think I may say, peace with honour.

(Impromptu speech from the steps of his railway carriage, Dover, on returning from the Congress of Berlin, 16 July 1878)

561 Lord Salisbury and myself have brought you back peace – and a peace, I hope, not without honour.

(Speech to the crowd outside 10 Downing Street, after completing his journey home from the Congress of Berlin, 16 July 1878)

562 [of Gladstone] A sophistical rhetorician, inebriated with the exuberance of his own verbosity, and gifted with an egotistical imagination that can at all times command an interminable and inconsistent series of arguments to malign an opponent and to glorify himself.

(Speech, Riding School, Knightsbridge, 27 July 1878)

563 What is at the bottom of this amendment is that principle of peace at any price which a certain party in this country upholds . . . That doctrine has done more mischief than any I can well recall that have been afloat in this country. It has occasioned more wars than any of the most ruthless conquerors. It has disturbed and nearly destroyed that political equilibrium so necessary to the liberties and the welfare of the world. It has dimmed occasionally for a moment even the majesty of England.

(Speech, H of L, 10 December 1878)

564 One of the great Romans, when asked what were his policies replied, '*Imperium et libertas*'. That would not make a bad programme for a British Ministry.

(Speech, Mansion House, London, 10 November 1879)

565 The key to India is London, the majesty of sovereignty, the spirit and vigour of your Parliament, the inexhaustible resources, the ingenuity and determination of your people – these are the keys of India.

(Speech, H of L, 4 March 1881; the suggestion that the 'key to India is London' had been made to Beaconsfield in conversation on the previous day by the Russian ambassador, Prince Lobanov)

566 Everyone likes flattery; and when you come to Royalty you should lay it on with a trowel.

(*Alleged remark to Matthew Arnold, ?1880)

567 We authors, ma'am . . .

(*Alleged remark in conversation with Queen Victoria)

568 Never complain and never explain.

(*Remark attributed by Gladstone to Disraeli, according to John Morley)

Milovan DJILAS (b. 1912): dissident Yugoslav socialist

569 Though man may endure his ordeal like Sisyphus, the time must come for him to revolt like Prometheus before his powers are exhausted by the ordeal.

(*The Unperfect Society*, 1969)

Stephen A. DOUGLAS (1813–61): US Senator

570 It matters not what way the Supreme Court may hereafter decide as to the abstract question whether slavery may or may not go into a Territory under the Constitution, the people have the lawful means to introduce it or exclude it as they please, for the reason that slavery cannot exist a day or an hour anywhere unless it is supported by local police regulations . . .

(Speech, in debate with Lincoln, at Freeport, Illinois, 27 August 1858)

Sir Francis DRAKE (?1540–96): English seaman, explorer and commander
[see also 85]

571 I must have the gentleman to haul and draw with the mariner, and the mariner with the gentleman . . . I would know him that would refuse to set his hand to a rope but I know there is not any such here.

(Speech to the crew off Puerto San Julian, May 1578)

572 The advantage of time and place in all practical actions is half a victory; which being lost is irrecoverable.

(Letter to Elizabeth I while awaiting news of the coming of the Armada, 1588)

573 There is plenty of time to win this game and to thrash the Spaniards too.

(*Alleged remark at Plymouth, 1588 – no contemporary evidence. 'The tradition goes, that Drake would needs see the game up: but was soon prevailed on to go and play out the rubbers with the Spaniards.': Oldys, 'Life of Ralegh', in Ralegh, *History of the World*, 1736)

574 There was never anything pleased me better than seeing the enemy flying with a southerly wind to the westwards. God grant you have a good eye to the Duke of Parma, for with the grace of God, if we live, I doubt not but ere it be long, so to handle the matter with the Duke of Sidonia as he shall wish himself at St Mary Port among his orange trees.

(Letter to Walsingham, 1588, while chasing the Armada)

575 Singeing the King of Spain's Beard.

(*Of expedition to Cadiz, 1587, cf. 85)

Michael DUCAS (?1400–?70): Byzantine historian

576 It would be better to see the royal turban of the Turks in the midst of the city [Constantinople] than the Latin mitre.

(Remark attributed to an official of the Byzantine Empire, after the Emperor Constantine XI's attempt to reunite his Church with Rome, 1452)

John Foster DULLES (1888–1959): US Secretary of State

577 Our capacity to retaliate must be, and is, massive in order to deter all forms of aggression.

(Speech, Chicago, 8 December 1955)

578 The ability to get to the verge of war without getting into war is the necessary art. If you cannot master it, you inevitably get into wars. If you try to run away from it, if you are scared to go to the brink, you are lost. We've had to look it square in the face – on the question of enlarging the Korean War, on the question of getting into the Indo-China war, on the question

of Formosa. We walked to the brink and we looked it in the face.

(Interview quoted in *Life Magazine*, 11 January 1956)

Charles F. du P. de M. DU-MOURIEZ (1739–1823): French General

579 The courtiers who surrounded him [Louis XVIII] have forgotten nothing and learnt nothing.

(*At the time of the Declaration of Verona, September 1795 [also attributed to Talleyrand])

John DUNNING, Baron Ashburton (1731–83): English lawyer and politician

580 The power of the Crown has increased, is increasing, and ought to be diminished.

(Motion passed in H of C, 6 April 1780)

John George Lambton, Earl of DURHAM (1792–1840): Governor-General of British provinces in North America

581 It will be observed by everyone who has observed the progress of Anglo-Saxon colonization in America that sooner or later the English race was sure to predominate even numerically in Lower Canada, as they predominate already by their superior

knowledge, energy, enterprise
and wealth.

(The 'Durham Report', 1839)

582 I believe that tranquillity can
only be restored by subjecting the
province of Lower Canada to the
vigorous rule of an English majority; and that the only effica-
cious government would be that
formed by a legislative union.

(Ibid.)

Anthony EDEN, Earl of Avon
(1898–1977): British Conservative Foreign Secretary and Prime
Minister

583 It is the appeasement of
Europe as a whole that we have
constantly before us ... I do not
intend to approach the problem
of the immediate future with the
idea of being bound to the di-
vergent policies of either France
or Germany. Our policy is the
Covenant and membership of the
League. We know our obligations
and are prepared to fulfil them.

(Speech, H of C, 26 March 1936)

584 We best avoid wars by taking
even physical action to stop small
ones. Everybody knows that the
United Nations is not in a position to do that. We and the
French have the forces available.
We must face the fact that the
United Nations is not yet the
international equivalent of our

own legal system and the rule of
law ... Police action there must
be to separate the belligerents
and to prevent a resumption of
hostilities.

(Speech, explaining the reasons
for Anglo-French intervention in
the Israeli-Egyptian conflict, H of
C, 1 November 1956)

EDGAR (944–75): King of England

585 And it is my will that secular
rights be in force among the
Danes [settled in England] according to as good laws as they
can best decide on. Among the
English, however, that is to be in
force which I and my councillors
have added to the decrees of my
ancestors for the benefit of all the
nation. Nevertheless, this measure is to be common to all the
nation, whether Englishmen,
Danes or Britons, in every province of my dominion to the end
that poor men and rich may possess what they rightly acquire and
that a thief may not find a place to
bring what he has stolen.

(Law issued 962/3)

EDWARD III (1312–77): King
of England

586 *Honi soit qui mal y pense* [Evil
be to him who evil thinks].

(*Alleged remark at the falling of
the Countess of Salisbury's

garter, presumably when the Order of the Garter was founded in 1344: no contemporary evidence whatsoever, but the traditional tale was current in Henry VIII's reign when Polydore Vergil wrote his *Anglicae Historiae*)

587 Let the boy win his spurs.

(Of the Black Prince at the Battle of Crecy, 26 August 1346. *This remark only appears in Froissart's Chronicle, based on oral traditions gathered at least fifteen years later, and is contradicted by other chroniclers)

EDWARD VI (1537–53): King of England

588 Methinks I am in prison. Here be no galleries nor no gardens to walk in.

(To his attendants at Windsor during the deposition of Somerset, autumn 1549)

589 For women, as far forth as ye may, avoid their company. Yet if the French King command you, you may sometimes dance, so measure be your mean. Else apply yourself to riding, shooting or tennis, with such honest games. Not forgetting sometime, when you have leisure, your learning, chiefly reading of the Scripture.

(Advice in a letter written, aged fourteen, to his friend, Barnaby

Fitzpatrick, at the French Court, 20 December 1551)

590 Little hath been done here since you went; but the duke's of Somerset arraignment of felonious treason, and the musters of the new erected gendarmery.

(Ibid.)

EDWARD VII (1842–1910): King of England

591 Because a man has a black face and a different religion from our own there is no reason why he should be treated as a brute.

(Letter from India to Lord Granville, 30 November 1875)

592 Mademoiselle, I remember applauding you in London where you represented all the grace and spirit of France.

(To the actress, Jeanne Granier, at the start of a visit to Paris which eased Anglo–French tension: 1 May 1903)

EDWARD VIII (1894–1972): King of England
[see also 729, 812, 1794]

593 Those works brought all these people here: something must be done to find them work.

(To officials accompanying him when he met unemployed Welsh miners outside a derelict steel

plant at Dowlais, 18 November
1936)

594 I have found it impossible to
carry the heavy burden of responsibility and to discharge my duties
as King as I would wish to do
without the help and support of
the woman I love.

(Radio speech, 11 December
1936)

Dwight D. EISENHOWER
(1890–1969): US General and
thirty-fourth President of USA
[see also 1516, 1826]

595 The eyes of the world are
upon you. The hopes and prayers
of liberty-loving people everywhere march with you.

(Order to his troops for D-Day, 6
June 1944)

596 History does not long entrust the care of freedom to the
weak or the timid.

(Inaugural address, 20 January
1953)

597 You have a row of dominoes
set up; you knock over the first
one, and what will happen to the
last one is that it will go over very
quickly.

(At Press Conference, on
south-east Asia after defeat of the
French by the Viet-Minh: 7 April
1954)

598 There can be no law if we
were to invoke one code of international conduct for those who
oppose us and another for our
friends.

(Broadcast speech, Suez Crisis,
31 October 1956)

ELIZABETH I (1533–1603):
Queen of England
[see also 222, 223, 225, 282, 816,
817, 871, 922, 923, 1038, 1555]

599 I give you this charge, that
you shall be of my Privy Council,
and content yourself to take pains
for me and my realm. This judgment I have of you, that you will
not be corrupted with any manner
of gift and that you will be faithful
to the state, and that, without
respect of my private will, you will
give me that counsel that you
think best.

(To William Cecil, later Lord
Burghley, 1558)

600 It is true that the world was
made in six days, but it was by
God, to Whose power the infirm-
ity of man is not to be compared.

(To the French ambassador, who
complained of being kept waiting
six days for an answer, 10 May
1565)

601 I thank God I am endued
with such qualities that if I were
turned out of the Realm in my

petticoat I were able to live in any place in Christendom.

(To Deputation of Lords and Commons, October 1566)

602 And you Madam I may not call you, and mistress I am ashamed to call you, so I know not what to call you, but yet I do thanke you.

(To the wife of Matthew Parker [Archbishop of Canterbury, 1558–75] after being entertained at his house; Queen Elizabeth disapproved of married clergy)

603 She supposed the King of Spain had not wished to write . . . thinking that, so soon after the death of the queen his wife, it would be most unseemly for him to send letters to a marriageable girl (*une fille à marier*) like herself.

(Comment on Philip II's failure to inform her of his third wife's death: as reported by the French ambassador in a letter to Catherine de Medici, 27 December 1568)

604 The daughter of debate, that eke discord doth sow.

(*Alleged reference to Mary, Queen of Scots, 1572)

605 I believe that, at the worst, God has not yet decided England shall cease to stand where she does; or, at least, that God has not given power to overthrow her

to those men who would like so to do.

(In conversation with the French ambassador, Christmas/New Year 1572/3, as reported by Bertrand de la Mothe Fenelon to Charles IX, 2 January 1573)

606 As for me, I see no such great cause why I should either be fond to live or fear to die. I have had good experience of the world, and I know what it is to be a subject and what to be a sovereign. Good neighbours I have had, and I have met with bad: and in trust I have found treason.

(Speech to deputation from Parliament, 12 November 1586)

607 I know I have the body of a weak and feeble woman, but I have the heart and stomach of a king, and of a king of England too; and think foul scorn that Parma or Spain, or any prince of Europe, should dare to invade the borders of my realm.

(Speech to troops at Tilbury, 8 August 1588)

608 God's death, my Lords, but I have been enforced this day to scour up my old Latin that hath lain long rusting.

(To her Council, after making an impromptu reply in Latin to complaints from a Polish envoy, July 1597)

609 Though God hath raised me high, yet this I count the glory of my crown: that I have reigned with your loves ... And though you have had, and may have, many mightier and wiser princes sitting in this seat; yet you never had, nor shall have any that will love you better.

(To the Speaker and Members of the H of C, 30 November 1601)

610 The word 'must' is not to be used to princes. Little man, little man, if your father had lived ye durst not have said so much; but ye know I must die and that makes you presumptuous.

(To Sir Robert Cecil, who had urged her to go to bed in her last illness, March 1603)

ELIZABETH II (b. 1926): Queen of England

611 I declare before you that my whole life, whether it be long or short, shall be devoted to your service and the service of our great Imperial Commonwealth to which we all belong.

(Broadcast speech to the Commonwealth, as Princess Elizabeth, from Cape Town on her 21st birthday, 21 April 1947)

612 I am sure that this, my Coronation, is not the symbol of a power and a splendour that are gone, but a declaration of our hopes for the future.

(Coronation Day speech, 2 June 1953)

613 I think people really will concede that, on this of all days, I should begin my speech with the words 'My husband and I'.

(Speech at banquet to celebrate her Silver Wedding, 20 November 1972)

ELIZABETH (b. 1900): Queen-Consort of England

614 I'm glad we've been bombed. It makes me feel I can look the East End in the face.

(In conversation after the bombing of Buckingham Palace, September 1940)

ELIZABETH (1596–1662): wife of the Elector Palatine and later Queen of Bohemia, only daughter of James I

615 I would rather eat sauer-kraut with a King than roast beef with an Elector.

(*Alleged remark to her husband, September 1619, on hearing he had been offered the crown of Bohemia by rebels against the Emperor)

Sir Thomas ELYOT (?1450–1522): English diplomat

616 [Football] wherein is nothing but beastly fury and extreme violence, whereof proceedeth hurt; and consequently rancour and malice do remain with them that be wounded.

(*Boke called the Governour*, 1531)

Ralph Waldo EMERSON (1803–82): American philosopher

617 That new saint, than whom nothing purer or more brave was ever led by love of men into conflict and death . . . will make the gallows glorious like the cross.

(Of John Brown's execution, December 1859)

Friedrich ENGELS (1820–95): German communist

618 The first act in which the state really comes forward as the representative of society as a whole – the taking possession of the means of production in the name of society – is at the same time its last independent act as a state . . . The state is not 'abolished', it withers away.

(*Anti-Dühring*, 1878)

619 The British Labour movement is today, and for many years has been, working in a narrow circle of strikes which are looked upon, not as an expedient, and

not as a means of propaganda, but as an ultimate aim.

(Letter to Eduard Bernstein, 17 June 1878)

Desiderius ERASMUS (1466/7–1536): Dutch scholar

620 In the midst stood Prince Henry, who showed already something of royalty in his demeanour, in which there was a certain dignity combined with singular courtesy.

(On first meeting the future Henry VIII, aged 8, at Eltham Palace, 1499)

621 How then is peace to be secured? . . . Let a king recall that to improve his realm is better than to increase his territory . . . Let the clergy absent themselves from silly parades and refuse Christian burial to those who die in battle. If we must fight, why not go against the common enemy, the Turk? But wait. Is not the Turk also a man and a brother?

(*Querela Pacis*, July 1517)

622 We have no right to despise the discoveries or improvements which have originated in the minds of our contemporaries; yet it is an unscrupulous intellect that does not pay to antiquity its due reverence . . . There are many kinds of genius; each age has its different gifts.

(Preface to his edition of *Works of Hilary*, 5 January 1523)

623 I replied that I wished to be a citizen of the world, not of a single city.

(Letter to Laurimus describing how he refused Zwingli's suggestion that he should be made a citizen of Zurich, 1 February 1523)

Robert Devereux, second Earl of ESSEX (1566–1601): Elizabethan soldier and courtier [see also 82, 218, 224]

624 I was never proud till you sought to make me too base. And now, since my destiny is no better, my despair shall be like my love was, without repentance.

(Letter to Elizabeth I after a quarrel in which she had boxed his ears, August 1598)

Robert Devereux, third Earl of ESSEX (1591–1646): soldier and supporter of the Parliamentarian cause

625 Stone dead hath no fellow.

(In conversation with Clarendon 'walking in the bowling-green at Piccadilly', of the bill of attainder on Strafford: 26 April 1641)

John EVELYN (1620–1706): English diarist

626 This fatal night about ten, began that deplorable fire near Fish Street in London ... oh the miserable and calamitous spectacle, such as happly the whole world had not seen the like since the foundation of it ... all the sky were of a fiery aspect, like the top of a burning Oven, and the light seen above 40 miles round about for many nights.

(Diary, 2/3 September 1666)

627 [Charles II] took delight to have a number of little spaniels follow him, and lie in his bed-chamber, where often times he suffered the bitches to puppy and give suck, which rendered it very offensive.

(Entry in Diary, after the death of Charles II, 4 February 1685)

628 The French persecution ... raging with the utmost barbarity, exceeded even what the very heathen us'd ... on a sudden demolishing all their churches, banishing, imprisoning and sending to the galleys all the ministers; plundering the common people ... taking away their children; forcing people to the Mass, and then executing them as relapsers; they burned their libraries ... and eat up their fields and substance.

(Of Louis XIV's persecution of the Huguenots, 3 November 1685)

629 [James II] brought people to so desperate a pass as with utmost expressions even passionately seen to long for and desire the landing of that Prince, whom they looked on as their deliverer from Popish tyranny, praying incessantly for an Easterly wind . . .

(Diary, 6 October 1688)

630 She came into Whitehall laughing and jolly, as to a wedding, so as to seem quite transported.

(Of Mary II's arrival in London; Diary, 21 February 1689: cf. Burnet, no. 252)

631 I went to Deptford to view how miserably the tzar of Moscovy [Peter the Great] had left my house after 3 months making it his court, having gotten Sir Christopher Wren his Majesty's Surveyor and Mr London his Gardner to go down and make an estimate of the repairs, for which they allowed 150 pounds.

(Diary, 9 June 1698)

Robert FABYAN (?–1511/12): English chronicler

632 This year, that is to mean ye 18 day of February, the Duke of Clarence and [second] brother to the king, then being prisoner in ye Tower, was secretly put to death and drowned in a barrel of malvesye within the said Tower.

(*Chronicle, 1478: also found in Chronicles of London – but unlikely)

Erich von FALKENHAYN (1861–1922): German General

633 There are objectives within our reach . . . for the retention of which the French General Staff would be forced to throw in every man they have. If they do so the forces of France will be bled to death, since there can be no question of a voluntary withdrawal, whether or not we reach our goal . . . The objectives of which I speak are Belfort and Verdun . . . The preference must be given to Verdun.

(Memorandum for Kaiser William II, early December 1915)

Lucius Cary, Viscount FALKLAND (1610–43): English politician and soldier
[see also 402]

634 When it is not necessary to change, it is necessary not to change.

(Speech, concerning Episcopacy, H of C, 22 November 1641)

Guy FAWKES (?–1606): conspirator
[see also 453, 900, 932]

635 Being thus taken in the fact, he both confessed and defended it; adding, 'That, if he had happened to be within the house, as he was without, he would, by putting fire to the train, have put an end to their inquiry'.

(*Attributed, at his arrest, 5 November 1605)

François de la Mothe-FÉNELON (1651–1715): Archbishop of Cambrai

636 Your peoples die of hunger. Agriculture is almost stationary, industry languishes everywhere, all commerce is destroyed. France is a vast hospital . . . It is you who have caused all this distress . . . Your victories no longer cause rejoicing. There is only bitterness and despair . . . You relate everything to yourself as though you were God on earth.

(*Lettre secrète à Louis XIV*, 1694(?)-5)

FERDINAND I (1503–64): Holy Roman Emperor

637 *Fiat justitia, et pereat mundus* [Let justice be done, though the world perish].

(Motto adopted in the early 1530s)

H. A. L. FISHER (1865–1940): English historian and Liberal politician

638 One intellectual excitement has . . . been denied me. Men wiser and more learned than I have discerned in history a plot, a rhythm, a predetermined pattern. These harmonies are concealed from me. I can see only one emergency following upon another as wave follows upon wave, only one great fact with respect to which, since it is unique, there can be no generalisations, only one safe rule for the historian: that he should recognize in the development of human destinies the play of the contingent and the unforeseen.

(Preface, *History of Europe*, 1935)

John FISHER (1469–1535): Bishop of Rochester

639 My lords, you see clearly what bills come hither from the Common House, and all is to the destruction of the Church . . . For God's sake, see what a realm the kingdom of Bohemia was, and when the Church went down, then fell the glory of the kingdom. Now, with the Commons is nothing but down with the Church!

(Speech, H of L, 1529)

Ferdinand FOCH (1851–1929): Marshal of France

640 My right gives way. My centre yields. Situation excellent. I shall attack.

(*Alleged message to General Joffre during Battle of Marne, September 1914)

Gerald FORD (b. 1913): thirty-seventh President of the USA

641 Truth is the glue that holds our government together . . . Our long national nightmare is over. Our constitution works.

(Speech on being sworn in as President after the resignation of Nixon because of the Watergate affair, 9 August 1974)

642 I am a Ford not a Lincoln.

(During Presidential campaign, 1976)

643 There is no Soviet domination of Eastern Europe and there never will be under a Ford administration.

(6 October 1976: in television debate with Carter)

Henry FORD (1863–1947): American industrialist

644 History is bunk.

(Giving evidence in a libel action against the *Chicago Tribune* at the Court House in Mt Clemens, Illinois, July 1919)

Sir George Eulas FOSTER (1847–1931): Canadian politician

645 In these somewhat troublesome days when the great Mother Empire stands splendidly isolated in Europe.

(Speech, Canadian H of C, 16 January 1896)

Joseph FOUCHÉ (1759–1820): Napoleon's Minister of Police [see also 356, 1757]

646 It was worse than a crime: it was a mistake.

(Comment on the execution of the abducted royalist émigré, the Duc d'Enghien, at Vincennes, 21 March 1804)

Charles James FOX (1744–1806): Leader of the English Whigs [see also 237, 709, 998, 1866]

647 Kings govern by popular assemblies only when they cannot do without them.

(Speech, H of C, 31 October 1776)

648 He was uniformly of an opinion which, though not a popular one, he was ready to aver, that the right of governing was not a property, but a trust.

(April 1785, on Pitt's scheme of Parliamentary Reform)

649 How much the greatest event it is that ever happened in the world! And how much the best!

(Letter to Richard Fitzpatrick on the fall of the Bastille, 30 July 1789)

650 The worst of revolutions is a restoration.

(Speech, H of C, 10 December 1785)

651 Is peace a rash system? Is it dangerous for nations to live in amity with each other? . . . Must the bowels of Great Britain be torn out – her best blood be spilt – her treasure wasted – that you may make an experiment? Put yourselves – oh! that you would put yourselves – in the field of battle, and learn to judge of the sort of horrors that you excite.

(Speech in favour of a peace with France, H of C, 3 February 1800)

George FOX (1624–91): Founder of Quakers

652 O Oliver, hadst thou been faithful . . . the King of France should have bowed his neck under thee, the Pope should have withered as in winter, the Turk in all his fatness should have smoked.

(To Cromwell, 1654/7)

653 Had you been faithful to the power of the Lord God which first carried you on, you had gone into the midst of Spain into their land, to require the blood of the innocent that there had been shed, and commanded them to have offered up their Inquisition to you, and gone over them as the wind, and knocked at Rome's gates before now, and trampled deceit and tyrants under.

(Letter to Council of officers of the Army and heads of the Nation against the cashiering of Quakers, 1657)

FRANCIS I (1494–1547): King of France

654 Out of all I had only honour remains, and my life, which is safe.

(Letter to his mother after losing the Battle of Pavia, February 1525: usually quoted as 'All is lost save honour – *Tout est perdu fors l'honneur*')

FRANCIS I (1768–1835): Austrian Emperor

655 But is he a patriot for me?

(Remark on being told of the patriotic qualities of a candidate for high office, *c.* 1821)

St FRANCIS of Assisi (1181/2–1226): founder of the Franciscan Order

656 My Lord, if we possessed property, we should have need of arms for its defence, for it is the source of quarrels and lawsuits, and the love of God and of one's neighbour usually finds many obstacles therein.

(To the Bishop of Assisi, ?1209/10)

657 Let the friars take care not to appear gloomy or as sad as hypocrites but rather let them be jovial and merry, showing that they rejoice in the Lord, and let them be pleasantly courteous.

(Injunction for the early brethren of Assisi, later adapted in modified form for the Franciscan rule, 1210?/11)

658 My lord, my brethren have been styled Lesser, that they may not presume to become Greater ... I pray you by no means let them rise to high office, lest their pride should be proportionate to their poverty and they should wax arrogant against the rest.

(To Cardinal Ugolino, later Pope Gregory IX, who wished him to unite his followers with the Dominican friars, ?1218)

659 If any of our ministers should give to any brother an order that is contrary to our life or his conscience, that brother is not bound to obey him.

(3rd Admonition, 1221)

FRANCIS JOSEPH (1830–1916): Emperor of Austria, King of Hungary

660 Nothing has been spared me in this world.

(On learning of the assassination of the Empress Elizabeth at Geneva, 10 September 1898)

661 You see in me the last monarch of the old school.

(In conversation with Theodore Roosevelt, 1910)

Benjamin   FRANKLIN (1706–90): American scientist and diplomat

662 Some punishment seems preparing for a People who are so ungratefully abusing the best Constitution and the best King any nation was ever blessed with.

(Comment while in London during the Wilkes riots of May 1768)

663 There never was a good war or a bad peace.

(Letter from England to Josiah Quincy, 11 September 1773)

664 We must indeed all hang together, or most assuredly, we shall all hang separately.

(To John Hancock, at signing of the Declaration of Independence, 4 July 1776)

665 But in this world nothing can be said to be certain, except death and taxes.

(Letter to Jean Baptiste Le Roy, 13 November 1789)

FREDERICK I (Barbarossa) (1122–90): Holy Roman Emperor

666 Will you know where the ancient glory of your Rome, the gravity of your senate ... the stainless and invincible courage in the conflict have gone? Look at our state. All these things are with us Germans. With us are your consuls, with us your senate, with us your soldiery.

(To envoys from the Senate of Rome after an anti-Papal revolution, 1155)

FREDERICK II (1194–1250): Holy Roman Emperor

667 We keep the students within view of their parents; we save them many toils and long foreign journeys; we protect them from robbers. They used to be pillaged while travelling abroad; now, they may study at small cost and short wayfaring, thanks to our liberality.

(Charter of foundation of the University of Naples, July 1224)

668 Our work is to present things that are as they are.

(Preface to *De Arte Venandi cum Avibus*, completed between 1244 and 1250)

FREDERICK II (1712–86): King of Prussia [see also 892, 1149, 1636]

669 It is a political error to practise deceit, if deceit is carried too far.

(*Antimachiavel*, 1740)

670 A crown is merely a hat that lets the rain in.

(Remark made in declining a formal coronation, 1740)

671 Gentlemen, I have no allies save your valour and your goodwill ... Our cause is just ... Farewell until we achieve the rendezvous with glory which awaits us.

(To his generals, 12 December 1740)

672 Rogues, would you live for ever?

(Rallying a Guard battalion, Kolin, 18 June 1757)

673 [Of George II of England and Frederick William I of Prussia] Although brothers-in-law, they could never abide each other even when children. The King of England used to style the King of Prussia, 'My brother the Sergeant' and the King of Prussia would call the King of England 'My brother the Dancing Master'.

(*Oeuvres*)

674 [Of George III] The King of England changes his ministers as often as he changes his shirts.

(Comment, 1783)

675 I was born much too soon, but I do not regret it: I have seen Voltaire.

(Remark, ?1778)

FREDERICK III (1415–93): Holy Roman Emperor

676 A.E.I.O.U. (*Alles Erdreich ist Oesterreich Untertan; Austria est Imperare Orbi Universo*) [The whole world is subject to Austria]

(Imperial motto, inscribed in books and on public buildings)

FREDERICK WILLIAM IV (1795–1861): King of Prussia

677 Henceforth Prussia merges into Germany.

(Proclamation in response to nationalistic revolutionary pressure, Berlin, 21 March 1848)

Hugh GAITSKELL (1906–63): Leader of British Labour Party

678 There are some of us, Mr Chairman, who will fight, fight and fight again to save the Party we love.

(Labour Party Conference, Blackpool, 5 October 1960)

679 Let us not forget that we can never go farther than we can persuade at least half of the people to go.

(Speech, Labour Party Conference, Brighton, 3 October 1961)

Galileo GALILEI (1564–1642): Italian scientist

680 Here I shall say what was agreed on by an ecclesiastic of the highest rank [note: Cardinal Baronio] – that it is the Holy Spirit's intention to teach us how to go to heaven, not how the heavens go.

(Letter to Cristina di Lorena, Grandduchess of Tuscany, 1615)

681 [I am blamed because] in my studies of astronomy and philosophy I hold this opinion about the universe, that the Sun remains fixed in the centre of the circle of heavenly bodies, without changing its place; and the Earth, turning upon itself, moves round the Sun.

(Ibid.)

682 It is not in the power of professors of demonstrative sciences to change their opinions at pleasure, and adopt first one side

and then the other ... no man doubts that his Holiness hath always an absolute power of admitting or condemning them [i.e. opinions of scientists] but it is not in the power of any creature to make them to be true or false, otherwise than as, in fact, they are.

(Ibid.)

683 Yet it does move [*E pur si muove*].

(*1632: no evidence of this saying before 1734)

Leopoldo GALTIERI (b. 1924): General, President of the Argentine Republic

684 Why are you telling me this? The British won't fight.

(In conversation with the US Secretary of State, Alexander Haig, 10 April 1982)

Léon GAMBETTA (1838–82): French radical leader

685 Let us never speak of it to the foreigner but see to it that he understands we think of it always.

(Speech at St Quentin, on the loss of Alsace-Lorraine to Germany, September 1871)

686 Clericalism – there is the enemy.

(Speech, Chamber of Deputies, 5 May 1877)

Indira GANDHI (1917–84): Indian Prime Minister

687 Even if I died in the service of the nation, I would be proud of it. Every drop of my blood, I am sure, will contribute to the growth of this nation and to make it strong and dynamic.

(Speaking in Delhi on 30 October 1984, the day before her assassination)

Mohandas Karamchand GANDHI (1869–1948): Indian Nationalist leader, and pacifist [see also 378, 466]

688 A post-dated cheque on a crashing bank.

(Comment on the British proposal that India would have an assembly with powers to draft a constitution, once the war was over – the abortive 'Cripps Mission' – March 1942)

689 Non-violence is not a garment to be put on and off at will. Its seat is in the heart and it must be an inseparable part of our very being.

(*Non-violence in War and Peace*, published posthumously, 1948)

James   A.   GARFIELD
(1831–81): twentieth President of
the USA

690 God reigns and the Government at Washington lives.

(Impromptu speech, as a
Congressman, to calm a crowd in
New York alarmed by the news of
Lincoln's assassination, April
1865)

691 My God! What is there in
this place that a man should ever
want to get in it?

(On White House, a few months
after his inauguration on 4
March 1881)

Giuseppe   GARIBALDI
(1807–82): Italian revolutionary
General and patriotic leader

692 I offer neither pay, nor
quarters, nor food; I offer only
hunger, thirst, forced marches,
battles and death. Let him who
loves his country with his heart,
and not merely with his lips,
follow me.

(Speech to the Garibaldi legion
besieged in Rome, 2 July 1849)

693 England is a great and powerful nation, foremost in human
progress, enemy to despotism,
the only safe refuge for the exile,
friend of the oppressed. If ever
England should be so circum-
stanced as to require the help of
an ally, cursed be the Italian who

would not step forward with me
in her defence.

(Letter to Joseph Cowen on
leaving Newcastle upon Tyne, 12
April 1854)

William Lloyd GARRISON
(1805–79): American slave abolitionist

694 I am in earnest – I will not
equivocate – I will not excuse – I
will not retreat a single inch – and
I will be heard!

(Salutatory address of *The
Liberator*, 1 January 1831)

695 Our country is the world –
our countrymen are all mankind.

(Prospectus of *The Liberator*, 15
December 1837)

696 The compact which exists
between the North and the South
is 'a covenant with death and an
agreement with hell'.

(Resolution adopted by
Massachusetts Anti-Slavery
Society, 27 January 1843)

Mrs Elizabeth GASKELL
(1810–65): English novelist

697 Numbers of [English]
people have *faith* in the North [in
the American Civil War]; but
cannot tell how to reply to questions based upon the weekday
bible, as *The Times* is sometimes
called.

(Letter to Charles E. Norton,
Professor of the History of Art at
Harvard, 4 July 1864)

698 My heart burnt within me
with indignation and grief; we
could think of nothing else . . . All
night long we had only snatches
of sleep, waking up perpetually to
the sense of a great shock and
grief. Every one is feeling the
same. I never knew so universal a
feeling . . . We do so want to
know what Johnson is really like.

(Letter to C.E. Norton, when the
news reached England of
Lincoln's assassination, 28 April
1865)

[Charles de Gaulle, *see* **DE
GAULLE]**

John GAULE (*flor.* 1640s–60s):
Vicar of Great Stoughton, Huntingdonshire

699 Every old woman with a
wrinkled face, a furr'd brow, a
hairy lip, a gobber tooth, a squint
eye, a squeaking voice, or a scold-
ing tongue . . . a dog or cat by her
side, is not only suspected but
pronounced for a witch.

(*Sermons on Witchcraft*, against the
activities of Matthew Hopkins,
q.v., 30 June 1646)

Sir Eric GEDDES (1875–1937):
British Conservative politician

700 We will get out of her [Ger-
many] all you can squeeze out of a
lemon and a bit more . . . I will
squeeze her until you can hear
the pips squeak . . . I would strip
Germany as she has stripped Belgium.

(Speech at the Guildhall,
Cambridge, 9 December 1918)

GENGHIS KHAN (?1155–
1227): Khan of Mongols

701 It is forbidden ever to make
peace with a monarch, a prince or
a people who have not submitted
. . .
Every man who does not go to
war must work for the empire,
without reward, for a certain time
. . .
No subject of the empire may
take a Mongol for servant or
slave. Every man, with rare ex-
ceptions, must join the army.

(*Laws*, ?1206)

702 The words of the lad Kublai
are well worth attention; see all of
you, that ye heed what he says!
One day he will sit in my seat and
bring you good fortune such as
you have had in my day.

(*On his deathbed, 1227)

Friedrich von GENTZ
(1764–1832): Austrian bureaucrat and publicist

703 The end of the Turkish monarchy could be survived by the Austrian for only a short time.

(Memorandum for Metternich, October 1814)

704 Metternich and Talleyrand held forth in their usual way, while I sensed as never before the futility of human endeavour, the failings of men who hold the fate of the world in their hands ... The fine-sounding nonsense of these gentlemen enveloped my mind in a fog of unreality.

(Diary, 12 January 1815, after entertaining to dinner the chief delegates to the Congress of Vienna)

GEORGE II (1683–1760): King of England
[see also 673]

705 [of Wolfe] Oh! He is mad, is he? Then I wish he would *bite* some other of my generals.

(*Reply to anonymous criticism of General Wolfe, ?1758)

706 No, I shall have mistresses [*Non, j'aurai des maîtresses*].

(Reply to his wife, Caroline of Anspach who, as she lay dying, advised him to marry again. Her own response is said to have been 'Heavens! That is no obstacle' [*Ah, mon Dieu! Cela n'empêche pas*]. The episode was recorded

by the Vice-Chamberlain of the Court, Lord Hervey, 1737)

GEORGE III (1738–1820): King of England
[see also 94, 254, 255, 662, 674, 809, 1690, 1857]

707 Born and educated in this country I glory in the name of Briton.

(First speech from the throne, 18 November 1760, printed version: manuscript says 'Britain')

708 Bloodshed is not what I delight in but it seems to me the only way of restoring a due obedience to the laws.

(Letter to Lord North, 10 May 1768)

709 [of C. J. Fox] That young man has so thoroughly cast off every principle of common honour and honesty, that he must become as contemptible as he is odious.

(Letter to Lord North, 16 February 1774)

710 I know that I am doing my duty and therefore can never wish to retract.

(Letter to Lord North, 26 July 1775)

711 I will rather risk my Crown than do what I think personally disgraceful, and whilst I have no wish but for the good and prosperity of my country, it is impossible that the nation shall not stand by me; if they will not, they shall have another King.

(To Lord North, 17 March 1778)

712 Experience has thoroughly convinced me that the Country gains nothing by granting to Her Dependencies indulgencies, for opening the Door encourages a desire for more which if not complied with causes discontent, and the former benefit is obliterated.

(Letter to Lord North, 12 November 1778)

713 I can never suppose this country so far lost to all ideas of self-importance as to be willing to grant America independence; if that could ever be adopted I shall despair of this country being ever preserved from a state of inferiority and consequently falling into a very low class among the European States.

(Letter to Lord North, 7 March 1780)

714 I cannot conclude without mentioning how sensibly I feel the dismemberment of America from this Empire, and that I should be miserable indeed if I did not feel that no blame on that account can be laid at my door, and did I not also know that knavery seems to be so much the

striking feature of its inhabitants that it may not in the end be an evil that they will become aliens to this Kingdom.

(Letter to Shelburne, 10 November 1782)

715 I was the last to consent to the separation, but the separation having been made and having become inevitable, I have always said that I would be the first to meet the friendship of the United States as an independent power.

(To John Adams, first ambassador from USA, 1 June 1785)

716 I never assent till I am convinced what is proposed is right, and then ... I never allow that to be destroyed by after-thoughts which on all subjects tend to weaken, never to strengthen, the original proposal.

(To the younger Pitt, 2 March 1797)

717 Should the implacable enemy so far succeed as to land, you will have an opportunity of showing your zeal at the head of your regiment. It will be the duty of every man to stand forward on such an occasion; and I shall certainly think it mine to set an example in defence of every thing that is dear to me and my people.

(Letter to the Prince of Wales, later George VI, when a

Napoleonic invasion seemed imminent, 7 August 1803)

GEORGE IV (1762–1830):
King of England
[see also 76, 209, 295, 460, 912]

718 Harris, I am not well, pray get me a glass of brandy.

(To James Harris, Lord Malmesbury, after first meeting Caroline of Brunswick, 5 April 1795, three days before their marriage)

719 I rejoice . . . at the great and glorious news from Russia of which I have, under Providence, the heartfelt consolation, without unbecoming vanity, to ascribe in a great degree to my own original and indefatigable endeavours in drawing that Power to those measures which have since been pursued.

(Private letter to his mother, Queen Charlotte, on news of Napoleon's retreat from Moscow, 6 December 1812)

720 Though I have now lived a good many years in the world, still I never thought that I should have lived to witness so much prevarication, so much lying, and so much wilful and convenient forgetfulness.

(Letter to the Duke of York, 7 October 1820, commenting on the evidence presented in Parliament on the personal conduct of his wife, Caroline)

721 No foreign dances. I dislike seeing anything in Scotland that is not purely national and characteristic.

(Instructions for the Caledonian Hunt Ball, August 1822)

722 . . . This untoward event . . .

(King's speech at opening of Parliament, 29 January 1828, written by the Prime Minister, Wellington, regretting the Russo-French-British naval action against the Turks at Navarino three months previously)

GEORGE V (1865–1936): King of England
[see also 1943, 1944]

723 I venture to allude to the impression which seemed generally to prevail among our brethren overseas, that the Old Country must wake up if she intends to maintain her old position of pre-eminence in her Colonial trade against foreign competitors.

(Speech, as Prince of Wales, after a tour of the Empire, Guildhall, London, 5 December 1901. The speech was reported in the popular Press under the headline 'Wake up, England!')

724 Prince Henry of Prussia [brother of Kaiser William II] came to see me ... He asked what England would do if there was a European war. I said 'I don't know what we shall do, we have no quarrel with anyone & I hope we shall remain neutral'. But if Germany declared war on Russia, & France joins Russia, then I am afraid we shall be dragged into it. But you can be sure that I & my Government will do all we can to prevent a European war.

(26 July 1914: note in Royal Archives, printed in H. Nicolson, *King George V*)

725 My God, Mr Page, what else could we do?

(In conversation with the American ambassador, Walter Page, two days after the declaration of war against Germany, 6 August 1914)

726 Today 23 years ago dear Grandmama [Queen Victoria] died. I wonder what she would have thought of a Labour Government.

(Diary entry, 22 January 1924, having invited Ramsay Macdonald to form the first Labour Government at noon)

727 If I may be regarded as in some true sense the head of this great family, sharing its life and

sustained by its affection, this will be a full reward for the long and sometimes anxious labours of my reign.

(Christmas Day broadcast, 1934)

728 I will not have another war ... If there is another one and we are threatened with being brought into it, I will go to Trafalgar Square and wave a red flag myself sooner than allow this country to be brought in.

(To Lloyd George in conversation: 10 May 1935)

729 After I am dead the boy will ruin himself in twelve months.

(In conversation about the future Edward VIII with Baldwin in 1935 as cited by Middlemas and Barnes, *Baldwin*)

GEORGE VI (1895–1952): King of England

730 The British Empire has advanced to a new conception of autonomy and freedom, to the idea of a system of British nations, each freely ordering its own individual life, but bound together in unity by allegiance to one Crown and co-operating in all that concerns the common weal.

(Speech, as Duke of York, at the opening of the first Australian Parliament to meet in Canberra, 9 May 1927)

731 London ... that Mother City of the Commonwealth which is proving herself to be built as a city at unity with itself. It is not the walls that make the city, but the people who live within them. The walls of London may be battered, but the spirit of the Londoner stands resolute and undismayed.

(Broadcast to the Empire during the German bomber offensive against London, 23 September 1940)

David Lloyd GEORGE (1863–1945): British Liberal politician and Coalition Prime Minister

732 Four spectres haunt the Poor – Old Age, Accident, Sickness and Unemployment. We are going to exorcise them. We are going to drive hunger from the hearth. We mean to banish the workhouse from the horizon of every workman in the land.

(Speech, Reading, Berkshire, 1 January 1910)

733 The House of Lords is not the watchdog of the constitution: it is Mr Balfour's poodle. It fetches and carries for him. It barks for him. It bites anybody that he sets it on to!

(Speech, H of C, 21 December 1908)

734 The Landlord is a gentleman ... who does not earn his wealth. He has a host of agents and clerks that receive for him. He does not even take the trouble to *spend* his wealth. He has a host of people around him to do the actual spending. He never sees it until he comes to enjoy it. His sole function, his chief pride, is the stately consumption of wealth produced by others.

(Speech on behalf of the 'People's Budget', Limehouse, 30 July 1909)

735 We are placing the burdens on the broadest shoulders ... I made up my mind that, in framing my Budget, no cupboard should be barer, no lot should be harder to bear.

(Ibid.)

736 A fully equipped duke costs as much to keep up as two Dreadnoughts; and dukes are just as great a terror and they last longer.

(Speech, Newcastle upon Tyne, 9 October 1909)

737 If a situation were to be forced upon us, in which peace could only be preserved by the surrender of the great and beneficent position Britain has won by centuries of heroism and achievement, by allowing Britain to be treated, where her interests were vitally affected, as if she were of no account in the Cabinet of Nations, then I say emphatically that peace at that price would be a humiliation intolerable for a great country like ours to endure.

(Speech, as Chancellor of the Exchequer, Mansion House, London, during the Agadir Crisis, 21 July 1911)

738 We have been too comfortable and too indulgent – many, perhaps, too selfish – and the stern hand of fate has scourged us to an elevation where we can see the great everlasting things which matter for a nation – the great peaks we had forgotten, of Honour, Duty, Patriotism, and clad in glittering white, the great pinnacle of Sacrifice pointing like a rugged finger to Heaven. We shall descend into the valleys again, but as long as men and women of this generation last, they will carry in their hearts the image of those great mountain peaks whose foundations are not shaken, though Europe rock and sway in the convulsions of a great war.

(Speech, Queen's Hall, London, 19 September 1914)

739 Diplomats were invented simply to waste time.

(Comment on preparations for the Peace Conference, November 1918)

740 What is our task? To make Britain a fit country for heroes to live in.

(Speech, Wolverhampton, 24 November 1918)

741 I should like to put each Member of this House under an examination. I am certain that I could not have passed it before I went to the Peace Conference. How many Members have heard of Teschen? I do not mind saying that I had never heard of it, but Teschen very nearly produced an angry conflict between two Allied States and we had to interrupt the proceedings to try and settle the affairs of Teschen.

(Speech, H of C, 16 April 1919)

742 I do not claim that the treaty [of Versailles] is perfect in all respects. Where it is not perfect, I look forward to the organisation of the League of Nations to remedy, to repair, and redress.

(Speech, H of C, 21 July 1919)

743 Without Russia, these three guarantees to Poland, to Roumania and to Greece are the most reckless commitments that any country has ever entered into. I will say more. They are demented pledges that cannot be redeemed with this enormous deficiency, this great gap between the forces arrayed on the other side and the forces which at the present moment we could put in.

(Speech, H of C, 8 May 1939)

744 It is the old trouble – too late in dealing with Czechoslovakia, too late with Poland, and certainly too late with Finland ... It is always too late, or too little, or both. That is the road to disaster.

(Speech criticizing Chamberlain Government, H of C, 13 March 1940)

Sir Humphrey GILBERT (1537[?1539]–83): English seaman and explorer

745 We are as near to heaven by sea as by land.

(During a storm on his last, and fatal, voyage back from Newfoundland, September 1583)

James GILLRAY (1757–1815): English political cartoonist

746 Political Ravishment, or The Old Lady of Threadneedle Street in Danger.

(Title of caricature about the Bank of England, February 1797)

William Ewart GLADSTONE (1809–98): British Liberal Prime Minister
[see also 363, 559, 562, 1043, 1144, 1373, 1847]

747 I, for my part, am of opinion that England will stand shorn of a chief part of her glory and her pride if she will be found to have separated herself, through the policy she preserves abroad, from the moral supports which the general and fixed convictions of mankind afford – if the day shall come in which she may continue to excite the wonder and the fear of other nations, but in which she shall have no part in their affection and their regard.

(Speech, in Don Pacifico debate, H of C, 27 June 1850)

748 It was in the Greek debate [Don Pacifico] of 1850, which involved the censure or acquittal of Lord Palmerston, that I first meddled in speech with foreign affairs, to which I had heretofore paid the slightest possible attention.

(Autobiographical note of 1897 included in Morley's *Gladstone*, Vol. 1)

749 This is the negation of God erected into a system of Government.

(First *Letter to Earl of Aberdeen on State Persecutions of Neapolitan Government*, 1851)

750 The best resistance to be offered to Russia is by the strength and freedom of those countries that will have to resist her. You want to place a living barrier between her and Turkey. There is no barrier like the breasts of freemen.

(Speech, H of C, 4 May 1858)

751 We may have our own opinions about slavery; we may be for or against the South; but there is no doubt that Jefferson Davis and other leaders of the South have made an army; they are making, it appears, a navy; and they have made what is more than either, they have made a nation.

(Speech, Newcastle upon Tyne, 7 October 1862)

752 I contend . . . that it is upon those who say it is necessary to exclude forty-nine fiftieths of the working classes [from the vote] . . . to show cause, and I venture to say that every man who is not presumably incapacitated by some consideration of personal unfitness or of political danger, is morally entitled to come within the pale of the constitution.

(Speech on Private Members' Bill for franchise reform, H of C, 11 May 1864)

753 You cannot fight against the future. Time is on our side.

(Speech on Reform Bill, H of C, 27 April 1866)

754 My mission is to pacify Ireland.

(Comment on receiving telegram at Hawarden indicating he was to form a government, 1 December 1868)

755 Let the Turks now carry away their abuses in the only possible manner, namely by carrying off themselves. Their Zaptiehs and their Mudirs, their Bimbashis and their Yuzbachis, their Kaimakans and their Pashas, one and all, bag and baggage, shall, I hope, clear out from the province they have desolated and profaned.

(Pamphlet, *The Bulgarian Horrors and the Question of the East,* published 6 September 1876)

756 Remember the rights of the savage, as we call him. Remember that the happiness of his humble home, remember that the sanctity of life in the hill villages of Afghanistan, among the winter snows, is as inviolable in the eye of Almighty God, as can be your own.

(Speech, Dalkeith, 26 November 1879)

757 The foreign policy of England should always be inspired by the love of freedom. There should be a sympathy with freedom, a desire to give it scope, founded not upon visionary ideas, but upon the long experience of many generations within the shores of this happy isle, that in freedom you lay the firmest foundations both of loyalty and order.

(Speech, West Calder, 27 November 1879)

758 If it shall appear that there is still to be fought a final conflict in Ireland between law on the one side and sheer lawlessness upon the other, if the law purged from defect and from any taint of injustice is still to be repelled and refused, and the first conditions of political society to remain unfulfilled, then I say, gentlemen, without hesitation, the resources of civilization against its enemies are not yet exhausted.

(Speech, Cloth Hall, Leeds, 8 October 1881)

759 All the world over, I will back the masses against the classes.

(Speech, Liverpool, 28 June 1886)

760 Oxford had not taught me, nor had any other place or person, the value of liberty as an essential condition of excellence in human things.

(Autobiographical note written in 1894 but referring to the late 1830s)

William Henry, Duke of GLOUCESTER (1743–1805): brother of King George III

761 Another damned, thick, square book! Always scribble, scribble, scribble! Eh! Mr Gibbon?

(To the historian, Edward Gibbon, ?1776)

Martin H. GLYNN (1891–1924): Governor of New York State

762 He kept us out of war!

(Speech praising Woodrow Wilson, Democratic National Convention, St Louis, 15 June 1916)

Joseph GOEBBELS (1897–1945): German Nazi Minister of Propaganda

763 Should the German people lay down arms, the Soviets ... would occupy all eastern and south-eastern Europe together with the greater part of the Reich. Over all this territory, which with the Soviet Union included, would be of enormous extent, an iron curtain [*ein eiserner Vorhang*] would at once descend.

(Article in Nazi propaganda weekly, *Das Reich*, 23 February 1945)

Hermann GOERING (1893–1946): German Nazi politician and Air Marshal

764 Our movement took a grip on cowardly Marxism and from it

extracted the meaning of socialism. It also took from the cowardly middle-class parties their
nationalism. Throwing both into
the cauldron of our way of life
there emerged, as clear as a crystal, the synthesis – German
National Socialism.

(Speech, Sports Palast, Berlin, 9
April 1933)

765 Our leader [Hitler] said in
Nuremberg, '. . . We have made
human beings once more of millions of people who were in
misery . . .' Anyone who will not
deny himself a pound of butter
for that is not worthy to be a
German.

(Speech on the Nazi Four Year
Plan, Sports Palast, Berlin, 28
October 1936)

766 Guns will make us powerful;
butter will only make us fat.

(*Alleged statement in a radio
broadcast on the Four Year Plan,
1936, probably based on the
phrases in 765)

**Johann   Wolfgang   von
GOETHE**   (1749–1832):
German man of letters

767 [Of Napoleon I] His life was
the stride of a demigod.

(Comment, 1828)

Oliver   GOLDSMITH
(?1730–74): Anglo-Irish writer

768 It is probable we shall hear
Russia, in future times, as formerly, called the officina gen-
tium. It was long the wish of
Peter, their great monarch, to
have a fort in some of the western
parts of Europe . . . A fort in the
power of this people would be
like the possession of a floodgate;
and whenever ambition, interest,
or necessity prompted, they might
then be able to deluge the whole
western world with a barbarous
inundation.

(A 'Chinese Letter' contributed
to the *Public Ledger*, 31 October
1760, and republished in *The
Citizen of the World*, 1762)

Barry   GOLDWATER   (b.
1909): US Senator

769 Extremism in the defense of
liberty is no vice. And . . . moderation in the pursuit of justice is
no virtue.

(Speech accepting Presidential
nomination, Republican National
Convention, Cow Palace, San
Francisco, 16 July 1964)

George   Peabody   GOOCH
(1873–1968): English historian
and Liberal MP

770 We can now look forward
with something like confidence to
the time when war between civil-

ized nations will be considered as antiquated as a duel.

(*History of Our Time*, 1911)

Godfrey   GOODMAN (1583–1656): Bishop of Gloucester

771 [Of James I and his consort, Anne of Denmark] They did love as well as man and wife could do, not conversing together.

(*The Court of King James I: c.* 1640)

George Joachim (Lord) GOSCHEN (1831–1907): English Conservative politician [see also 364]

772 We have stood alone in that which is called isolation – our splendid isolation, as one of our colonial friends was good enough to call it.

(Speech, Lewes, 26 February 1896, cf. 645)

Ulysses S. GRANT (1822–85): General and eighteenth President of the USA

773 No terms except an unconditional and immediate surrender can be accepted.

(To General Buckner, whom he was besieging at Fort Donelson, Tennessee, 16 February 1862)

774 What General Lee's feelings were I do not know ... My own feelings, which had been quite jubilant ... were sad and depressing. I felt like anything rather than rejoicing at the downfall of a foe who had fought so long and gallantly ... The much talked of surrendering of Lee's sword and my handing it back, this and much more that has been said about it is the purest romance.

(Description of Lee's surrender at Appomattox, 9 April 1865, *Personal Memoirs of Ulysses S. Grant*, written 1885)

775 I know no method to secure the repeal of bad or obnoxious laws so effective as their stringent execution.

(Inaugural Address, 4 March 1869)

776 Let no guilty man escape, if it can be avoided ... No personal considerations should stand in the way of performing a public duty.

(Endorsement of a letter relating to the Whiskey Ring, 29 July 1875)

777 I feel we are on the eve of a new era, when there is to be great harmony between the Federal and the Confederate.

(Written in the last week of his life, July 1885, *Personal Memoirs of Ulysses S. Grant*)

GREGORY VII (?1020–85): Pope

778 Suddenly, while our late master the pope was being carried to his tomb in the Saviour's church, there arose a great confusion and shouting of the people; and they rushed upon me like madmen, leaving me no opportunity or time to speak or take advice. They dragged me with violent hands to the place of apostolic rule, for which I am so unfitted.

(Letters to Wibert of Ravenna and Desiderius of Casino, recounting his election to the Papacy on 22, 24 and 26 April 1073)

779 There for three days, before the castle gate, he laid aside all his royal gear; barefoot and wearing coarse wool, he stood pitifully, and did not stop begging for our apostolic help and compassion, until he had moved everyone there, or who heard tell of this, to great reverence and pity.

(Letter to German princes, describing the penance of Emperor Henry IV at Canossa, ?28 January 1077)

780 It is the custom of the Roman Church which I unworthily serve with the help of God, to tolerate some things, to turn a blind eye to some, following the spirit of discretion rather than the rigid letter of the law.

(Letter, 9 March 1078)

781 Who does not know that kings and rulers sprang from men who were ignorant of God, who assumed because of blind greed and intolerable presumption to make themselves masters of other men, their equals, by means of pride, violence, bad faith, murder, and almost every kind of crime? Surely the devil drove them on.

(Letter to Hermann, Bishop of Metz, about the right of the Pope to excommunicate the Holy Roman Emperor, 15 March 1801)

782 I have loved justice and hated iniquity: therefore I die in exile.

(*Attributed last words, Salerno, 25 May 1085)

George GRENVILLE (1712–70): English Tory Prime Minister

783 It is clear that both England and America are now to be governed by the mob.

(After the Government of which he was Prime Minister had been forced to repeal the Stamp Act and embarrassed by popular support for John Wilkes, July 1765)

Sir Thomas GRESHAM
(1519–79): English financier

784 The exchange is the chiefest and richest thing only above all other, to restore your Majesty and your Realm to fine gold and silver, and is the meane that makes all foreign commodities and your own commodities with all kinds of victuals good cheap, and likewise keeps your fine gold and silver within your Realm.

(Advice to Queen Elizabeth I, ?autumn 1558)

Charles (Earl) GREY
(1764–1845): British Liberal Prime Minister

785 The only way with newspaper attacks is, as the Irish say, 'to keep never minding.' This has been my practice through life.

(In conversation during his final months as Prime Minister; summer 1834)

Sir Edward GREY (Viscount Grey of Fallodon) (1862–1933): British Foreign Secretary

786 If there is war, there will be Labour Governments in every country, and quite right too.

(In conversation with the Italian ambassador and others, London, late July 1914)

787 I ask the House . . . to consider what is at stake. If France is beaten . . . to her knees . . . I do not believe, for a moment, that at the end of this war, even if we stood aside and remained aside, we should be in a position, a material position, to use our force decisively to undo what had happened in the course of the war, to prevent the whole of Western Europe opposite to us – if that had been the result of the war – falling under the domination of a single power, and I am quite sure that our moral position would be such as to have lost us all respect.

(Speech, informing H of C of Germany's invasion of Belgium, 3 August 1914)

788 The lamps are going out all over Europe; we shall not see them lit again in our lifetime.

(Remark on standing by the window of the Foreign Secretary's room in the Foreign Office, dusk, 3 August 1914)

789 In 1914 Europe had arrived at a point in which every country except Germany was afraid of the present, and Germany was afraid of the future.

(Speech, H of L, 24 July 1924)

Lady Jane GREY (1537–54): 'Nine Days Queen' of England (1553), great-niece of Henry VIII

790 One of the greatest benefits, that ever God gave me, is, that he sent me so sharp and severe parents, and so gentle a schoolmaster.

(To the humanist, Roger Ascham, on the eve of his departure for Germany, 1550 [her parents were the Duke of Suffolk and Lady Frances Brandon: her schoolmaster was John Aylmer, later Bishop of London])

Franz   GRILLPARZER (1791–1872): Austrian bureaucrat, poet and dramatist

791 In Thy camp lies Austria [*In deinem Lager ist Oesterreich*].

(From a laudatory ode to Marshal Radetzky on the eve of the counter-revolutionary campaign in northern Italy, 8 June 1848)

Wilhelm GROENER (1867–1939): German General

792 Sire you no longer have an army. The army will march home under its leaders and commanding Generals, but not under Your Majesty's command, for it no longer stands behind Your Majesty ... Today the oath on the colours is mere fiction.

(To Kaiser William II at headquarters in Spa, 9 November 1918)

Rees Howell GRONOW (1795–1865): Guards officer, spendthrift, Tory MP and social observer

793 How unspeakably odious ... were the dandies of forty years ago ... Why they arrogated to themselves the right of setting up their own fancied superiority on a self-raised pedestal, and despising their betters, Heaven only knows. They were generally middle-aged ... had large appetites and weak digestions, gambled freely and had no luck. They hated everybody, and abused everybody, and would sit together in White's bay window, or the pit boxes at the Opera, weaving tremendous crammers. They swore a good deal, never laughed, looked hazy after dinner, and had most of them been patronized at one time or other by Brummel and the Prince Regent.

(*Reminiscences*, Vol. I, written mid-1850s, published 1895)

Robert   GROSSETESTE (?1175–1253): Bishop of Lincoln

794 [of Franciscans] They illuminate our whole country with the bright light of their preaching and teaching.

(Letter to Pope Gregory IX, 1238)

795 Apart from the common faith owed by all princes as sons of the church, [Henry III] is particularly bound to loyalty, at risk of very serious penalties, by the charter and oath of his father, the famous King John . . . it will be a good plan if the Queen of England, your niece, may be persuaded . . . to try to change our lord King's heart for the better in this respect.

(To Boniface, Archbishop of Canterbury, 1243)

796 We hear that the clergy also perform the plays, which they call 'Miracles' and other games, such as 'Bringing in May' . . . [these] you shall do away with utterly, as you can easily do, and you shall try to prevent Christians and Jews from living together, as far as you are able.

(Letter to the Archdeacons, about abuses in his Diocese of Lincoln, ?1244)

797 Because of this [murder] the University is so disturbed that the Oxford students are giving up all their lectures, ordinary and special; they have sworn that, unless sufficient punishment is exacted (for if it is not, this sort of thing may happen frequently) they will leave off study entirely.

(To his official, Robert de Marisco; a student at Oxford had been murdered by townspeople, 1248)

François GUIZOT (1787– 1874): French Prime Minister and historian

798 The spirit of revolution, the spirit of insurrection is a spirit radically opposed to liberty.

(Speech, Paris, 29 December 1830)

799 Only after I had taken part in the government of men did I learn to be just to the Emperor Napoleon.

(*Mémoires*, Vol. 1, written early 1850s, published 1858)

GUSTAVUS ADOLPHUS (1594–1632): King of Sweden [see also 1394]

800 I have taken the water from them; I would take the air if I could.

(To Louis de Geer who had tried to persuade him to lift the blockade of Gdansk during the Swedish–Polish conflict, 1627)

801 God be my witness, you are yourselves the destroyers, wasters and spoilers of your Fatherland. My heart is sickened when I look upon any one of you.

(To officers of his German Protestant allies who had stolen cattle during his invasion of Bavaria, September 1632)

Nell GWYNNE (*c*. 1650–87): English actress, mistress of King Charles II [see also 348, 1435]

802 Good people, let me pass, I am the *Protestant* whore.

(To an angry crowd during the 'Popish Terror', 1681)

803 Shall the dog lie where the deer once couched?

(*Alleged rejection of a lover after Charles II's death, 1685)

Douglas Haig, Earl HAIG (1861–1928): British Field-Marshal

804 With our backs to the wall, and believing in the justice of our cause, each one of us must fight on to the end. The safety of our Homes and the Freedom of mankind alike depend on the conduct of each one of us at this critical moment.

(Order to British troops on the Western Front, 12 April 1918)

Richard HAKLUYT (?1552–1616): geographer

805 Through our long peace and seldom sickness we are grown more populous than ever heretofore . . . many thousands of idle persons are within this realm which, being no way to be set on work, be either mutinous and seek alteration in the state or at least very burdensome to the common wealth and often fall to pilfering and thieving and other lewdness, whereby all the prisons of the land are daily pestered and stuffed full of them.

(*Particular Discourse of Western Planting*, ?1584)

Viscount HALIFAX (1881–1959): Lord Privy Seal (later Foreign Secretary) and Chancellor of Oxford University

806 I often think how much easier the world would have been to manage if Herr Hitler and Signor Mussolini had been at Oxford.

(Speech, York, 4 November 1937)

Alexander HAMILTON (1755–1804): American statesman
[see also 1888]

807 Let Americans disdain to be the instruments of European greatness. Let the Thirteen States, bound together in a strict and indissoluble union, concur in erecting one great American system, superior to the control of all transatlantic force or influence, and able to dictate the terms of the connection between the old and the new world!

(*Federalist Papers*, XI, November 1787)

808 To model our political systems upon speculations of lasting tranquillity is to calculate on the weaker springs of the human character.

(Ibid., XXXIV, December 1787)

John HANCOCK (1737–93): American Revolutionary leader

809 There, I guess King George will be able to read that.

(On being the first man to sign the Declaration of Independence, Philadelphia, 2 August 1776)

Marcus HANNA (1837–1904): Republican Party 'boss'

810 [of Theodore Roosevelt] I told William McKinley it was a mistake to nominate that wild man [as Vice-President] at Philadelphia ... Now, look, that damned cowboy is President of the United States.

(To H. H. Kohlstat while travelling to President McKinley's funeral, September 1901)

Wal HANNINGTON (b. 1896): British communist

811 Led by a piper's band, we set out to blaze the trail for over five hundred miles on the roads of Britain, calling upon the workers of the land to stir their slumbering souls and to rise against the callous governing class responsible for the terrible plight of the unemployed.

(Account of Glasgow to London hunger march, 23 January 1929, *Unemployed Struggles, 1919–1936*)

James   Keir   HARDIE (1856–1915): pioneer British socialist

812 From his childhood onwards this boy will be surrounded by sycophants and flatterers ... In due course, following the precedent which has already been set, he will be sent on a tour of the world and probably rumours of a morganatic marriage alliance will follow and the end of it will be the country will be called upon to pay the bill.

(Speech opposing a motion congratulating Queen Victoria on the birth of the future Edward VIII [Duke of Windsor], H of C, 28 June 1894)

813 I now understand what Christ suffered in Gethsemane as well as any man living.

(To friends in his Merthyr Tydfil constituency after being howled down at Aberdare for speaking against the War, 6 August 1914)

Warren Gamaliel HARDING (1865–1923):   twenty-ninth President of the USA

814 America's present need is not heroics but healing; not nostrums but normalcy; not revolution but restoration.

(Speech, Boston, June 1920)

Sir John HARINGTON (1561–1612): translator, Elizabeth I's godson

815 His guard for the most part were beardless boys without shirts, who, in the frost, wade as familiarly through rivers as water-spaniels. With what charm such a master makes them love him I know not, but, if he bid them come, they come; if go, they do go; if he say do this, they do it.

(On Tyrone, Irish rebel leader, in his camp, 1599: *Nugae Antiquae*, pub. 1779)

816 She walks much in her privy chamber, and stamps with her feet at ill news, and thrusts her rusty sword at times into the arras in great rage.

(On Elizabeth I's reaction to Essex's behaviour, 1600; Ibid.)

James HARRINGTON (1611–77): English political writer

817 [of Elizabeth I] The balance of the Commonwealth was too apparently in the popular party to be unseen by the wise council of Queen Parthenia [Elizabeth] who, converting her reign through the perpetual love-tricks that passed between her and her people into a kind of Romance, wholly neglected the Nobility.

(*The Commonwealth of Oceana*, 1656)

818 No man can be a Politician, except he be first an Historian or a Traveller; (for except he can see what Must be, or what May be, he is no Politician).

(Ibid.)

819 For the Colonies in the Indies, they are yet babes that cannot live without sucking the breasts of their mother-Cities, but such as, I mistake, if when they come of age they do not wean themselves.

(Ibid.)

820 Well, the King will come in. Let him come in, and call a Parliament of the greatest Cavaliers in England, so they be men of Estates, and let them sit but seven years and they will all turn Commonwealth's men.

(Comment at the breaking-up of his political club, the Rota, for excessive republicanism; Turk's Head, New Palace Yard, Westminster: 20/21 February 1660, as recorded by John Aubrey who was there: *Brief Lives*)

William HARRISON (1534–93): Anglican clergyman, chronicler

821 Most nations do not unjustly deride us as also for that we do seem to imitate all nations round about us, wherein we be like to the polypus or chameleon, and thereunto bestow most cost upon our arses and much more than upon all the rest of our bodies, as women do likewise upon their heads and shoulders ... I have met with some of these trulls in London so disguised that it hath passed my skill to discern whether they were men or women.

(*Description of England*: intro. to Holinshed's *Chronicles*, 1577)

Sir William HARVEY (1578–1657): pioneer medical scientist

822 [of Francis Bacon, formerly his patient] He writes Philosophy like a Lord Chancellor ... I have 'cured' him.

(In conversation with John Aubrey, ?1654/7)

Sir Christopher HATTON (1540–91): Lord Chancellor of England

823 Shall we now suffer ourselves with all dishonour to be conquered? England hath been accounted hitherto the most renowned kingdom for valour and manhood in all Christendom, and shall we now lose our old reputation? If we should, it would have been better for England we had never been born.

(First speech in Parliament after the defeat of the Spanish Armada: a call for additional taxation, 4 February 1589)

Robert Stephen HAWKER (1803–75): English poet and Cornish vicar

824 [of Bishop Sir Jonathan Trelawny, one of the Seven Bishops charged with seditious libel by James II, June 1688]
    And shall Trelawny die?
    Here's twenty thousand
        Cornish men
    Will know the reason why!

(*Song of the Western Men*, 1845, based on a Cornish ballad traditional since 1688)

John HAY (1838–1905): US diplomat and Secretary of State

825 All who think cannot but see there is a sanction like that of religion which binds us in partnership in the serious work of the World ... We are joint ministers in the same sacred mission of Freedom and Progress.

(Speech, as ambassador in London, on Anglo–American relations, 21 April 1898)

Rutherford B. HAYES (1822–93): nineteenth President of the USA

826 He serves his party best who serves his country best.

(Inaugural message, 5 March 1877)

827 Many, if not most, of our Indian wars have had their origin in broken promises and acts of injustice on our part.

(Message to Congress, 4 December 1877)

Edward HEATH (b. 1916): British Conservative politician and Prime Minister

828 I cannot promise to stop roaring inflation overnight but I will give it priority.

(Election broadcast, 27 May 1970)

829 [with reference to possible tax cuts and a halt in the prices charged by the nationalized industries] This would, at a stroke, reduce the rise of prices, increase productivity and reduce unemployment.

(Press release by the Conservative Central Office during the election campaign, 16 June 1970)

830 It is the unpleasant and unacceptable face of capitalism, but we should not suggest that the whole of British industry consists of practices of this kind.

(Answering questions about the high emoluments of directors of the Lonrho international trading group during a period of governmental counter-inflation policy: H of C, 15 May 1973)

831 If you want to see the acceptable face of capitalism, go out to an oil rig in the North Sea.

(Election campaign speech, Edinburgh, 18 February 1974)

832 We are the trade union for pensioners and children, the trade union for the disabled and the sick ... the trade union for the nation as a whole.

(Election campaign speech, Manchester, 20 February 1974)

George Wilhelm HEGEL (1770–1831): German philosopher

833 Political genius consists in identifying oneself with a principle.

(*Constitution of Germany*, 1802)

834 Experience and history teaches us this: that people and governments have learnt nothing from history, nor acted on principles deduced from it.

(*The Philosophy of History*, 1807)

835 World-historical men – the Heroes of an epoch – must be recognized as its clear-sighted ones: their deeds and their words are the best of their time.

(Ibid.)

836 The history of the World is the World's court of justice.

(*The Philosophy of Right*, 1821 [Phrase apparently borrowed from Schiller: see 1672])

837 The State is the march of God through the World.

(Ibid.)

838 In England even the poorest of people believe they have Rights: this is very different from what satisfies the poor in other lands.

(Ibid.)

HENRY I (1068–1135): King of England

839 An illiterate king is a crowned ass [*Rex illiteratus, asinus coronatus*].

(A proverb said, by the contemporary chronicler William of Malmesbury, to have been used by Henry in his youth)

HENRY II (1133–89): King of England
[see also 137, 1100]

840 I have nourished and raised up in my Kingdom indolent and wretched fellows, faithless to their master whom they allow to be mocked so shamefully by a certain low-born clerk.

(To his court, referring to the behaviour of Thomas Becket, Archbishop of Canterbury, December 1170. Often misquoted as: 'Who will rid me of this turbulent priest?')

841 Meanwhile the boldness of this man [Becket] wore out his victims, and others in England; they fell upon him and killed him (I say it with sorrow). I fear the anger I had recently shown against him may have been the cause of this misdeed. I call God to witness that I am extremely disturbed, but more with anxiety about my reputation than qualms of conscience.

(Letter to Pope Alexander III, 1171)

HENRY III (1207–72): King of England
[see also 795]

842 All these things shall I keep faithfully and undiminished, as a man, as a Christian, as a soldier, and as a king, crowned and anointed.

(On taking an oath to uphold Magna Carta, 1253)

HENRY V (1387–1422): King of England

843 If God wills and I keep my life and health, in a few months, I shall play such a ball-game with the French in their own courtyards, that they will lose their fun in the end and win grief instead of the game.

(To ambassadors returning from France with an insulting gift of tennis balls, 1414)

844 You speak like a fool, for by God in Heaven ... I should not wish to have even a single man more than I have now, if I could. For this is God's people whom I have and whom he thinks it right for me to have at this time. Do you not believe that the Almighty, with this small force of men on his side, can conquer the hostile arrogance of the French, who pride themselves on their numbers and their own strength?

(Before the Battle of Agincourt, on being asked if he did not wish for more troops, October 1415)

845 Everyone knows that I act in everything with kindness and mercy, for I am forcing Rouen into submission by starvation, not by fire, sword or bloodshed.

(To an envoy from Rouen, during the siege, 1418)

HENRY VIII (1491–1547): King of England
[see also 174, 487, 620, 1210, 1279, 1280, 1972, 1983]

846 [of John Colet, Dean of St Paul's, London] Let every man have his own doctor and everyone follow his liking, but this is the doctor for me.

(After Colet had been accused of heresy by Bishop Fitzjames of London, 1512)

847 We are, by the sufferance of God, King of England; and the Kings of England in times past never had any superior but God. Wherefore know you that we will maintain the rights of the Crown ... as any of our progenitors.

(To Wolsey, refusing to allow a dispute over an ecclesiastic to be referred to Rome, 1515)

848 We are so much bounden to the See of Rome that we cannot do too much honour to it ... for we received from that See our Crown Imperial.

(To Thomas More [who was trying to persuade Henry not to support the Pope's authority so strongly in his book *A Defence of the Seven Sacraments*, 1521])

849 My book maketh substantially for my matter; in looking whereof I have spent above IV hours this day, which caused me now to write the shorter letter to you at this time, because of some pain in my head, wishing myself (specially an evening) in my sweetheart's arms, whose pretty dukkys I trust shortly to kiss.

(Letter to Anne Boleyn, August 1528. The 'book' Henry was preparing questioned the canonical validity of his marriage to a deceased brother's widow)

850 No more to you, at this present, mine own darling, for lack of time; but that I would you were in mine arms, or I in yours; for I think it long since I kissed you. Written after the killing of an hart, at XI of the clock.

(Letter to Anne Boleyn, September 1528)

851 I perceive that that man [Cranmer] hath the sow by the right ear: and if I had known this device but two years ago, it had been in my way a great piece of money, and had also rid me out of much disquietness.

(Letter to Edward Foxe and Stephen Gardiner, 3 August 1529)

852 Three may keep counsel if two be away; and if I thought that my cap knew my counsel, I would cast it into the fire and burn it.

(To George Cavendish, servant of the late Cardinal Wolsey, 6 December 1530)

853 Let him [i.e. the Pope] not suppose that either the King or his nobles will allow the fixed laws of his kingdom to be set aside.

(To Pope Clement VII, 6 December 1530)

854 We at no time stand so highly in our estate royal as in the time of Parliament, wherein we as head and you as members are conjoined and knit together into one body politic, so as whatsoever offence or injury (during that time) is offered to the meanest member of the House is to be judged as done against our person and the whole Court of Parliament.

(Speech to a deputation from the H of C, Whitehall, 31 March 1543)

855 I see and hear daily that you of the Clergy preach one against another, teach one contrary to another, inveigh one against another without charity or discretion. Some be too stiff in their old mumpsimus, others be too busy and curious in their new sumpsimus. Thus all men almost be in variety and discord . . .

(Speech to Parliament, 24 December 1545)

856 I am very sorry to know and hear how unreverently that most precious jewel, the Word of God, is disputed, rhymed, sung and jangled in every ale-house and tavern, contrary to the true meaning and doctrine of the same.

(Ibid.)

857 No prince in the world more favoureth his subjects than I do you, nor no subjects or Commons more love and obey their Sovereign Lord than I perceive you do me; for whose defence my treasure shall not be hidden, nor if necessity require my person shall not be unadventured.

(Ibid.)

HENRY IV (1533–1610): King of France

858 I regret only two things I have had to leave behind in Paris, the Mass and my wife: I can manage without the first, but not without the second.

(Remark, 1576)

859 Those who follow their conscience directly are of my religion; and, for my part, I am of the same religion as all those who are brave and true.

(Letter to M. de Batz, 1577)

860 Paris is well worth a mass [*Paris vaut bien une messe*].

(*Attributed. No evidence at all for this traditional remark. Péréfixe, in his history of Henry IV in 1681, records that 'the Politiques . . . said to him that of

all canons, the Canon of the Mass was the best to reduce the towns of his kingdom')

861 [of James I] The wisest fool in Christendom.

(*Alleged comment on hearing that James was seeking a reversal of English foreign policy which would have favoured Spain at the expense of France, 1604)

862 What! If they ruin my people, who will feed me, who will pay the expenses of the State, who will pay your pensions, gentlemen! God's life, to rob my people is to rob me.

(On hearing that his own troops were plundering Champagne, 1610)

863 I will make sure that there will be no labourer in my kingdom without the means of having a chicken in his pot.

(Remark recorded by the contemporary lawyer, Pierre de l'Estoile, 1546–1611)

HENRY, Prince of Wales (1594–1612): first-born son of James I

864 Who but my father would keep such a bird in a cage?

(Of the imprisonment of Sir Walter Raleigh, 1611)

Patrick HENRY (1736–99):
American Revolutionary leader

865 Caesar had his Brutus:
Charles the First, his Cromwell:
and George III ... ('Treason',
the Speaker intervened) ... may
profit by their example. If *this* be
treason, make the most of it.

(Speech, Virginia House of
Delegates, 1765)

866 I am not a Virginian, but an
American.

(Speech, Continental Congress, 5
September 1774)

867 I know not what course
others may take; but as for me,
give me liberty, or give me death!

(Speech, Virginia House of
Delegates, 23 March 1775)

868 I have the highest veneration
for those gentlemen the authors
of the US Constitution; but, Sir,
give me leave to demand, What
right had they to say 'We, the
People'? My political curiosity,
exclusive of my anxious solicitude
for the public welfare, leads me to
ask, Who authorized them to
speak in the language of 'We, the
People', instead of, 'We, the
States'? States are the characteristics and the soul of a confederation.

(Speech against ratification of the
US Constitution, Virginia House
of Delegates, 4 June 1788)

869 To erect and concentrate
and perpetuate a large monied
interest ... must in the course of
human events produce one or
other of two evils, the prostration
of agriculture at the feet of commerce, or a change in the present
form of federal government, fatal
to the existence of American
liberty.

(Remonstrance to Virginia House
of Delegates, 23 December 1790)

Paul HENTZNER (*flor.* 1590s):
German tutor

870 [The English] are powerful
in the field, successful against
their enemies, impatient of anything like slavery, vastly fond of
great noises that fill the ear, such
as the firing of cannons, drums,
and the ringing of bells, so that it
is common for a number of them,
that have a glass in their heads, to
go up into some belfrey and ring
the bells for hours together for
the sake of exercise. If they see a
Foreigner, very well made or particularly handsome, they will say
'It is a pity he is not an Englishman'.

(*Journey into England*, 1598)

871 [of Queen Elizabeth I] Next
came the Queen ... her face
oblong, fair but wrinkled; her
eyes small, yet black and pleasant;
her nose a little hooked, her lips
narrow and her teeth black (a
defect the English seem subject

to from their too great use of sugar) . . . She wore false hair and that red . . . her air was stately, her manner of speaking mild and obliging.

(Ibid.)

Sidney HERBERT (1810–61): 1st Baron Herbert of Lea, British Secretary for War

872 I suppose Lizzy [his wife] told you of my interview with the Pope. Nothing could be better than his tone and language on the subject of Ireland.

(Letter to his mother, Countess of Pembroke, after meeting Pius IX during Herbert's honeymoon in Rome, 1847)

873 Upon the whole it was worth seeing; one has the feeling that it is history, though not history of a very high class, or giving any precedents which will be useful to mankind except as warnings.

(Remark after attending first meeting of new French Senate, 1852)

Alexander HERZEN (1812–70): Russian writer

874 I think there is a certain basis of truth in the fear which the Russian government is beginning to have of communism: for communism is Tsarist autocracy turned upside down.

(*My Past and Thoughts*, written ?*c.* 1854–5)

William HICKEY (?1749–1830): English traveller

875 The Americans (whom the Chinese distinguish by the expressive title 'second chop Englishmen') have also a flag [here].

(At Canton, 1809, *Memoirs*)

Sir Michael HICKS BEACH (1837–1916): British Conservative Chancellor of the Exchequer

876 The country has put its foot down. If, unhappily, another view should be taken elsewhere, we, the Ministers of the Queen, know what our duty demands. It would be a great calamity . . . But there are greater evils than war.

(Speech during Fashoda Crisis, North Shields, 19 October 1898)

877 The Hon. Member for King's Lynn was good enough to suggest that we should tax diamonds, pearls, feathers and lace in a way which made me doubt whether he sufficiently realized that two of the highest and holiest feelings in woman's nature are the love of diamonds and the love of smuggling.

(Speech, H of C, 19 March 1900)

Paul von HINDENBURG
(1847–1934): German Field
Marshal and President

878 As an English General has
very truly said, 'The German
army was stabbed in the back'.

(Statement read to a Reichstag
Committee of Inquiry, 18
November 1919. There is no
evidence to show whom
Hindenburg thought he was
citing)

Adolf HITLER (1889–1945):
German Nazi politician and dictator
[see also 66, 151, 331, 765, 806,
1299, 1700, 1945]

879 If today I stand here as a
revolutionary, it is as a revolutionary against the Revolution.
There is no such thing as high
treason against the traitors of
1918.

(Defence speech when tried for
treason, Munich, 26 February
1924)

880 The broad masses of a population are more amenable to the
appeal of rhetoric than to any
other force. All great movements
are popular movements. They are
the volcanic eruptions of human
passions and emotions, stirred
into activity by the ruthless God-
dess of Distress or by the torch of
the spoken word cast into the
midst of the people.

(*Mein Kampf*, Vol. 1, Ch. 3,
written 1924, published 1925)

881 The fact that England did
not possess a national army
proved nothing ... England has
always had the armament which
she needed. She always fought
with those weapons which were
necessary for success.

(Discussion of the German
misunderstanding of Britain's
military potential in 1914, Ibid.,
Ch. 4)

882 In the big lie, there is always
a certain force of credibility ... In
the primitive simplicity of their
minds, the great masses of the
people more readily fall victims to
the big lie than to the small lie.

(Ibid.: Vol. 1, Ch. 10)

883 Whoever lights the torch of
war in Europe can wish for nothing but chaos.

(Speech, Reichstag, 21 May
1935)

884 I go the way that Providence
dictates with the assurance of a
sleepwalker.

(Speech, Munich, 15 March
1936)

885 Mussolini, make no mistake
about it, Christianity is the Bol-
shevism of the Classical Age.

(In conversation reported by a British diplomat, Rome, 4 May 1938)

886 Before us stands the last problem that must be solved and will be solved. It is the last territorial claim which I have to make in Europe, but it is the claim from which I will not recede.

(Speech, Berlin Sportpalast, 26 September 1938)

887 With regard to the problem of the Sudeten Germans, my patience now is at an end.

(Ibid.)

888 As England, despite her hopeless military position, still shows no sign of willingness to come to terms, I have decided to prepare, and if necessary carry out, a landing operation against her. The aim of this enterprise is to eliminate the English mother-country as a base for continuance of the war against Germany.

(Directive No. 16, 16 July 1940)

889 The German armed forces must be prepared to crush Soviet Russia in a quick campaign even before the end of the war against England ... Preparations requiring more time to start are to be begun now ... and completed by 15 May, 1941 ... The ultimate objective of the operation is to

establish a defence line against Asiatic Russia from a line running approximately from the river Volga to Archangel.

(Directive No. 21, for 'Operation Barbarossa', 18 December 1940)

890 I am convinced that 1941 will be the crucial year of a great New Order in Europe. The world shall open up for everyone.

(Speech, Berlin Sportpalast, 30 January 1941)

891 A historical revision on a unique scale has been imposed on us by the Creator.

(Speech, announcing Germany's declaration of war on America, 11 December 1941)

892 All coalitions in history have disintegrated sooner or later ... We will continue this battle until, as Frederick the Great said, one of our damned enemies gets too tired to fight any more. We will fight until we get a peace which secures the life of the German people for the next fifty or a hundred years, a peace which above all does not shame our honour a second time, as in 1918.

(Speech in military conference, 31 August 1944)

Thomas HOBBES (1588–1679): English political philosopher
[see also 74]

893 During the time men live without a common power to keep them all in awe ... the life of man [is] solitary, poor, nasty, brutish, and short.

(*Leviathan* Pt 1, Ch. 13, written *c.* 1650)

894 War consisteth not in battle only, or the act of fighting; but in a tract of time, wherein the will to contend by battle is sufficiently known.

(Ibid.)

895 Covenants without the sword are but words and of no strength to secure a man at all.

(Ibid., Pt 2, Ch. 17)

896 The obligation of subjects to the sovereign is understood to last as long, and no longer, than the power lasteth by which he is able to protect them.

(*Leviathan*, Pt 2, Ch. 21)

897 The Papacy is no other than the ghost of the deceased Roman empire, sitting crowned upon the grave thereof.

(Ibid., Pt 4, Ch. 47)

898 After the Bible was translated into English every man, nay every boy and every wench that could read English, thought they spoke with God Almighty and understood what he said ...

Every man became a judge of religion and an interpreter of the Scriptures to himself.

(*Behemoth, or a dialogue on the Civil Wars*, written in the late 1670s)

John Cam HOBHOUSE, Baron Broughton (1786–1869): British radical politician

899 It is said to be hard on His Majesty's Ministers to raise objections to this proposition. For my part, I think it no more hard on His Majesty's Opposition to compel them to take this course.

(First recorded use of 'His Majesty's Opposition'; speech, H of C, 27 April 1826)

Sir Edward HOBY (1560–1617): English diplomat and politician

900 On the 5th of November we began our Parliament, to which the King should have come in person, but refrained, through a practice but that morning discovered. The plot was to have blown up the King ... at one instant and blast to have ruined the whole estate and kingdom of England.

(Letter to Sir Thomas Edmondes, ambassador in Brussels, 19 November 1605)

Raphael HOLINSHED (?–d. by 1582): chronicler

901 When I came to consider of the histories of Ireland I found myself so unprovided of helps to set down any particular discourse thereof that I was in despair.

(*Description of Ireland, Chronicles,* 1577: Edmund Campion wrote the Irish history for Holinshed)

Herbert HOOVER (1874–1964): thirty-first President of the USA

902 Our country has deliberately undertaken a great social and economic experiment, noble in motive and far-reaching in purpose [i.e. 18th Amendment on Prohibition].

(Letter to Senator W. H. Borah, 28 February 1928)

903 When the war closed . . . we were challenged with a peacetime choice between the American system of rugged individualism and a European philosophy of diametrically opposed doctrines – doctrines of paternalism and State socialism.

(Presidential Campaign speech, Madison Square Garden, New York, 22 October 1928)

904 We are nearer today to the ideal of the abolition of poverty and fear from the lives of men and women than ever before in any land.

(Ibid.)

905 In no nation are the fruits of accomplishment more secure . . . I have no fears for the future of our country. It is bright with hope.

(Inaugural address, 4 March 1929)

Matthew HOPKINS (?–1647): self-appointed Witch-Finder General

906 I have this day received a letter to come to a town called Great Stoughton, to search for evil disposed persons called witches . . . It shall be tenne to one but I will come to your town first; but I would certainly know afore, whether your towne affords many sticklers for such cattell, or willing to give us good welcome and entertainment . . . with thanks and recompence.

(Letter to a parishioner of Great Stoughton, Huntingdonshire, 1645/6, cf. 699)

Samuel HORSLEY (1733–1806): Bishop of Rochester

907 The mass of the people have nothing to do with the laws but to obey them.

(Speech, H of L, 1795)

Henry HOWARD (1540–1614): Earl of Northampton

908 It falls out in a better consequence, that the skull of faithless

Percy should stand sentinel where he was once a captain pioneer; and Lambeth should now be Catesby's horizon, that was his arsenal.

(Speech at trial of Father Garnet, March 1606, for complicity in Gunpowder Plot: The heads of Jocelyn Percy and Robert Catesby, two other plotters, were exposed on Westminster Bridge)

William Morris HUGHES (1864–1952): Australian Prime Minister

909 Without the Empire we should be tossed like a cork in the cross current of world politics. It is at once our sword and our shield.

(Speech to the Australian Historical Society, Melbourne, 1926)

Alexander von HUMBOLDT (1769–1859): Prussian writer

910 Diplomacy today is a collective education in fear [*C'est l'enseignement mutuel de la peur*].

(Conversation with Maréchal de Castellane: Castellane, *Journal* II, 1832)

G. W. HUNT (*flor.* 1870s): English song-writer

911 We don't want to fight, but, by jingo if we do,

We've got the ships, we've got the men, we've got the money too.
We've fought the Bear before, and while Britons shall be true,
The Russians shall not have Constantinople.

(English music-hall song popularized in 1878 by James MacDermott)

J. H. Leigh HUNT (1784–1859): English radical essayist and poet

912 [of the Prince Regent] This delightful, blissful, wise, pleasurable, honourable, virtuous, true and immortal Prince was a violator of his word, a libertine over head and ears in debt and disgrace, a despiser of domestic ties, the companion of gamblers and demireps, a man who has just closed half a century without one single claim on the gratitude of his country or the respect of posterity.

(*The Examiner*, 22 March 1812, commenting on a passage in the *Morning Post* which had called the Regent 'the Maecenas of the Arts' and 'an Adonis in loveliness'. Hunt was prosecuted, fined and imprisoned for two years for the libellous attack in *The Examiner*)

Francis   HUTCHESON
(1694–1746): Scottish Professor
of Moral Philosophy

913 That action is best which
procures the greatest happiness
for the greatest numbers.

(*An Inquiry into the Original of our
Ideas of Beauty and Virtue*, 1725,
cf. 129)

**Dolores IBARRURI ('La Pas-
ionaria')** (b. 1895): Spanish
communist

914 It is better to die on your feet
than to live on your knees.

(Speech on behalf of Spanish
Republicans, Paris, 3 September
1936)

INNOCENT III (1160–1216):
Pope

915 Just as the moon receives its
light from the sun, which is greater by far, owing to the quantity
and quality of its light, so the
royal power takes all its reputation and prestige from the pontifical power.

(Letter to recteurs of Tuscany,
1198)

916 It is a much more serious
thing to offend the divine majesty
than to offend the temporal
majesty.

(Letter, 25 March 1199)

917 Nothing which happens in
the world should escape the
notice of the supreme pontiff.

(Letter, 1199)

918 You are aware ... of the
evils that have come ... as a
consequence of the dispute
which, as retribution for sin, has
arisen between you and our well-
beloved son in Christ, John, the
illustrious king of the English.
Look around you! Because of
your conflict churches are destroyed, the rich impoverished and
the poor oppressed; and, since
neither religion nor sex is spared,
religious men who formerly devoted themselves to prayer are
now forced to beg, and women
who had vowed chastity to the
creator of chastity are now – we
say with grief – being prostituted
to the lust of brigands.

(Letter to Philip II of France
appealing for a truce between the
French and English in
Normandy, 21 May 1203)

919 The King of kings and Lord
of lords, Jesus Christ ... has
established in the Church His
kingdom and His priesthood ...
and over all He has set up one
whom He has appointed as His
Vicar on earth, so that, as every
knee is bowed to Jesus ... so all
men should obey His Vicar and
see to it that there may be one
fold and one shepherd. For the
sake of God all secular kings so

venerate this Vicar that unless they strive to serve him devotedly they doubt that they are reigning properly. To this, most beloved son, you have wisely attended . . .

(Letter to King John of England rejoicing in his acceptance of a position of fealty to the Holy See, 21 April 1214)

920 This charter [Magna Carta] has been forced from the king. It constitutes an insult to the Holy See, a serious weakening of the royal power, a disgrace to the English nation, a danger to all Christendom, since this civil war obstructs the crusade. Therefore . . . we condemn this charter and forbid the king to keep it, or the barons and their supporters to make him do so, on pain of excommunication.

(Papal Bull, 24 August 1215)

IVAN IV, 'the Terrible' (1530–84): Tsar of Russia

921 We are furthermore willing that you send unto us your ships and vessels, when and as often as they may have passage, with good assurance on our part to see them harmless. And if you send one of your Majesty's Counsell to treat with us whereby your Country Merchants may with all kinds of wares and where they will make their Market in our Dominions, they shall have their free Mart with all free liberties, through my whole Dominions.

(Letter to Edward VI establishing trade relations, February 1554 [version as printed by Samuel Purchas (q.v.) in 1625])

922 The Emperor requireth earnestly that there may be assurance made by oath and faith betwixt the Queen's Majesty and him that if any misfortune might fall or chance upon either of them to go out of their countries, that it might be lawful to either of them to come into the other's country for the safeguard of themselves and their lives.

(Secret message to Elizabeth I, conveyed by Anthony Jenkinson, from Moscow, November 1567)

923 We had thought that you had been ruler over your land and had sought honour to yourself and profit to your country, and therefore we did pretend those weighty affairs between you and us; but now we perceive that there be other men that do rule, and not men but bowers and merchants the which seek not the wealth and honour of our majesties, but they seek their own profit of merchandize.

(Letter to Elizabeth I, 24 October 1570)

924 The autocracy of this Russian kingdom of veritable Orthodoxy, by the will of God, has its beginning from the great tsar Vladimir, who enlightened the whole Russian land with holy baptism, and the great tsar Vladimir Monomach . . . and the brave and great sovereign, Alexander Nevsky, who won a victory over the godless Germans . . . and [autocracy] has come down even to us, the humble sceptre-bearer of the Russian kingdom.

(Letter to the rebellious boyar, Prince Kurbsky, September 1577)

925 Did I ascend the throne by robbery or armed bloodshed? I was born to rule by the grace of God; and I do not even remember my father bequeathing the kingdom to me and blessing me – I grew up upon the throne.

(Ibid.)

Andrew JACKSON (1767– 1845): seventh President of the USA

926 Our Federal Union: it must be preserved.

(Toast at Jefferson Birthday Celebration, 13 April 1830)

JAMES I (1566–1625): King of Scotland and England
[see also 771, 861, 1555, 1678]

927 Ye wad na that your King suld appear a scrub on sic an occasion?

(Reported appeal for silk stockings to wear at his wedding, 1589)

928 [England and Scotland] now in the end and fullness of time united, the right and title of both in my Person, alike lineally descended of both the Crowns, whereby it is now become like a little World within itself, being entrenched and fortified round about with a natural, and yet admirable strong pond or ditch, whereby all the former fears of this Nation are now quite cut off.

(First speech to Parliament, 19 March 1603)

929 His Majesty concluded this point . . . with the short aphorism: 'No Bishop, no King'.

(Contemporary report by William Barlow of the King's speech at the Hampton Court Conference on possible Church reform, 14 January 1604)

930 I have peppered them [the Puritans] soundly . . . They fled me so from argument to argument . . . as I was forced at last to say unto them that if any of them had been in a College disputing with their scholars, if any of their disciples had answered them in that sort, they would have fetched him up in place of a reply, and so should the rod have plied upon the poor boy's buttocks.

(Letter describing the Hampton Court Conference, 16 January 1604)

931 A custom loathsome to the eye, hateful to the nose, harmful to the brain, dangerous to the lungs, and in the black, stinking fume thereof, nearest resembling the horrible Stygian smoke of the pit that is bottomless.

(*A Counterblast to Tobacco*, 1604)

932 [of Guy Fawkes] When the party himself was taken, he was but new come out of his house from working, having his Firework for kindling ready in his pocket, wherewith as he confesseth, if he had been taken but immediately before when he was in the House, he was resolved to have blown up himself with his Takers.

(Speech in Parliament, December 1605)

933 The state of monarchy is the supremest thing upon earth: for kings are not only God's Lieutenants upon earth, and sit upon God's throne, but even by God himself they are called Gods.

(To Parliament, 21 March 1609)

934 I never mean wittingly and willingly to bear any man's sins but my own . . . I will never care to lose the hearts of any for justice sake.

(Letter to ex-favourite Somerset just before his arrest for murder of Overbury, 1615)

935 That is done to-day with a penny, that will not be done here-after with an hundred pounds, and that will be mended now in a day, which hereafter will not be mended in a year; and that in a year, which will not be done in our time, as we may see by Paul's Steeple.

(Of mending highways and bridges: Speech in Star Chamber, 20 June 1616)

936 For it is possible but the Country must diminish, if London do so increase, and all sorts of people do come to London? and where doth this increase appear? not in the heart of the City, but in the suburbs; not giving wealth or profit to the City, but bringing misery and surcharge both to City and Court.

(Of new buildings in London, Ibid.)

937 [On his favourite, George Villiers, Duke of Buckingham] Christ had his John and I have my George.

(Reported remark, 1616)

938 Our pleasure likewise is, that after the end of divine service our good people be not disturbed . . . from any lawful recreation, such as dancing ... archery for men, leaping, vaulting ... but withal we do here account still as prohibited all unlawful games to be used upon Sundays only, as bear and bull-baiting, interludes, and ... bowling.

(*The Book of Sports*, 1618)

JAMES II (1633–1701): King of England
[see also 247, 251, 344, 346, 629, 1111, 1214, 1386, 1441]

939 [The Duke of York said] it was the interest of an English Parliament to encourage the navy for the sake of their younger sons, who might be bred to the business thereof.

(To Pepys at Newmarket, October 1681)

940 This is a standard of rebellion.

(On receiving a petition from Seven Bishops protesting against his Second Declaration of Indulgence, ?2 June 1688)

941 Things being come to the extremity that I have been forced to send away the Queen and my son, the Prince of Wales, that they might not fall into my enemy's hands, which they must have done, had they stayed, I am obliged to do the same thing ... If I could have relied upon all my troops I might not have been put to this extremity I am in.

(To Lord Feversham, night of 10/11 December 1688: final message before his flight from London to France)

JAMES V (1512–42): King of Scotland

942 Adieu, farewell, it came with a lass, it will pass with a lass.

(December 1542: said when James, defeated in the battle of Solway Moss and dying, heard of the birth of his daughter Mary, later Queen of Scots)

Jean JAURÈS (1859–1914): French socialist leader

943 You [Radical deputies] have wrested the people away from the protection of the Church and its teachings ... You have silenced the old song which lulled human misery; and human misery awakens and cries out. It rises before you, and now demands its place.

(Speech, Chamber of Deputies, 21 November 1893)

944 There is, then, over the affairs of the army a universal conspiracy of silence, of childlike mysteries, of clannishness, routine and intrigue.

(*L'Armée Nouvelle*, originally written 1910)

945 It is the duty of everyone of you not to miss any opportunity to show that you belong to that international socialist party which, at this hour when the storm is breaking, represents the sole prospect of maintaining peace or of restoring peace.

(Speech at Vaise, 24 July 1914)

Thomas JEFFERSON (1743–1826): third President of the USA

946 We hold these truths to be sacred and undeniable; that all men are created equal and independent, that from that equal creation they derive rights inherent and inalienable, among which are the preservation of life, and liberty, and the pursuit of happiness.

(Original draft for Declaration of Independence, ?1775)

947 The whole commerce between master and slave is a perpetual exercise of the most boisterous passions, the most unremitting despotism on the one part, and degrading submissions on the other. Our children see this, and learn to imitate it; for man is an imitative animal ... The parent storms, the child looks on, catches the lineaments of wrath, puts on the same airs in the circle of smaller slaves, gives a loose to the worst of passions, and thus nursed, educated and daily

exercised in tyranny, cannot but be stamped by it with odious peculiarities. The man must be a prodigy who can retain his manners and morals undepraved by such circumstances.

(*Notes on the State of Virginia,* Query XVIII, written 1781)

948 I tremble for my country when I reflect that God is just; that his justice cannot sleep forever; that considering numbers, nature and natural means only, a revolution of the wheel of fortune, an exchange of situation is among possible events; that it may become probable by supernatural interference.

(Ibid. The context refers to the master–slave relationship in Virginia)

949 The tree of liberty must be refreshed from time to time with the blood of patriots and tyrants. It is its natural manure.

(Letter to W. S. Smith, 13 November 1787)

950 A bill of rights is what the people are entitled to against every government on earth, general or particular and what no just government should refuse or rest on inference.

(Letter to James Madison, 20 December 1787)

951 There is not a single crowned head in Europe whose talents or merits would entitle him to be elected a vestryman by the people of any parish in America.

(Letter to George Washington, from Paris, 2 May 1788)

952 Tranquillity is now restored to the capital: the shops are again opened; the people resuming their labours, and if the want of bread does not disturb our peace, we may hope a continuance of it. The demolition of the Bastille is going on.

(Letter from Paris to John Jay, 19 July 1789)

953 Equal and exact justice to all men ... freedom of religion, freedom of the press, freedom of person under the protection of the habeas corpus; and trial by juries impartially selected – these principles form the bright constellation which has gone before us.

(First Inaugural Address, 4 March 1801)

954 Peace, commerce and honest friendship with all nations, entangling alliances with none.

(Ibid.)

955 If a due participation of office is a matter of right, how are vacancies to be obtained? Those by death are few; by resignation, none. [Usually quoted as 'Few die and none resign'.]

(Letter to Elias Shipman and others of New Haven, Connecticut, 12 July 1801)

956 When a man assumes a public trust, he should consider himself as public property.

(To Baron von Humboldt, 1807)

957 [of Tsar Alexander I of Russia] A more virtuous man, I believe, does not exist, nor one who is more enthusiastically devoted to better the condition of mankind.

(Letter to William Duane, 20 July 1807)

958 Some men look at constitutions with sanctimonious reverence and deem them like the ark of the covenant, too sacred to be touched.

(Letter to Samuel Kercheval, 12 July 1816)

959 This momentous question, like a firebell in the night, awakened and filled me with terror. I considered it at once as the knell of the Union.

(Letter to John Adams, April 1820, over imposition by Congress of the Missouri Compromise)

960 Our first and fundamental maxim should be never to entangle ourselves in the broils of Europe. Our second, never to suffer Europe to intermeddle with cis-Atlantic affairs.

(Letter to James Monroe, 24 October 1823)

George (Baron) JEFFREYS (1648–89): English Chief Justice and Lord Chancellor

961 [of his Assize in the West of England after Monmouth's rebellion, 1685] I was not half bloody enough for him who sent me thither.

(To the Chaplain of the Tower of London shortly before his death, April 1689)

St JOAN of Arc (1412–31): French patriotic leader

962 Good prince, why do you not believe me. I tell you God pities you, He pities your kingdom and your people; for Saint Louis and Charlemagne are on their knees before Him, praying for you.

(To the Dauphin after her arrival at Chinon, March 1429)

963 King of England, and you duke of Bedford ... give up to the Maid sent here by the King of Heaven the key of all the noble cities of France you have taken and ravaged ... I have come here ... to drive you man for man from France ... If you will not believe the Maid's message from God, wherever you happen to be we ... shall make such a great hahaye as has not been made in France these thousand years.

(Letter to the English besieging Orleans, 22 March 1429)

964 If I said that God did not send me, I should condemn myself; truly God did send me ... all this I have done, I did for fear of the fire and my retraction was against the truth ... I prefer to do penance once, by dying, rather than suffer longer punishment in prison.

(At her trial, when retractions did not set her free, 28 May 1431)

JOHN III Sobieski (1674–96): King of Poland

965 The immortal God ... has blest us with so signal a victory as scarce the memory of man can equal. Thanks be to Heaven, now the Half-Moon triumphs no longer over the Cross.

(Letter to his wife after routing the Turks and raising the siege of Vienna, ?16 September 1683)

JOHN PAUL II (born 1920): Pope

966 To the see of Peter in Rome there succeeds today a Bishop who is not a Roman, a Bishop who is a son of Poland. But from this moment he too becomes a Roman.

(Homily at his Inauguration Mass, 22 October 1978)

967 The command 'Thou shalt not kill' must be binding on the conscience of humanity if the terrible tragedy and destiny of Cain is not to be repeated.

(Homily delivered at Drogheda, Ireland, 29 September 1979)

968 Violence is a lie, for it goes against the truth of our faith, the truth of our humanity . . . Violence is a crime against humanity, for it destroys the very fabric of society . . . On my knees I beg you to turn away from the paths of violence.

(Ibid.)

969 War should belong to the tragic past, in history. It should find no place on humanity's agenda for the future.

(Address at Coventry, 30 May 1982)

JOHN   of   Winterthur
(?1300–?44): German chronicler

970 In the year 1315, a certain rustic people, who live in the valleys called 'Swiz' and are almost surrounded by high mountains, trusted in the strong bul-

wark and protection of their mountains; they gave up the obedience, payments, and customary services which they owed to Duke Leopold [Hapsburg] and prepared to resist him.

(Chronicle, 1315)

971 They wore on their feet some kind of iron chains, as is their custom, with which they easily fixed their steps on the mountains, however steep they might be, while the enemy and the enemy's horse could not keep their footing at all. The Swiss also wielded a spear-like, lethal weapon, called in their vernacular 'halberd'.

(Description of Battle of Morgarten, 15 November 1315)

Lyndon   B.   JOHNSON
(1908–73): thirty-sixth President of the USA
[see also 1518]

972 [with reference to the Vice-Presidency] Power is where power goes.

(At Democratic Convention, Los Angeles, 14 July 1960)

973 This Administration here and now declares unconditional war on poverty in America.

(State of Union message to Congress, 8 January 1964)

974 The challenge of the next half century is whether we have the wisdom to use wealth to enrich and elevate our national life – and to advance the quality of American civilization – for in your time we have the opportunity to move not only toward the rich society and the powerful society but upward to the Great Society.

(Speech, University of Michigan, Ann Arbor, 22 May 1964)

975 We are not going to send American boys nine or ten thousand miles away from home to do what Asian boys ought to be doing for themselves.

(Campaign speech, 21 October 1964)

976 When I was a boy growing up we never had these issues of our relations with other nations so much. We didn't wake up with Vietnam and have Cyprus for lunch and the Congo for dinner. All we knew because the folks that kind of moulded the opinion and contributed to the political atmosphere – well, they just kept us debating whether we were 'wet' or 'dry', whether we were prohibitionists or anti-prohibitionists.

(Informal talk in White House, Washington, 1 March 1965)

977 A rioter with a Molotov cocktail on his hands is not fighting for civil rights any more

than a Klansman with a sheet on his back and a mask on his face.

(Speech, Washington DC, 20 August 1965)

978 It is the genius of our Constitution that under its shelter of enduring institutions and rooted principles there is ample room for the rich fertility of American political invention.

(Message to Congress, 12 January 1966)

Samuel JOHNSON (1709–84): English writer

979 *Excise.* A hateful tax levied upon commodities.

(*Dictionary of the English Language,* 1755)

980 *Pension.* An allowance made to anyone without an equivalent. In England it is generally understood to mean pay given to a state hireling for treason to his country.

(Ibid.)

981 *Whig.* The name of a faction.

(Ibid.)

982 *Johnson:* 'Rousseau, Sir, is a very bad man. I would sooner sign a sentence for his transportation than that of any felon who has gone from the Old Bailey these many years. Yes, I should like to have him work in the Plantations.'

Boswell: 'Sir, do you think him as bad a man as Voltaire?'

Johnson: 'Why, Sir, it is difficult to settle the proportion of iniquity between them.'

(Boswell, *Life*, 15 February 1766)

983 It was not for me to bandy civilities with my Sovereign.

(Ibid., February 1767)

984 [to Sir Adam Fergusson] Sir, I perceive you are a vile Whig.

(Ibid., 31 March 1772)

985 I would not give half a guinea to live under one form of government rather than another. It is of no moment to the happiness of an individual.

(Ibid., 31 March 1772)

986 I am always sorry when any language is lost, because languages are the pedigree of nations.

(Boswell, *Tour to Hebrides*, 18 September 1773)

987 George the First knew nothing, and desired to know nothing; did nothing, and desired to do nothing; and the only good thing that is told of him is, that he wished to restore the crown to its hereditary successor.

(Boswell, *Life*, 6 April 1775)

988 Patriotism is the last refuge of a scoundrel.

(Ibid., 7 April 1775)

989 Politics are now nothing more than a means of rising in the world.

(Ibid., 11 April 1775)

990 How is it that we hear the loudest yelps for liberty among the drivers of negroes?

(*Taxation No Tyranny*, 1775)

991 It is better that some should be happy than that none should be happy, which would be the case in a general state of equality.

(Boswell, *Life*, 7 April 1776)

992 When a man is tired of London, he is tired of life; for there is in London all that life can afford.

(Ibid., 20 September 1777)

993 John Wesley's conversation is good, but he is never at leisure. He is always obliged to go at a certain hour. This is very disagreeable to a man who loves to fold his legs and have out his talk, as I do.

(Ibid., 31 March 1778)

994 Sir, there are rascals in all countries. [To Boswell, who was surprised at finding a Whig in Staffordshire.] I have always said, the first Whig was the Devil.

(Ibid., 28 April 1778)

995 [of Lord North] He fills a chair.

(Ibid., 1 April 1781)

996 A wise Tory and a wise Whig, I believe, will agree. Their principles are the same, though their modes of thinking are different.

(Ibid., May 1781)

997 Your levellers wish to level *down* as far as themselves; but they cannot bear levelling *up* to themselves.

(Ibid., 21 July 1763)

998 [of C. J. Fox] He talked to me at club one day concerning Catiline's conspiracy – so I withdrew my attention, and thought about Tom Thumb.

(*Johnsonian Miscellanies*, 1897)

999 [of Burke] You could not stand five minutes with that man beneath a shed while it rained, but you must be convinced you had been standing with the greatest man you had ever yet seen.

(Ibid.)

1000 [on his Parliamentary reports] I took care that the *Whig Dogs* should not have the best of it.

(Ibid.)

J. Paul JONES (1747–92): American naval commander

1001 I have not yet begun to fight.

(Response to Captain of HMS *Serapis* who wished to know if he was striking his colours as his vessel appeared to be sinking after an action off Flamborough Head, 23 September 1779)

JOSEPH II (1741–90): Emperor and King of Hungary

1002 Convinced on the one hand of the perniciousness of all restraints on conscience and, on the other, of the great benefits accruing to religion and the State from true Christian tolerance, we are moved to grant the right of private worship to the Lutheran, Calvinist and non-Uniat Greek religions everywhere, without regard to whether or not it had previously been customary or introduced . . .

(Edict of Toleration, 13 October 1781)

JULIUS II (1443–1513): Pope

1003 Nay, give me a sword, for I am no scholar.

(To Michelangelo who, while carving a statue at Bologna to commemorate Julius's capture of the city, asked the Pope what he should place in his hand, 1506)

'JUNIUS' (*flor.* 1769–71)

1004 The liberty of the press is the *Palladium* of all the civil, political and religious rights of an Englishman.

(Dedicatory notice in the *Letters of Junius*, 1772: author was probably Philip Francis, 1740–1818)

John KEBLE (1792–1866): English churchman and leader of the Oxford Movement

1005 The point to be considered is whether ... the fashionable liberality of this generation be not ascribable ... to the same temper which led the Jews voluntarily to set about degrading themselves to a level with the idolatrous Gentiles? And if it be true anywhere that such enactments are forced on the legislature by public opinion is Apostasy too hard a word to describe the temper of the nation?

(Assize Sermon, St Mary's, Oxford, 14 July 1833)

John F. KENNEDY (1917–63): thirth-fifth President of the USA [see also 1178]

1006 We stand today on the edge of a new frontier – the frontier of the 1960s – a frontier of unknown opportunities and perils – a frontier of unfulfilled hopes and threats.

(Speech accepting presidential nomination, Democratic Convention, Los Angeles, 13 July 1960)

1007 My fellow Americans, ask not what your country can do for you; ask what you can do for your country. My fellow citizens of the world, ask not what America will do for you, but what together we can do for the freedom of man.

(Inaugural Address, 20 January 1961)

1008 Let us never negotiate out of fear. But let us never fear to negotiate.

(Ibid.)

1009 Let the word go forth from this time and place, to friend and foe alike, that the torch has been passed to a new generation of Americans, born in this century, tempered by war, disciplined by a hard and bitter peace, proud of our ancient heritage, and unwilling to witness or permit the slow undoing of those human rights to which this nation has always been committed, and to which we are committed today at home and around the world.

(Ibid.)

1010 The great battleground for the defence and expansion of freedom today is the whole southern half of the globe . . . the lands of the rising peoples. Their revolution is the greatest in human history. They seek an end to injustice, tyranny and exploitation. More than an end, they seek a beginning.

(Supplementary State of the Union Message to Congress, 25 May 1961)

1011 I believe that this nation should commit itself to achieving the goal, before this decade is out, of landing a man on the Moon and returning him safely to earth.

(Ibid.)

1012 Now we have a problem in making our power credible and Vietnam is the place.

(*Alleged remark to James Reston, after meeting Khrushchev, June 1961)

1013 Today every inhabitant of this planet must contemplate the day when this planet may no longer be habitable. Every man, woman and child lives under a nuclear sword of Damocles, hanging by the slenderest of threads, capable of being cut at any moment by accident or miscalculation or madness.

(Address to the United Nations Assembly, New York, September 1961)

1014 History teaches us that enmities between nations . . . do not last for ever . . . We must conduct our affairs in such a way that it becomes in the Communists' interests to agree on a genuine peace . . . to let each nation choose its own future, so long as that choice does not interfere with the choices of others . . . If we cannot now end our differences, at least we can help make the world safe for diversity.

(Speech, primarily on Russo–American relations, the American University, Washington DC, 10 June 1963)

1015 We are confronted primarily with a moral issue. It is as old as the scriptures and is as clear as the American Constitution. The heart of the question is whether all Americans are to be afforded equal rights and equal opportunities, whether we are going to treat our fellow Americans as we want to be treated.

(Broadcast after race riots in Alabama, 11 June 1963)

1016 There are no 'white' or 'colored' signs on the foxholes or graveyards of battle.

(Message to Congress over civil rights, 19 June 1963)

1017 As a free man I take pride in the words, '*Ich bin ein Berliner*' [I am a Berliner].

(Speech, West Berlin, 26 June 1963)

Jomo KENYATTA (*c.* 1897–1978): leader of the Kenya national movement and first President of the Republic of Kenya

1018 God said this is our land, land in which we flourish as a people . . . We want our cattle to get fat on our land so that our children grow up in prosperity; and we do not want the fat removed to feed others.

(Speech, Nyeri, Kenya, 26 July 1952)

John Maynard KEYNES (1883–1946): British economist

1019 One could not despise Clemenceau or dislike him, but only take a different view as to the nature of civilized man, or indulge, at least, a different hope.

(*The Economic Consequences of the Peace*, 1919)

1020 England still stands outside Europe. Europe's voiceless tremors do not reach her. Europe is apart and England is not of her flesh and body.

(Ibid.)

1021 I offer it as a thesis for examination by those who like such generalisations that by far the larger proportion of the world's greatest writers and artists have flourished in the atmosphere of buoyancy, exhilaration and the freedom from economic cares felt by the governing class, which is engendered by profit inflation.

(*Treatise on Money*, Vol. 2, 1930)

Nikita KHRUSHCHEV (1894–1971): Soviet political leader

1022 [on the possibility of the Soviet Union rejecting communism] Those who wait for that must wait until a shrimp learns to whistle.

(Comment, 18 September 1955)

1023 Whether or not you like it, history is on our side. We will bury you.

(To Western diplomats, Kremlin, Moscow, 26 November 1956)

1024 Revolutions are not made for export.

(Speech, 21st Congress, Communist Party, Moscow, 27 January 1959)

1025 Politicians are the same all over: they promise to build a bridge even where there is no river.

(At press conference, Glen Cove, New York, October 1960)

Francis KILVERT (1840–79): Anglican country vicar

1026 At eleven o'clock this morning Napoleon III passed away at Camden House, Chislehurst ... It has been a life of marvellous vicissitudes and the most wonderful romance since that of Charles Edward.

(*Diary*, 9 January 1873)

1027 A satisfactory lecture. I spoke about Noah's vineyard and drunkenness, the Tower of Babel, Babylon and the confusion of tongues, the Tongue Tower, the death of the Emperor Napoleon III and the Great Coram Street Murder.

(*Diary*, 15 January 1873)

Martin Luther KING (1929–68): Negro civil rights leader

1028 Alone for days in a narrow jail cell, long thoughts, long thoughts ... We were here before the mighty words of the Declaration of Independence were etched across the pages of history. Our forebears labored without wages. They made cotton 'king'. And yet out of a bottomless vitality, they continued to thrive and develop. If the cruelties of slavery could not stop us,

the opposition we now face will surely fail. So let us march, let us go on freedom rides, prayer pilgrimages to city-hall. And we will reach the goal in Birmingham and all over the nation. Because the goal of America is freedom, abused and scorned tho' we may be, our destiny is tied up with America's destiny.

(Letter to a group of white clergymen from the city jail of Birmingham, Alabama, April 1963)

1029 I have a dream that my four little children will one day live in a nation where they will not be judged by the color of their skin but by the content of their character.

(Speech, civil rights demonstration, Washington, 15 June 1963)

1030 We have genuflected before the god of science only to find that it has given us the atomic bomb, producing fears and anxieties that science can never mitigate.

(*Strength through Love*, Ch. 13, 1963)

A. W. KINGLAKE (1809–91): English historian

1031 A crowd of monks with bare foreheads stood quarrelling for a key at the sunny gates of a church in Palestine.

(*The Invasion of the Crimea*, 1863)

Rudyard **KIPLING** (1865–1936): English writer

1032 Take up the White Man's burden –
Send forth the best ye breed –
Go, bind your sons to exile
To serve your captives' need.

('The White Man's Burden', *Barrack Room Ballads*, 1892)

Henry **KISSINGER** (b. 1923): American historian and Secretary of State

1033 It is not often that nations learn from the past, even rarer that they draw the correct conclusions from it. For the lessons of historical experience, as of personal experience, are contingent. They teach the consequences of certain actions, but they cannot force a recognition of comparable situations.

(*A World Restored*, 1957)

1034 We have no intention of buying an illusory tranquillity at the expense of our friends. The United States will never knowingly sacrifice the interests of others. But the perception of common interests is not automatic; it requires constant re-definition.

(Speech, New York, 23 April 1973)

1035 The pursuit of peace must . . . begin with the pragmatic concept of existence – especially in a period of ideological conflict.

(Address on 'Moral Purposes and Policy Choices', Washington DC, 8 October 1973)

Horatio Herbert (Earl) **KITCHENER** (1850–1916): British Field Marshal

1036 You are ordered abroad as a soldier of the King to help our French comrades against the invasion of a common enemy . . . Remember that the honour of the British Army depends on your individual conduct . . . In this new experience you may find temptations both in wine and women. You must entirely resist both temptations, and, while treating all women with perfect courtesy, you should avoid any intimacy. Do your duty bravely. Fear God. Honour the King.

(Message handed to every soldier in the British Expeditionary Force, August 1914)

John **KNOX** (?1505–72): Scottish religious reformer

1037 To promote a Woman to bear rule, superiority, dominion or empire, above any Realm,

Nation, or City, is repugnant to Nature; contumely to God, a thing most contrarious to his revealed will and approved ordinance, and finally it is the subversion of good Order, of all equity and justice.

(Opening sentence of the *First Blast of the Trumpet against the Monstrous Regiment of Women*, 1558)

1038 Ungrate ye shall be proved ... if ye transfer the glory of that honour in which ye now stand to any other thing, than to the dispensation of His mercy which only maketh that lawful to your grace which nature and law denieth to all woman.

(Declaration to Queen Elizabeth I, 20 July 1559)

Lajos KOSSUTH (1802–94): Hungarian revolutionary patriot

1039 Seven weeks back I was a prisoner in Kiutayah in Asia Minor. Now I am a free man. I am a free man because glorious England chose it. That England chose it which the genius of mankind selected for the resting monument of its greatness and the spirit of freedom for his happy home.

(Speech, in English, upon arrival at Southampton, 13 October 1851)

1040 Despotism and oppression never yet were beaten except by heroic resistance ... I hope the people of the United States will remember that in the hour of their nation's struggle it received from Europe more than kind wishes. It received aid from others in times past and it will, doubtless, now impart its mighty agency to achieve the liberty of other lands.

(Speech, on landing in the USA, Staten Island, 5 December 1851)

Mikhail KUTUZOV (1745–1813): Russian Marshal

1041 Napoleon is a torrent which as yet we are unable to stem. Moscow will be the sponge that will suck him dry.

(Address to the Russian army commanders at Fili, 13 September 1812)

Henry LABOUCHERE (1831–1912): British radical politician

1042 Nothing has conduced more to shake that decent respect for the living symbol of the State which goes by the name of royalty than the ever-recurring rattle of the money-box.

(*Fortnightly Review*, February 1884)

1043 [of Gladstone] He did not

object, he once said, to Gladstone's always having the ace of trumps up his sleeve, but only to his pretence that God had put it there.

(*Dict. Nat. Biog. 1912–21*)

Fiorello LA GUARDIA (1882–1947): Mayor of New York City

1044 Ticker tape ain't spaghetti.

(Speech to UN Relief and Rehabilitation Commission, New York, 29 March 1946)

Alphonse de Prat de LAMARTINE (1790–1869): French Romantic poet, historian and Foreign Minister in 1848

1045 France is revolutionary or she is nothing at all. The Revolution of 1789 is her political religion.

(*Histoire des Girondins*, 1847)

1046 At its birth the Republic gave voice to ... three words 'Liberty, Equality, Fraternity!' ... If Europe is wise and just, each of these words signifies Peace.

(*A Manifesto to the Powers*, 4 March 1848)

Stephen LANGTON (*c.* 1150–1228): Archbishop of Canterbury

1047 We earnestly beg that no one among you be an accomplice of evil, as administrator or counsellor or servant ... Any service rendered to the temporal king to the prejudice of the eternal king is, without doubt, an act of treachery. My beloved children, Holy Church decrees that, if a rebel persists in schism, his men are absolved from that fealty which they owe him as a just retribution.

(Letter from exile to the baronage of England during the period of Interdict imposed on King John, 1207)

Thomas LANGTON (?1440–1501): Bishop of St David's

1048 [of Richard III] He contents the people where he goes best that ever did Prince, for many a poor man that hath suffered wrong many days has been relieved and helped by him ... God hath sent him to us for the weal of us all.

(1484)

Robert Cavalier de LA SALLE (1643–87): French explorer

1049 [I] do now take, in the name of his Majesty and of his successors to the crown, possession of this country of Louisiana, the seas, harbours, ports, bays, adjacent straits, and all the nations, peoples, provinces, cities, towns, villages, mines, minerals, fisheries, streams and rivers, within the extent of the said Louisiana, from the mouth of the great river St Louis, otherwise called the Ohio ... as also along the river Colbert or Mississippi.

(Proclamation on reaching the mouth of the Mississippi, 9 April 1682)

Bartolomé de LAS CASAS (1474–1566): Spanish historian and Bishop of Chaipa

1050 Here the men could bear no more; they complained of the length of the voyage. But the Admiral Columbus encouraged them as best as he could, holding out high hopes of the gains they could make. He added that it was no use their complaining, because he had reached the Indies and must sail on until with the help of our Lord he discovered land.

(Digest of Columbus's log-book, 10 October 1492: land was sighted next day)

Hugh LATIMER (1485–1555): Bishop of Worcester

1051 Be of good comfort Master Ridley, and play the man. We shall this day light such a candle by God's grace in England, as I trust shall never be put out.

(Final words at stake in Oxford to Bishop Ridley of London, 16 October 1555)

William LAUD (1573–1645): Archbishop of Canterbury [see also 53]

1052 And for the State indeed, my Lord, I am for Thorough, but I see that both thick and thin stays somebody, where I conceive it should not; and it is impossible for me to go thorough alone.

(To Thomas Wentworth [Strafford], Lord Deputy in Ireland, 9 September 1633)

1053 But all that I laboured for in this particular was, that the external worship of God in this Church might be kept up in uniformity and decency and some beauty of holiness.

(In answer to Articles brought against him in Parliament, February 1641)

1054 I laboured nothing more than that the external public worship of God, too much slighted in most parts of this kingdom, might be preserved and that with as much decency and uniformity as might; being still of opinion that Unity cannot long continue in the Church, when Uniformity is shut out at the Church door.

(At his trial, 12 March 1644)

1055 This is an uncomfortable time to preach ... the poor Church of England ... hath flourished and been a shelter to other neighbouring Churches, when storms have driven upon them. But alas! now it is in a storm itself ... that Church, which all the Jesuits' machinations could not ruin, is fallen into danger by her own.

(On the scaffold, 10 January 1645)

Arthur Bonar LAW (1858–1923): British Conservative Prime Minister
[see also 61]

1056 I can imagine no length of resistance to which Ulster can go in which I should not be prepared to support them, and in which, in my belief, they would not be supported by the overwhelming majority of the British people.

(Speech as leader of the Conservative–Unionist Party during the Irish Home Rule crisis; Blenheim Palace, Oxfordshire, 27 July 1912)

James LAWRENCE (1781–1813): American naval commander

1057 Don't give up the ship.

(Orders when mortally wounded as Captain of USS *Chesapeake* in battle with HMS *Shannon*, 1 June 1813)

T. E. LAWRENCE (1888–1935): 'of Arabia', English soldier and writer

1058 I was sitting alone in my room ... when the Muedhins began to send their call of last prayer through the moist night ... One, with a ringing voice of special sweetness, cried into my window from a near mosque ... 'God alone is great: there is no god – but God' ... and softly added 'And he is very good to us this day, O people of Damascus'.

(*Seven Pillars of Wisdom*, written 1919–20, describing the capture of Damascus on 1 October 1918)

Emma LAZARUS (1849–87): American poet

1059 Give me your tired, your poor,
Your huddled masses yearning to breathe free,
The wretched refuse of your teeming shore,
Send these, the homeless, tempest-tossed to me;
I lift my lamp beside the golden door.

(Verses inscribed at foot of the Statue of Liberty, New York harbour, 1886)

Mary Elizabeth LEASE (1853–1933): American popular agrarian reformer

1060 The farmers of Kansas must raise less corn and more Hell.

(Campaign speech, 1890)

1061 The people are at bay, let the bloodhounds of money beware.

(Campaign speech, Wichita, Kansas, October 1894(?))

Edmond LEBOEUF (1809–88): Marshal of France

1062 The army is ready down to the last gaiter-button.

(Verbal assurance, as Minister of War, to a parliamentary commission, Paris, 15 July 1870)

Henry LEE (1756–1818): American soldier and Congressman

1063 [of Washington] First in war, first in peace, first in the hearts of his countrymen.

(Resolution in House of Representatives on death of Washington, 26 December 1799)

Richard Henry LEE (1732–94): American Revolutionary patriot and Senator

1064 That these United Colonies are, and of right ought to be, free and independent states.

(Motion proposed in the Continental Congress at Philadelphia, 7 June 1776)

H. B. LEES-SMITH (1878–1941): British Labour politician

1065 Security can only be obtained by a scheme by which the nations of Europe and outside agree together that all will guarantee each and each will guarantee all. The purposes of the War will be attained if there is a League of Nations with an absolute and decisive veto upon any mere aggression, and consideration of any legitimate claims which any of the countries engaged in the War may be able to make good.

(Speech, H of C, 21 October 1916: earliest parliamentary reference to the League)

Vladimir Ilyitch LENIN (1870–1924): Russian revolutionary leader
[see also 372, 1723, 1805]

1066 A small, compact core, consisting of reliable, experienced and hardened workers, with responsible agents ... connected by all the rules of strict secrecy with the organizations of revolutionists, can, with the wide support of the masses and without an elaborate set of rules, perform *all* the functions of a trade union organization.

(Pamphlet, *What is to be done?*,
1902: *Selected Works*, Vol. 2)

1067 Dear comrades, soldiers,
sailors and workers! I am happy
to greet in you the victorious
Russian Revolution! I greet you
as the advance guard of the world
proletarian army ... The hour is
not far off when at the summons
of our comrade Karl Liebknecht,
the German people will turn their
weapons against their capitalist
exploiters. The sun of the world
socialist revolution has already
risen.

(Speech, Finland Station,
Petrograd, 16 April 1917)

William   LENTHALL
(1591–1662): Speaker of the
House of Commons

1068 May it please Your
Majesty, I have neither eye to see
nor tongue to speak in this place
but as this House is pleased to
direct me, whose servant I am.

(To Charles I, seeking to arrest
five members in the H of C, 4
January 1642) (cf. 336, 1642)

LEO X (1475–1521): Pope

1069 [The Pope said that] the
Imperial electors would soon go
to Frankfurt, and that he was of
opinion the crown would be put
up to auction, so that the highest
bidder would be elected King of
the Romans.

(To the Venetian envoy, Marco
Minio, about the election of the
Holy Roman Emperor, 29
January 1519)

1070 As for the Catholic king
[the future Charles V] on no account would we have him [as
Emperor]. Do you know how
many miles hence the borders of
his territory are? Only forty!

(To Marco Minio about the
election of the Holy Roman
Emperor, 13 March 1519)

1071 Arise, O Lord, plead
Thine own cause; remember how
the foolish man reproacheth
Thee daily; the foxes are wasting
Thy vineyard, which Thou hast
given to Thy Vicar Peter, the boar
out of the wood doth waste it, and
the wild beast of the field doth
devour it.

(Preface to Bull 'Exsurge,
Domine' against Luther, 15 June
1520)

LEONARDO da VINCI
(1452–1519): Italian artist and
inventor

1072 I will make covered cars,
safe and unassailable, which will
enter among the enemy with their
artillery, and there is no company
of men at arms so great that they
will not break it.

(Letter to Ludovico [Sforza] il
Moro of Milan, offering his
services, 1483)

1073 Also I can carry out sculp-
ture in marble, bronze or clay and
also I can do in painting whatever
can be done, as well as any other,
whoever he be.

(Ibid.)

1074 A man with wings large
enough and duly attached might
learn to overcome the resistance
of the air, and conquering it succeed in subjugating it and raise
himself upon it.

(*Flight of Birds*, 1505)

David LESLIE (1601–82):
Scottish Parliamentary General

1075 How glorious it would be,
in the eyes of God and men, if we
managed to hunt the Catholics
from England, follow them to
France and, like the bold King of
Sweden, rouse the Protestants in
France, plant our religion in
Paris, by agreement or force, and
go from there to Rome to chase
the Antichrist and burn the town
whence superstition comes.

(To Lord Hume at Council of
Scottish nobles, August 1643)

**Charles-Joseph, Prince de
LIGNE** (1735–1814): diplomat
and soldier in Austrian service

1076 At table yesterday . . .
[dining with Catherine II of
Russia] . . . a deluge of thee-ings
and thou-ings, each more funny
than the others . . . But in spite of
it all, her thee-ing and thou-ing
and thee'd and thou'd Majesty
still wore the air of the auto-
cratess of All the Russias, and of
nearly all the rest of the world.

(Letter from Kherson in the
Crimea to the Marquise de
Coigny, May 1787)

1077 [Potemkin] . . . shows himself to his army with the air of an
Agamemnon amid the kings of
Greece. What is his magic?
Genius, and then genius, and
again genius; natural intelligence,
an excellent memory, elevation of
soul, malice without malignity,
craft without cunning, a happy
mixture of caprices, of which the
good when they are uppermost
win him all hearts . . .

(Letter to Count de Ségur,
describing the hospitality given to
him by Potemkin in the Crimea,
10 August 1788)

1078 [Of Napoleon I] One could
forgive the fiend for becoming a
torrent, but to become an earth-
quake was really too much.

(Comment, 1814)

1079 The Congress is getting
nowhere, it dances [*Le Congrès ne
marche pas, il danse*].

(Comment on the apparent
frivolity of the Congress of
Vienna, November 1814)

Thomas LINACRE (?1460–
1524): English humanist and
physician

1080 Either this is not the
Gospel or we are not Christians.

(*Attributed remark, said
towards the end of his life, on
reading the Gospels for the first
time)

Abraham LINCOLN (1809–
65): sixteenth President of the
USA
[see also 698, 1734]

1081 No man is good enough to
govern another man without that
other's consent.

(Speech, Peoria, Illinois, 16
October 1854, in the first of the
so-called Lincoln–Douglas
debates)

1082 'A house divided against
itself cannot stand.' I believe this
government cannot endure per-
manently, half slave and half
free. I do not expect the union to
be dissolved – I do not expect
the house to fall – but I do
expect it will cease to be divided.
It will become all one thing, or
all the other.

(Speech, Springfield, Illinois, 16
June 1858)

1083 You can fool all the people
some of the time, and some of the
people all the time, but you
cannot fool all the people all of
the time.

(Speech, Clinton, 8 September
1858)

1084 Our reliance is in the love
of liberty which God has planted
in us. Our defence is in the spirit
which prized liberty as the heritage of all men, in all lands everywhere.

(Speech, Edwardsville, Illinois,
13 September 1858)

1085 What is conservatism? Is it
not adherence to the old and
tried, against the new and un-
tried?

(Speech, New York, 27 February
1860)

1086 Let us have faith that right
makes might; and in that faith let
us to the end, dare to do our duty
as we understand it.

(Ibid.)

1087 I take the official oath
to-day with no mental reserva-
tions, and with no purpose to
construe the Constitution or laws
by any hypercritical rules.

(First Inaugural Address, 4
March 1861)

1088 The power confided to me
will be used to hold, occupy and

possess the property and places belonging to the government, and to collect the duties and imposts.

(Ibid.)

1089 [addressing himself to the Southern States] In *your* hands my dissatisfied fellow-countrymen, and not in *mine*, is the momentous issue of civil war. The government will not assail *you*.

(Ibid.)

1090 My paramount object in this struggle is to save the Union, and is not either to save or to destroy slavery.

(Letter to Horace Greeley, 22 August 1862)

1091 In giving freedom to the slave, we assure freedom to the free – honourable alike in what we give and what we preserve.

(Annual Message to Congress, 1 December 1862)

1092 I have placed you at the head of the army of the Potomac ... Yet I think it best for you to know that there are some things in regard to which I am not quite satisfied with you ... I have heard ... of your recently saying that both the army and the government needed a dictator. Of course, it was not for this, but in spite of it, that I have given you the command. Only those gene-

rals who gain successes can set up dictators. What I now ask of you is military successes, and I will risk the dictatorship ... I much fear that the spirit which you have aided to infuse into the army, of criticising their commander and withholding confidence from him, will now turn upon you. I shall assist you as far as I can to put it down. Neither you nor Napoleon, if he were alive again, could get any good out of an army while such a spirit prevails in it.

(Letter to General Joseph Hooker, 26 January 1863)

1093 Fourscore and seven years ago our fathers brought forth upon this continent a new nation, conceived in liberty and dedicated to the proposition that all men are created equal ... that we here highly resolve that the dead shall not have died in vain, that this nation, under God, shall have a new birth of freedom; and that government of the people, by the people, and for the people, shall not perish from the earth.

(Address at dedication of National Cemetery at Gettysburg, 19 November 1863)

1094 With malice toward none; with charity for all; with firmness in the right, as God gives us to see the right.

(Second Inaugural Address, 4 March 1865)

1095 Enough lives have been sacrificed. We must extinguish our resentments if we expect harmony and union.

(Speech to his Cabinet, 14 April 1865, a few hours before he was shot at Ford's Theater in Washington)

[Lloyd George, *see* GEORGE]

John LOCKE (1632–1704): English philosopher

1096 Government has no other end but the preservation of property.

(*Second Treatise on Civil Government*, written 1681, published 1690)

1097 Freedom of men under government is to have a standing rule to live by, common to every one of that society, and made by the legislative power vested in it; a liberty to follow my own will in all things, when the rule prescribes not, and not to be subject to the inconstant, uncertain, unknown, arbitrary will of another man.

(Ibid.)

1098 A sound mind in a sound body, is a short but full description of a happy state in this world. He that has these two, has little more to wish for; and he that wants either of them, will be little the better for anything else.

(*Thoughts concerning Education*, 1693)

Huey LONG (1893–1935): American demagogue and Governor of Louisiana

1099 Where are the schools that you have waited for your children to have, that have never come? Where are the roads and highways that you sent your money to build, that are no nearer now than ever before? Where are the institutions to care for the sick and the disabled? Evangeline wept bitter tears in her disappointment, but it lasted only through one lifetime. Your tears in this country, around this oak, have lasted for generations. Give me the chance to dry the tears of those who still weep here!

(Campaign speech, around the oak tree alleged to have inspired Longfellow's 'Evangeline', for Louisiana State Governorship, November 1928)

LOUIS VII (1120–80): King of France

1100 But your lord, the King of England [Henry II], who wants for nothing and has men, horses, gold, silk, jewels, fruit, game and everything else. And we in France have nothing but bread and wine and gaiety.

(In conversation with the chronicler, Walter Map, who was

staying in Paris on his way to
Rome, *c.* 1179)

St LOUIS IX (1214–70): King of France

1101 I would rather have a Scot
come from Scotland to govern the
people of this kingdom well and
justly than that you should govern
them ill in the sight of all the
world.

(To his son Louis, during the
king's illness at Fontainebleau,
?1244)

1102 No one, unless he is an
expert theologian, should argue
with these people [the Jews]. But
a layman, whenever he hears the
Christian religion abused, ought
not to defend its tenets, except
with the sword.

(To de Joinville between 1240
and 1254)

1103 There is very great honour
for me in the peace which I am
making with the King of England,
since he is now my vassal, which
before he was not.

(Discussing the Treaty of Paris
made with Henry III of England,
1259)

1104 Our clothing and our
armour ought to be of such a kind
that men of mature experience
will not say we have spent too

much on them, nor younger men
say we have spent too little.

(?Whitsunday, at Corbeil: no
date)

LOUIS XI (1423–83): King of France

1105 I have chased the English
out of France more easily than my
father ever did, for my father
drove them out by force of arms,
whereas I have driven them out
with venison pies and good wine.

(After Treaty of Picquigny [29
August] and celebration banquet
at Amiens, September 1475)

LOUIS XIV (1638–1715): King of France
[see also 173, 437, 636, 1385,
1388, 1597]

1106 I am the State [*L'État c'est
moi*].

(*Alleged remark to Parlement of
Paris, 13 April 1655: no
contemporary evidence)

1107 Everyone knows how much
trouble your meetings have
caused in my State and how many
dangerous results they have had. I
have learnt that you intend to
continue them ... I have come
here expressly to forbid you to do
this, which I do absolutely.

(To the Parlement of Paris, 13 April 1655)

1108 The function of kings consists primarily of using good sense, which always comes naturally and easily. Our work is sometimes less difficult than our amusements.

(*Mémoires for the Instruction of the Dauphin*, 1661)

1109 [The Holy Roman Emperors today] are in no way comparable to the old Roman Emperors, nor to Charlemagne and his first successors. For, to give them their due, they can be considered merely as heads, or captains-general, of a German republic, rather new by comparison with many other states.

(Ibid.)

1110 Every time I fill an empty position, I make a hundred men discontented and one ungrateful.

(After the disgrace of the Duke de Lauzun, ?1669)

1111 The best that I can wish you is that we shall never see each other again.

(To James II, who was leaving for Ireland in an attempt to regain his throne, March 1689)

1112 Love the Spanish and all your subjects attached to your crown and person ... give

thought to trade and continue in a close union with France, nothing being so advantageous to our two powers as such a union which nothing can resist.

(To grandson Philip V on his becoming King of Spain, 16 November 1700)

1113 You will soon be king of a great kingdom ... Try to keep peace with your neighbours. I have loved war too much; do not copy me in that nor in my extravagance ... Relieve your people as soon as you can, and do what I have been too unlucky to do.

(To his grandson [future Louis XV] on his deathbed, 26 November 1715)

1114 When you are considering the State, you are working for yourself; the good of the one becomes the glory of the other. When the State is happy, famous, and powerful, the King is glorious.

(Manuscript found in his papers after his death)

LOUIS XVI (1754–93): King of France

1115 *Rien* [Nothing].

(Diary entry made at Versailles on the evening of 14 July 1789)

1116 I pray to God that the blood you are now going to shed may never be visited on France.

(Last words before execution: 21 January 1793)

LOUIS XVIII (1755–1824): King of France
[see also 579, 1756]

1117 Have I not always been?

(At Hartwell, Buckinghamshire, on being told that, after Napoleon's abdication, he was now King of France, April 1814)

1118 Punctuality is the politeness of kings [*L'exactitude est la politesse des rois*].

(*Attributed remark, ?1814)

LOUIS PHILIPPE (1773–1850): King of the French
[see also 556]

1119 Henceforth the Charter will be a Truth.

(Proclamation to the people of Paris at his accession, 31 July 1830: refers to the Charter of Ghent, nominally accepted by Louis XVIII in 1814)

1120 Died, has he? Now I wonder what he meant by that.

(*Alleged comment on being informed of the death of Talleyrand, 18 March 1838)

George LOVELESS (1805–18??): Dorset farm-labourer and Trade Unionist

1121 My Lord, if we have violated any law it was not done intentionally. We have injured no man's reputation, character, person, or property. We were meeting together to preserve ourselves, our wives, and our children, from utter degradation and starvation.

(Statement on behalf of 'Tolpuddle martyrs', Dorchester Assizes, March 1833)

Robert LOWE (1811–92): English Whig politician
[see also 202]

1122 With our own rash and inconsiderate hands we are about to pluck down on our heads the venerable temple of our liberty and our glory.

(Speech against Gladstone's Parliamentary Reform Bill, H of C, 26 April 1866)

1123 I believe it will be absolutely necessary that you should prevail on our future masters to learn their letters.

(Speech on passage of Second Reform Act, H of C, 15 July 1867 [Apparent origin of ascribed remark, 'We must educate our masters'])

St Ignatius LOYOLA (1491–1556): Spanish soldier and founder of Jesuit Order

1124 I have never left the army: I have only been seconded for the service of God.

(*Alleged remark while in Rome to submit the foundation rules of the Society of Jesus to Paul III, 1539)

1125 To arrive at the truth in all things, we ought always to be ready to believe that what seems to us white is black if the hierarchical Church so defines it.

(*Rules for Thinking with the Church*, XIII, from *Spiritual Exercises*, first used in 1522)

1126 A sound mind in a sound body is the most useful instrument wherewith to serve God.

(Letter to Francis Borgia, 1548/9)

Erich   LUDENDORFF (1865–1937): German General

1127 I could not suppose that it [the Russian Revolution] would become the tomb of our own might.

(Discussing the decision to allow Lenin to cross Germany in returning to Russia, 1917, *War Memoirs*, II, 1919)

1128 August 8 [1918] was the black day of the German army in the history of the war. This was the worst experience that I had to go through, except for the events

that, from September 15 onwards, took place on the Bulgarian Front and sealed the fate of the Quadruple Alliance.

(Ibid.)

Raymond LULL (1235–1315): Spanish mystic and missionary

1129 The Christians build hospitals in which they receive the poor, the sick, and travellers, and in each city they have one, two or even three hospitals. But I never heard that the Saracens have more than two hospitals, one at Tunis and the other at Alexandria.

(*Dispute between Raymond the Christian and Hama the Saracen*, 1308)

Martin LUTHER (1483–1546): German theologian and reformer [see also 349, 1071]

1130 No. 51. Christians are to be taught that the pope would and should wish to give of his own money, even though he had to sell the basilica of St Peter, to many of those from whom certain hawkers of indulgences cajole money.

(Ninety-five theses, Wittenberg, 31 October 1517)

1131 I shall never be a heretic, I may err in dispute; but I do not wish to decide anything finally; on the other hand, I am not bound by the opinions of men.

(Letter to George Spalatin, Chaplain to Elector of Saxony, 28 August 1518)

1132 I cannot and I will not recant anything, for to go against conscience is neither right nor safe. (Here I stand. I cannot do otherwise. God help me. Amen.)

(Speech at the Diet of Worms, 18 April 1521, the section in brackets added in Luther's handwriting to the first printed version)

1133 The Devil knows I would have gone into Worms though there were as many devils as tiles on the roof . . . I would ride into Leipzig now, though it rained Duke Georges for nine days.

(Letter to Frederick, Elector of Saxony, who tried to persuade Luther to stay in hiding: spring 1522)

1134 Anyone who can be proved to be a seditious person is an outlaw before God and the emperor; and whoever is the first to put him to death does right and well . . . Therefore let everyone who can, smite, slay and stab, secretly or openly, remembering that nothing can be more poisonous, hurtful, or devilish than a rebel.

(*Against the Robbing and Murdering Hordes of Peasants*, May 1525)

1135 In my opinion it is better that all of these peasants should be killed rather than that the sovereigns and magistrates should be destroyed, because the peasants take up the sword without God's authorization.

(Letter to Nicholas von Ansdorf, 30 May 1525)

Douglas MACARTHUR (1880–1964): American General [see also 190]

1136 I shall return.

(Message on leaving Corregidor, Philippines, 11 March 1942)

1137 People of the Philippines, I have returned.

(Broadcast after landing on Leyte, 20 October 1944)

1138 A great tragedy has ended. A great victory has been won . . . A new era is upon us . . . We have had our last chance. If we do not devise some greater and more equitable system, Armageddon will be at our door.

(Broadcast, on surrender of Japan, 2 September 1945)

1139 When I joined the army, even before the turn of the century, it was the fulfilment of all my boyish hopes and dreams . . .

Like the old soldier of the ballad,
I now close my military career
and just fade away.

(Address to Congress, 19 April
1951)

**Thomas Babington (Lord)
MACAULAY** (1800–59): English historian and Whig politician
[see also 55, 1237, 1711]

1140 The gallery in which the
reporters sit has become a fourth
estate of the realm.

(*Edinburgh Review*, September
1828)

1141 We know no spectacle so
ridiculous as the British public in
one of its periodical fits of morality.

(Ibid., June 1830)

1142 At present . . . we drive
over to the side of revolution
those whom we shut out from
power . . . Turn where we may,
within, around, the voice of great
events is proclaiming to us,
Reform, that you may preserve!

(Speech on Reform Bill, H of C,
2 March 1831)

1143 Dark and terrible beyond
any season within my remem-
brance of political affairs was the
day of their flight. Far darker and
far more terrible will be the day of
their return.

(Speech, on defeat of Tory
government, November 1830, H
of C, 20 September 1831)

1144 [of Gladstone] The rising
hope of those stern and unbend-
ing Tories.

(*Historical Essays: Gladstone on
Church and State*, April 1839)

1145 They [the Nabobs] raised
the price of everything in their
neighbourhood, from fresh eggs
to rotten boroughs.

(*Historical Essays: Lord Clive*,
January 1840)

1146 [of Clive] A savage old
Nabob, with an immense fortune,
a tawny complexion, a bad liver
and a worse heart.

(Ibid.)

1147 [The Roman Catholic
Church] . . . may still exist in
undiminished vigour, when some
traveller from New Zealand shall,
in the midst of a vast solitude,
take his stand on a broken arch of
London Bridge to sketch the
ruins of St Paul's.

(Essay on Ranke's 'History of the
Popes', *Edinburgh Review*,
October 1840)

1148 [of Warren Hastings] The
Great Proconsul.

(*Historical Essays: Warren
Hastings*, October 1841)

1149 [of Frederick the Great] We hardly know any instance of the strength and weakness of human nature so striking, and so grotesque, as the character of this haughty, vigilant, resolute, sagacious blue-stocking, half Mithridates and half Trissotin, bearing up against a world in arms, with an ounce of poison in one pocket and a quire of bad verses in the other.

(*Historical Essays: Frederick the Great*, April 1842)

1150 I hardly know which is the greater pest to society, a paternal government, that is to say a prying, meddlesome government, which intrudes itself into every part of human life, and which thinks it can do everything for everybody better than anybody can do anything for himself; or a careless, lounging government, which suffers grievances, such as it could at once remove, to grow and multiply, and which to all complaint and remonstrance has only one answer: 'We must let things take their course; we must let things find their own level'.

(Speech, on Ten Hours Bill, H of C, 22 May 1846)

1151 It is pleasing to reflect that the public mind of England has softened while it has ripened, and that we have, in the course of ages, become, not only a wiser, but also a kind people ... The more we study the annals of the past, the more shall we rejoice in a merciful age, in an age in which cruelty is abhorred, and in which pain, even when deserved, is inflicted reluctantly and from a sense of duty.

(*History of England*, written 1848)

1152 Persecution produced its natural effect on them. It found them a sect; it made them a faction.

(Ibid.: Refers to the early Puritans).

1153 There were gentlemen and there were seamen in the navy of Charles the Second. But the seamen were not gentlemen; and the gentlemen were not seamen.

(Ibid.)

1154 The history of England is emphatically the history of progress.

(Ibid.)

1155 Let no damned Tory index my *History*.

(*Alleged remark to the publishers of his *History of England*, 1848)

J. Ramsay MACDONALD (1866–1937): British Labour Prime Minister [see also 1739]

1156 The League of Nations grows in moral courage. Its frown will soon be more dreaded than a nation's arms, and when that happens you and I shall have security and peace.

(Speech, Guildhall, London, 9 November 1929)

Niccolò   **MACHIAVELLI** (1469–1527): Italian political theorist

1157 War should be the only study of a prince. He should look upon peace only as a breathing time which affords him the leisure to contrive, and furnishes him with ability to execute military plans.

(*The Prince*, 1513)

1158 A prince who desires to maintain his position must learn to be not always good, but to be so or not as needs may require.

(Ibid.)

1159 We Italians then owe to the Church of Rome and to her priests our having become irreligious and bad, but we owe her a still greater debt, and one that will be the cause of our ruin, namely that the Church has kept and still keeps our country divided.

(*Discourses on First Ten Books of Livy*, written 1513/14)

1160 But we must assume, as a general rule, that it never or rarely happens that a republic or monarchy is well constituted, or its old institutions entirely reformed, unless it is done by only one individual.

(Ibid.)

Maurice de **MACMAHON** (1808–93): Marshal of France

1161 Here I am, here I stay [*J'y suis, j'y reste*].

(On capturing Malakoff Fort, 8 September 1855)

Harold   **MACMILLAN**   (b. 1894):   British   Conservative Prime Minister
[see also 179]

1162 We have not overthrown the divine right of kings to fall down for the divine right of experts.

(Speech, Strasbourg, 16 August 1950)

1163 Let's be frank about it; most of our people have never had it so good. Go around the country, go to the industrial towns, go to the farms, and you will see a state of prosperity such as we have never had in my lifetime – nor indeed ever in the history of this country.

(Speech, Bedford, 20 July 1957: this passage in the speech occurs in the context of a general warning over the folly of inflation)

1164 Little local difficulties ...

(Description of the crisis caused by the resignation of three Treasury ministers, January 1958)

1165 At home you always have to be a politician. When you're abroad you almost feel yourself a statesman.

(Speech, during the first visit of a British prime minister to Australia, Melbourne, 17 February 1958)

1166 The most striking of all the impressions I have formed since I left London a month ago is of the strength of African national consciousness. In different places it may take different forms, but it is happening everywhere. The wind of change is blowing through the continent. Whether we like it or not the growth of national consciousness is a political fact.

(Speech to South African Parliament, Cape Town, 3 February 1960)

1167 Are we so sure that with fifteen representatives ... in NATO, acting under the unanimity rule, the deterrent would

continue to deter? There might be one finger on the trigger, but there will be fifteen fingers on the safety catch.

(Speech, arguing against handing over Britain's independent nuclear deterrent to NATO control, H of C, 30 May 1960)

James MADISON (1751–1836): fourth President of USA

1168 The diversity in the faculties of men, from which the rights of property originate, is not less an insuperable obstacle to an uniformity of interests. The protection of these faculties is the first object of government.

(*Federalist Papers*, X, November 1787)

1169 The proposed [US] Constitution ... is, in strictness, neither a national nor a federal constitution; but a composition of both.

(Ibid., XXXIX, January 1788)

1170 What is government itself but the greatest of all reflections on human nature? If men were angels, no government would be necessary. If angels were to govern men, neither external nor internal controls on government would be necessary.

(Ibid., XLVII, January 1788)

MAGNA CARTA (1215)

1171 Except by the lawful judgment of his peers and by the law of the land . . .

(Article 39)

1172 To no one will we sell, to no one will we refuse or delay right or justice.

(Article 40)

1173 It shall be lawful in future for anyone to leave our kingdom and return safely and securely, by land and water, save, in the public interest, for a short period in time of war.

(Article 42)

Françoise de MAINTENON (1635–1719): second wife of Louis XIV
[see also 1385]

1174 You must make use of people according to their abilities, and realize that absolutely no one is perfect.

(Letter to Count d'Aubigne, 25 September 1679)

William of MALMESBURY (*c.* 1090–*c.* 1143): monastic chronicler

1175 [Of King Ethelred the Unready's reluctance to resist the Danish invaders] The King, readily and admirably suited for

sleeping, postponed all such matters and yawned, and if he ever recovered his senses enough to raise himself upon his elbow, he immediately sank back into wretchedness, either from a burden of apathy or from the adversities of fortune.

(*Gesta Regum Anglorum*)

Thomas Robert MALTHUS (1766–1834): English economist

1176 Population, when unchecked increases in a geometrical ratio. Subsistence only increases in an arithmetical ratio.

(*The Principle of Population*, 1798)

Henry Edward MANNING (1808–92): Cardinal, Archbishop of Westminster

1177 To put labour and wages first and human or domestic life second is to invert the order of God and of nature.

(On social obligations, after the first London Dock Strike, in 1889, which he helped to resolve)

Michael J. MANSFIELD (b. 1903): US Senator

1178 A piece of each of us died at that moment.

(Eulogy for President Kennedy after the Dallas assassination, US Senate, 24 November 1963)

William Murray, Lord MANS-FIELD (1705–93): Lord Chief Justice

1179 We must not regard political consequences, however formidable they may be; if rebellion was the certain consequence we are bound to say, '*Justitia fiat, ruat coelum*' ['Let Justice be done, though the skies fall'].

(In hearing an appeal by John Wilkes against a sentence of outlawry for publishing the *North Briton*, 28 April 1758)

1180 Every man who comes to England is entitled to the protection of the English law, whatever oppression he may heretofore have suffered, and whatever may be the colour of his skin, whether it is black or whether it is white.

(Judgment in the Habeas Corpus Case concerning the slave Somersett, May 1772)

MAO TSE-TUNG (1893–1976): Chinese communist leader

1181 A single spark can start a prairie fire ... Our forces, although small at present, will grow rapidly.

(Letter to combat pessimism within the Chinese Communist Party, 5 January 1930)

1182 If you want to know the taste of a pear, you must change the pear by eating it yourself ... If you want to know the theory and methods of revolution, you must take part in revolution. All genuine knowledge originates in direct experience.

(Address on the relation between knowledge and practice, Anti-Japanese Military and Political College, Yenan, July 1937)

1183 We should assimilate what is useful for us today, not only from present-day socialist and new democratic cultures, but also from the earlier cultures of other nations, such as the various capitalist states in the Age of Enlightenment. However we should not gulp any of this foreign material but rather we must treat it as we do our food ... before it is capable of nourishing us.

(*New Democracy*, 1940)

1184 Letting a hundred flowers blossom and a hundred schools of thought contend is the policy for promoting the progress of the arts and the sciences and a flourishing culture in our land.

(Speech on the handling of contradictions among the people, Peking, 27 February 1957)

1185 All the so-called powerful reactionaries are no more than paper tigers, for they are cut off from their people. Think of Hitler: was he not a paper tiger

and was he not overthrown? I
have said that the Tsar of Russia,
the Emperor of China and the
imperialism of Japan were all
paper tigers. As we know, they
were all overthrown. US imperialism has not yet been overthrown, and it has atomic bombs.
But I believe it, too, will be overthrown. It, too, is a paper tiger.

(Speech to international
Congress of Communist and
Workers' Parties, Moscow,
November 1957)

1186 Politics is war without
bloodshed: war is politics with
bloodshed.

(*Quotations from Chairman Mao,*
published 1966)

1187 We Communists are like
seeds and the people are like the
soil. Wherever we go, we must
unite with the people, take root,
and blossom among them.

(Ibid.)

MARIA THERESA (1717–80):
Empress in Austria, Queen of
Hungary

1188 Forsaken by all, we place
our sole resource in the fidelity,
arms, and long-tried valour of the
Hungarians ... In regard to
ourself, the faithful states and
orders of Hungary shall experience our hearty cooperation in all
things which may promote the
pristine happiness of this ancient

kingdom and the honours of the
people.

(To the Hungarian Diet, 11
September 1741)

1189 I confess that I prefer the
least of the Italians to all our
composers ... For instrumental
music there is a certain Haydn,
who has some peculiar ideas, but
he is only just beginning.

(Letter to Archduchess Marie
Beatrix, 1772)

MARIE   ANTOINETTE
(1755–93): Queen of France
[see also 239]

1190 Let them eat cake [*Qu'ils
mangent de la brioche*].

(*Attributed remark during the
bread-shortage of 1789: no
evidence that she used the
phrase, although a similiar phrase
is mentioned as common in
France by Rousseau in 1740)

**John   Churchill,   Duke   of
MARLBOROUGH** (1650–
1722): British military commander

1191 I have not time to say more,
but to beg you will give my duty to
the Queen, and let her know her
army has had a glorious victory.
Monsieur Tallard and two other
generals are in my coach, and I
am following the rest ...

(Note to his wife, Duchess Sarah, written on a tavern bill, giving news of the victory of Blenheim, 13 August 1704)

MARTIN IV (1210–85): Pope

1192 I wish I were a stork and the Germans were frogs in the marshes, so I could devour them all; or else a pike in a lake and they fish, so I could eat them this way.

(*Attributed saying, ?1284)

Peter MARTYR (Vermigli) (1500–62): Italian-born Protestant reformer

1193 Hitherto the popish party [in England] has been defeated and the palm rests with our friends, but especially with the Archbishop of Canterbury [Cranmer], whom they till now were wont to traduce as a man ignorant of theology, and as being only conversant with making of government; but now ... he has shown himself so mighty a theologian against them as they would rather not have proof of, and they are compelled against their inclination to acknowledge his learning and power and dexterity in debate.

(Letter from Oxford to the German Protestant, Martin Bucer, in Wittenberg, 28 December 1548)

Andrew MARVELL (1621–78): English poet

1194 [of Charles I's execution]
He nothing common did or
    mean
Upon that memorable scene
. . . But bowed his comely head
Down as upon a bed.

(*Horatian Ode upon Cromwell's return from Ireland*, summer, 1650)

1195 And now the Irish are ashamed
    To see themselves in one
        year tamed.

(Ibid.)

1196 The lands that were formerly given to superstitious uses, having first been applied to the publick revenue, and afterwards by several alienations and contracts distributed into private possession, the alteration of religion would necessarily introduce a change of property.

(*Account of the Growth of Popery and Arbitrary Government in England*, 1677)

Karl MARX (1818–83): German-born political theorist

1197 Religion is the sigh of the oppressed creature, the feelings of a heartless world and the spirit of conditions which are unspiritual. It is the opium of the people.

(Preface to *A Critique of Hegel's Philosophy of Right*, originally published in 1844 in the Parisian journal *Deutsch-Französische Jahrbücher*)

1198 The Democrats of Belgium and the Chartists of England are the real democrats, and the moment they carry the six points of their Charter, the road to liberty will be opened to the world. Effect this grand object, you workmen of England, and you will be hailed as the saviours of the whole human race.

(Speech at the Congress of the Communist League, London, 1847, as reported in the *Northern Star*, 4 December 1847)

1199 A spectre is haunting Europe – the spectre of communism. All the powers of old Europe have entered into a holy alliance to exorcise this spectre: Pope and Tsar, Metternich and Guizot, French Radicals and German police-spies.

(Opening paragraph of *The Communist Manifesto*, 1848)

1200 The history of all hitherto existing society is the history of class struggles.

(*The Communist Manifesto*, 1848)

1201 Let the ruling classes tremble at a communist revolution. The proletarians have noth-ing to lose but their chains. They have a world to win. Working men of all countries, unite!

(Ibid.)

1202 What I did that was new was to prove: (i) that the existence of classes is only bound up with particular, historic phases in the development of production; (ii) that the class struggle necessarily leads to the dictatorship of the proletariat; (iii) that this dictatorship itself only constitutes the transition to the abolition of all classes and to a classless society.

(Private letter from Marx to Weydemeyer, 5 March 1852, *Correspondence of Marx–Engels 1846–1895*, p. 67)

1203 [of the French Second Republic in 1852] Liberty, Equality, Fraternity! – when what this republic really means is Infantry, Cavalry, Artillery!

(*18th Brumaire of Louis Bonaparte*, 1852)

1204 The centralization of the means of production and the socialization of labour reach a point where they prove incompatible with their capitalist husk. This bursts asunder. The knell of private property sounds. The expropriators are expropriated.

(*Das Kapital*, I, 1867)

1205 Capitalist   production

develops technology solely by sapping the original sources of all wealth – the soil and the labourer.

(Ibid.)

1206 [of Adolphe Thiers] Even now, while playing the part of a French Sulla, Thiers cannot help setting off the abomination of his deeds by the ridicule of his ostentation.

(Printed address, on the suppression of the Paris Commune, to the International Working Men's Association, *The Civil War in France*, 30 May 1871)

1207 The Second Empire was the jubilee of cosmopolitan blackleggism, the rakes of all countries rushing in at its call for a share in its orgies and in the plunder of the French people.

(Ibid.)

1208 Only in a higher phase of communist society ... can the narrow horizon of bourgeois right be crossed in its entirety and society inscribe on its banners: From each according to his ability, to each according to his needs!

(*Critique of the Gotha Programme*, May 1875)

1209 Between capitalist and communist society lies the period of the revolutionary transformation of the one into the other.

Corresponding to this is also a political transition period in which the state can be nothing but the revolutionary dictatorship of the proletariat.

(Ibid.)

MARY I (1516–58): Queen of England

1210 And though you esteem little the Emperor, yet should you show more favour to me for my father's sake, who made the more part of you almost of nothing.

(To Privy Councillors who ordered her to use the Book of Common Prayer, 28 August 1551)

1211 And, as for your new books, I thank God I never read any of them; I never did, nor ever will do ... My Lord, for your gentleness to come and see me, I thank you; but for your offering to preach before me, I thank you never a whit.

(To Bishop Nicholas Ridley, ?8 September 1552)

1212 I cannot tell how naturally the mother loveth the child, for I was never the mother of any, but certainly if a prince and governor may as naturally and earnestly love her subjects as the mother doth love the child, then assure yourselves that I, being your lady and mistress, do as earnestly and tenderly love and favour you.

(Speech, Guildhall, London, during Wyatt's rebellion, 1 February 1554)

1213 Not that only, but when I am dead and opened you shall find Calais lying on my heart.

(*On being asked if she were sad because of the departure of her husband, Philip of Spain, November 1558. Calais, an English possession for more than two hundred years, was captured by the French on 7 January 1558)

MARY II (1662–94): Queen of England
[see also 252, 630]

1214 Many people have the fortune to be able to talk of things about which I have to be silent. You must not doubt the sincerity of my feelings when I say that I cannot forget my father, and I grieve for his misfortune.

(To Electress Sophia of Hanover after her coronation, 13 April 1688)

MARY Stuart (1542–87): Queen of Scots
[see also 604, 942]

1215 No more tears now; I will think upon revenge.

(On hearing of Riccio's death, 9 March 1566)

1216 (She appealeth to the commissioners, desiring them to) look into their consciences in the respect of God, and unto their honours in regard of the world; for England is not all the world.

(During the preliminaries to her trial at Fotheringay [according to Scottish State Papers], 13 October 1586)

1217 In my end is my beginning.

(Motto on her canopy of state, embroidered by herself while captured in England after 1568)

MARY (1867–1953): Queen-Consort of England

1218 God grant we may not have a European War thrust upon us, and for such a stupid reason too, no I don't mean stupid, but to have to go to war on account of tiresome Servia beggars belief.

(Letter to her aunt, Grand-Duchess of Mecklenburg-Strelitz, 28 July 1914)

Tomaš MASARYK (1850–1937): first President of Czechoslovakia

1219 Our whole history inclines us towards the democratic Powers. Our renaissance is a logical link between us and the democracies of the West.

(Inaugural Presidential message, 23 December 1918)

1220 Perhaps, in half a century, our times will appear to people living then in such a haze of splendour that they will almost envy us.

(In conversation with the Czech dramatist and author Karel Capek, 1936)

MATHIAS I Corvinus (1440–90): King of Hungary

1221 For centuries we have been famed for our skill in horsemanship, so that the Magyar has no need to have his horses dance with crossed legs, Spanish fashion.

(To his father-in-law, the King of Naples, who had sent him a Spanish riding-master: no date, but after 1476)

1222 *Bella gerant fortes; tu, felix Austria, nube* [Let the strong wage war; you marry, lucky Austria].

(*Attributed)

J. Frederick Denison MAURICE (1805–72): English Christian socialist

1223 We will help you in fighting against the greatest enemy you have, your own self-will and selfishness ... That is what is meant by Christian Socialism.

(*Tracts on Christian Socialism*, 1850)

MAXIMILIAN I (1459–1519): Holy Roman Emperor

1224 Since Christendom comprehends only a small part of the globe, should not everyone who believes in a God be saved by his own religion?

(To Abbot Tritemius, 1508)

1225 No marriage seems to us higher, greater, or richer than with the Kings of Hungary and Denmark, to whom they are united ... four or five great kingdoms to which King Louis of Bohemia [and Hungary] is rightful heir ... similarly there are three fine old kingdoms, over which the King of Denmark is Lord, although their subjects are all rough and uncouth.

(Letter to his daughter Margaret, asserting that his daughters Mary and Isabelle were well married, 1 January 1516)

1226 My child, you are about to cheat the French and I the English, or at least I shall do my best.

(To his grandson Charles, later Emperor Charles V, after Treaty of Noyon, spring 1517)

1227 The king of France is called the most Christian King, but this does him injustice, for he

never did a Christian thing. I am
called the most Invincible King,
but I have often been overcome.
The Pope is called his Holiness
but he is the biggest scoundrel on
earth. You are called the richest
king, and this is true.

(To Henry VIII of England:
*attributed by Martin Luther, in
his tabletalk, April–June 1542)

Jules, Cardinal MAZARIN
(1602–61): Italian-born statesman, chief minister of King Louis
XIV in his minority

1228 The French are nice
people. I allow them to sing and
to write, and they allow me to do
whatever I like.

(*Attributed, by Elizabeth
Charlotte, Duchess of Orléans, in
letter of 25 October 1715)

1229 [In France] a woman will
not go to sleep until she has
talked over affairs of state with
her lover or her husband.

(*Attributed remark, c. 1650)

1230 I owe you everything, Sire,
but I believe I can pay some of my
debt with this gift – Colbert.

(To Louis XIV, just before
Mazarin's death, 1661)

Giuseppe MAZZINI (1805–
72): Italian republican leader and
political theorist

1231 A nation is the universality
of citizens speaking the same
tongue.

(*La Giovine Italia*, written 1832)

MEHEMET ALI (1769–1849):
Pasha of Egypt

1232 If this Canal be made
which nation of Europe would
make most use of it for their
ships? Will it not be the English,
in passing from their own country
to their Indian empire and back
again? And do you not think that
when they come to see this
beautiful garden of Egypt which
is now my own, they will envy me
its possession ... and by using
their ships ... take possession of
Egypt as they have done of India?

(In conversation with Captain J.
S. Buckingham, R.N., September
1814: noted in his journal and
printed in this form in his
Autobiography, Vol. 2, 1855)

**William Lamb, Viscount
MELBOURNE** (1779–1848):
English Whig Prime Minister

1233 What I like about the
Order of the Garter is that there
is no damned merit about it.

(*Attributed remark soon after
becoming Prime Minister, 1835)

1234 I hardly make out what
Puseyism is. Either I am dull or
its apostles are very obscure. I

have got one of their chief Newman's publications with an ap-
pendix of four hundred and
forty-four pages. I have read
fifty-seven and cannot say I
understand a sentence or any idea
whatever.

(To Lord Holland, ?1839/40)

1235 Damn it all, another
Bishop dead – I verily believe
they die to vex me.

(*Alleged comment as Prime
Minister over the difficulties of
making ecclesiastical appoint-
ments, *c.* 1837)

1236 Now is it to lower the price
of corn, or isn't it? It is not much
matter which we say, but mind,
we must all say *the same.*

(*Alleged remark at a Cabinet
Meeting, March 1841)

1237 [of Macaulay] I wish I was
as cocksure of anything as Tom
Macaulay is of everything.

(As reported by his nephew Earl
Cowper in 1889)

Clement   METTERNICH
(1773–1859): Austrian diplomat
and Chancellor
[see also 704, 1348]

1238 Such men as M. de Talleyrand are like sharp-edged instruments with which it is dangerous to play but for great evils
drastic remedies are necessary

and whoever has to treat them
should not be afraid to use the
instrument which cuts the best.

(Report, as ambassador in Paris,
to the Austrian foreign minister,
24 September 1808)

1239 My life has coincided with
a wretched epoch. I came into the
world too soon or too late; today I
know I can do nothing. Earlier I
should have enjoyed the pleas-
ures of my age; later I should
have helped in reconstruction.
Now I spend my life in propping
up buildings mouldering in
decay. I ought to have been born
in 1900 and to have had the
twentieth century before me.

(Letter to Dorothea Lieven, 6
October 1820)

1240 Europe has for a long time
held for me the essence of a
fatherland [*Depuis   longtemps
l'Europe a pris pour moi la valeur
d'une patrie*].

(Letter to the Duke of
Wellington, 10 June 1824)

1241 When   Paris   sneezes,
Europe catches cold.

(Comment, 1830)

1242 Italy is a geographical expression.

(Letter, 6 August 1847)

1243 Error has never come into
my mind.

(On meeting Guizot on the steps of the British Museum when both men were in exile, summer 1848)

Adam MICKIEWICZ (1798–1855): Polish patriot and poet

1244 For the universal war to free the nations, we beseech thee, O Lord!

(*The Books of the Polish Nation and the Polish Pilgrims*, 1832)

Draža MIHAILOVIĆ (1893–1946): Yugoslav General, leader of the Serbian Chetniks

1245 A merciless fate threw me into this maelstrom. I wanted much, I began much, but the gale of the world carried away me and my work.

(Final defence plea at his trial, Belgrade, 15 July 1946)

John Stuart MILL (1806–73): English political philosopher

1246 When the land is cultivated entirely by the spade and no horses are kept, a cow is kept for every three acres of land.

(*Political Economy*, 1848, discussing farming in Flanders)

1247 If all mankind minus one, were of one opinion, and only one person were of the contrary opinion, mankind would be no more justified in silencing that one person, than he, if he had the power, would be justified in silencing mankind.

(*On Liberty*, 1859)

1248 A party of order or stability, and a party of progress or reform, are both necessary elements of a healthy state of political life.

(Ibid.)

1249 Every one who receives the protection of society owes a return for the benefit, and the fact of living in society renders it indispensable that each should be bound to observe a certain line of conduct towards the rest. This conduct consists, first, in not injuring the interests of one another . . . and secondly, in each person's bearing his share . . . of the labours and sacrifices incurred for defending the society or its members from injury and molestation.

(Ibid.)

1250 The worth of a State, in the long run, is the worth of the individuals composing it.

(Ibid.)

1251 It is in general a necessary condition of free institutions, that the boundaries of governments should coincide in the main with those of nationalities.

(Representative Government,
written 1861)

**Alfred (later, Viscount)
MILNER** (1854–1925): British
Imperial statesman

1252 The spectacle of thousands
of British subjects kept per-
manently in the position of helots,
constantly chafing under undoubted grievances, and calling
vainly to Her Majesty's Government for redress, does steadily
undermine the influence and
reputation of Great Britain and
the respect for the British Government within its own dominions.

(Despatch to Joseph Chamberlain from Cape Town on conditions in the Transvaal, 4 May
1899)

1253 If we believe a thing to be
bad, and if we have a right to
prevent it, it is our duty to try to
prevent it and to damn the consequences.

(Speech, Glasgow, 26 November
1909, on House of Lords and the
Budget)

John MILTON (1608–74): English poet and pamphleteer

1254 It would not be the first or
second time ... that England
hath had this honour vouchsafed
from heaven, to give out reformation to the world ... Let not

England forget her precedence of
teaching nations how to live.

*(The Doctrine and Discipline of
Divorce,* 1643)

1255 For this is not the liberty
which we can hope, that no griev-
ance ever should arise in the
Commonwealth, that let no man
in this world expect; but when
complaints are freely heard,
deeply considered and speedily
reformed, then is the utmost
bound of civil liberty attained that
wise men look for.

(Areopagitica, a speech for the
Liberty of Unlicensed Printing to
the Parliament of England, 1644)

1256 I cannot praise a fugitive
and cloistered virtue, unexercised
and unbreathed, that never sallies
out and seeks her adversary, but
slinks out of the race where that
immortal garland is to be run for,
not without dust and heat.

(Ibid.)

1257 God is decreeing to begin
some new and great period in His
Church, even to the reforming of
Reformation itself. What does He
then but reveal Himself to His
servants, and as His manner is,
first to His Englishmen?

(Ibid.)

1258 Give me the liberty to know,
to utter, and to argue freely ac-

cording to conscience, above all liberties.

(Ibid.)

1259 Methinks I see in my mind a noble and puissant nation rousing herself like a strong man after sleep, and shaking her invincible locks.

(Ibid.)

1260 New Presbyter is but old Priest writ large.

('On the New Forcers of Conscience under the Long Parliament', ?1645)

1261 No man who knows aught, can be so stupid to deny that all men naturally were born free.

('The Tenure of Kings and Magistrates', 1649)

1262 The power of kings and magistrates is nothing else, but what only is derivative, transformed and committed to them in trust from the people to the common good of them all, in whom the power yet remains fundamentally, and cannot be taken from them, without a violation of their natural birthright.

(Ibid.)

1263 Peace hath her victories
      No less renowned than war.
      Help us to save free conscience from the paw

Of hireling wolves, whose
      gospel is their maw.

(Sonnet XIX, 'To the Lord General Cromwell, May 1652')

1264 [The blood of the Indians] has been so unjustly, so cruelly, and so often shed by the hands of the Spaniards: since God has made of one blood all nations of men for to dwell on all the face of the earth ... All great and extraordinary wrongs done to particular persons ought to be considered as in a manner done to all the rest of the human race.

(Manifesto to the Lord Protector to justify war against Spain, 1655)

Honoré Gabriel, Count MIRABEAU (1749–91): French aristocratic Revolutionary

1265 Should Prussia perish, the art of government would return to its infancy.

(*Monarchie Prussienne*, 1788)

1266 I tremble for the royal authority [in France] ... No National Assembly ever threatened to be so stormy as that which will decide the fate of the monarchy, and which is gathering in such haste, and with so much distrust on both sides.

(Letter to one of the King's ministers, Montmorin, 6 December 1788)

1267 To administer is to govern: to govern is to reign. That is the essence of the problem.

(Memorandum, 3 July 1790)

Emilio MOLA (1887–1937): Spanish Nationalist General

1268 The Fifth Column [*La quinta columna*].

(To Press Conference, when asked which of his four army columns would capture Madrid, indicating he believed the city would fall from disruptive elements already within its defences, October 1937)

V. M. MOLOTOV (b. 1890): Soviet Prime Minister and Foreign Minister

1269 To Soviet patriots the homeland and communism become fused in one inseparable whole ... We Bolsheviks have sprung from the bowels of the people, and we prize and revere the glorious deeds in our people's history.

(Speech to the Supreme Soviet, 6 November 1939)

James MONROE (1758–1831): fifth President of the USA

1270 The mention of Greece fills the mind with the most exal-ted sentiments and arouses in our bosoms the best feelings of which our nature is susceptible.

(President's message to Congress, December 1822)

1271 The American continents, by the free and independent condition which they have assumed and maintain, are henceforth not to be considered as subjects for future colonization by any European powers ... In the wars of the European powers in matters relating to themselves we have never taken any part, nor does it comport with our policy to do so.

(Message to Congress, 2 December 1823, the 'Monroe Doctrine')

Simon de MONTFORT, Earl of Leicester (?1208–65): leader of the English baronial reformers in Henry III's reign

1272 By the arm of St James, they are coming on cleverly; they did not learn this method of themselves, they learnt it from me.

(On seeing Prince Edward's army approaching to attack him at Battle of Evesham, 4 August 1265)

Bernard (Viscount) MONT-GOMERY of Alamein (1887–1976): British Field-Marshal

1273 Let no man surrender so long as he is unwounded and can fight.

(Message to 8th Army on eve of Battle of El Alamein, 30 October 1942)

Anne-Marie-Louise, Duchess of MONTPENSIER (1627–93): niece of Louis XIII

1274 I paid a visit of condolence to the Queen of England. Her husband had been beheaded by order of the British parliament. The [French] court did not go into general mourning on this occasion, for want of funds. I found her not so deeply affected as she should have been.

(*Mémoires*, February 1649)

1275 When I thought, that evening and many times afterwards, how I had saved our fine army from destruction, I confess that I experienced a great wonder and thankfulness ... I had all those poor dead in my mind, while I could hear the cry of the returning soldiers, 'Long live the Granddaughter of France! Mademoiselle is at the gate: she will have it opened for us.'

(On the day on which she prevented the King's troops from keeping Paris closed to Condé's army in the second Fronde, *Mémoires*, 2 July 1652)

Jeremy MOORE (born 1928): Major-General commanding land forces in the Falklands campaign

1276 The Falkland Islands are once more under the Government desired by their inhabitants. God save the Queen.

(Message sent from Port Stanley to London, 14 June 1982)

Sir (St) Thomas MORE (1478–1535): Lord Chancellor of England
[see also 350]

1277 When I consider and weigh in my mind all those commonwealths which nowadays anywhere do flourish, so God help me, I can perceive nothing but a certain conspiracy of rich men procuring their own commodities under the name and title of the Commonwealth.

(*Utopia*, Book 1, 1516)

1278 For this is one of the ancientest laws among them; that no man shall be blamed for reasoning in the maintenance of his own religion.

('Of the Religions in Utopia', Ibid., Book 2)

1279 [of Henry VIII] The King has a way of making every man feel that he is enjoying his special favour, just as the London wives pray before the image of Our

Lady by the Tower till each of them believes it is smiling upon her.

(Letter to Bishop John Fisher, 1518)

1280 [of Henry VIII] If a lion knew his own strength, hard were it for any man to rule him.

(In conversation with Thomas Cromwell, May [?June] 1532)

1281 [comforting his wife who was sad to see him imprisoned in the Tower of London, 1535] 'Is not this house', quoth he, 'as nigh heaven as mine own?' To whom she, after her accustomed homely fashion, not liking such talk, answered, 'Tilly vally, Tilly vally'.

(Roper [his son-in-law], *Life of Sir Thomas More*)

1282 I pray you, I pray you, Mr Lieutenant, see me safe up, and for my coming down let me shift for myself.

(To the Governor of the Tower of London on ascending the scaffold at his execution, 7 July 1535)

Henry **MORGAN** (*flor.* 1580s): Purser of the barque *Sunshine* on the second expedition of John Davis in search of the north-west passage

1283 Divers times they [Eskimos] did weave us on shore to play with them at the football, and some of our company went on shore to play with them, and our men did cast them down as soon as they did come to strike the ball.

(Gilbert's Sound (64′ 15′), 21 August 1586. Hakluyt, *Voyages and Discoveries*)

Karl Philipp **MORITZ** (1756–93): German Lutheran pastor

1284 In England, more than in any other land, living hedges mark the limits of green cornfields so that all the countryside within sight is given the appearance of a large and majestic garden.

(Letter to a friend in Berlin, 1782, *Reisen eines Deutschen in England* (1792))

1285 When you see how in this happy country the lowest and poorest member of society takes an interest in all public affairs; when you see how high and low, rich and poor, are all willing to declare their feelings and convictions; when you see how a carter, a common sailor, a beggar is still a man, nay, even more, an Englishman – then, believe me, you find yourself very differently affected from the experience you feel when staring at our soldiers drilling in Berlin.

(Ibid.: Letter to a friend after observing a Westminster by-election, 1782)

William MORRIS (1834–96): English Utopian socialist

1286 The Socialist papers ... came out full to the throat of well-printed matter ... admirable and straightforward expositions of the doctrines and practice of Socialism, free from haste and spite and hard words [which] came upon the public with a kind of May-day freshness, amidst the worry and terror of the moment.

(*News from Nowhere*, written 1890, predicting an English communistic revolution in the early 1950s)

1287 Between complete Socialism and Communism there is no difference whatever in my mind. Communism is in fact the completion of Socialism; when that ceases to be militant and becomes triumphant, it will be communism.

(Lecture to Hammersmith Socialist Society, 1893)

Herbert MORRISON, Lord Morrison of Lambeth (1888–1965): British Labour politician

1288 Work is the call. Work at War Speed ... Go to it!

(First broadcast as Minister of Supply in Churchill's coalition government, 22 May 1940)

1289 War is an endurance test and we, who know that right is on our side, will last out longest. Keep at it!

(Broadcast message, 9 August 1940)

Fynes MORYSON (1566–1630): traveller, writer

1290 A man in those days might more easily lead bears and lions than the Irish ... [they are] most obedient ... under a hard hand, but stubborn and froward towards their master as soon as they are well clothed and set on horseback, for they are all in their opinion, and they all will be gentlemen, which poverty made them forget.

('Of the Commonwealth of Ireland' in his *Itinerary*, 1617)

Earl MOUNTBATTEN of Burma (1900–79): Admiral of the Fleet

1291 As a military man who has given half a century of active service, I say in all sincerity that the nuclear arms race has no military purpose. Wars cannot be fought with nuclear weapons; their existence only adds to our perils because of the illusions which they have generated.

(Speech, Strasbourg, 11 May 1979)

Georg (Count) MÜNSTER (1794–1868): Hanoverian diplomat

1292 An intelligent Russian once remarked to us: 'Every country has its own constitution; ours is absolutism moderated by assassination.'

(*Political Sketches of the State of Europe 1814–1867*, 1868)

Benito MUSSOLINI (1883–1945): Italian Fascist politician and dictator
[see also 885, 1513, 1613]

1293 I could have transformed this grey assembly hall into an armed camp of Blackshirts, a bivouac for corpses. I could have nailed up the doors of Parliament.

(First speech, Italian Lower House, after becoming Prime Minister, 16 November 1922)

1294 My ambition, Honourable Senators, is one and one only. To achieve it, I do not care if I work fourteen or sixteen hours a day. And it would not matter were I to lose my life, for I would not consider that a greater sacrifice than is due. My ambition is this: I want to make the people of Italy strong, prosperous and free.

(Speech, Italian Senate, 8 June 1923)

1295 If I advance, follow me: if I retreat, kill me; if I die, avenge me.

(To Fascist officials after an assassination attempt, 6 April 1926)

1296 War alone brings up to their highest tension all human energies and imposes the stamp of nobility upon the peoples who have the courage to make it.

(Article on 'The Political and Social Doctrine of Fascism', *Enciclopedia Italiana*, 1932)

1297 The keystone of the Fascist doctrine is its conception of the State, of its essence, its functions, and its aims. For Fascism the State is absolute, individuals and groups relative.

(*Fascism, Doctrine and Institutions*, 1935)

1298 This Berlin–Rome connection is not so much a diaphragm as an axis, around which can revolve all those states of Europe with a will towards collaboration and peace.

(Speech, Piazza del Duomo, Milan, 1 November 1936)

1299 I knew that my friend Adolf Hitler would not desert me.

(To Otto Skorzeny, commander of the German airborne troops which rescued him from

internment on the Gran Sasso
mountain, 12 September 1943)

Charles   James   NAPIER
(1782–1853): British General

1300 *Peccavi!* [I have sinned!]

(Punning message announcing
the successful military occupation
of the Indian province of Sind,
February 1843)

NAPOLEON I (1769–1821):
Emperor of the French
[see also 22, 23, 24, 111, 124,
134, 135, 172, 178, 285, 767,
1041, 1078, 1759, 1842, 1907,
1909]

1301 The last Austrians are expelled from Italy! Our outposts
are in the mountains of Germany!
I shall not list the names of the
men who distinguished themselves by acts of bravery: I would
have to cite every grenadier and
rifleman in the vanguard. They
play with death and laugh at it . . .

(Letter to The Directory from
Peschiera, 1 June 1769)

1302 As the battle was about to
begin, Napoleon pointed to the
Pyramids and said to his troops,
'Soldiers, forty centuries are
looking down upon you.'

(22 July 1798 note in Vol. IV of
the official *Correspondance de
Napoleon I*)

1303 Citizens, the Revolution
has been made fast to the principles which inspired it. The
Revolution is at an end.

(Proclamation, 15 December
1799)

1304 Power is my mistress. I
have worked too hard in conquering her to allow anyone to
take her from me or even to covet
her.

(In conversation with
Pierre-Louis Roederer, 1804;
Roederer, *Journal*)

1305 I am the successor, not of
Louis XVI, but of Charlemagne.

(To Pope Pius VII on his
Coronation Day, 1 December
1804)

1306 People complain that we
have no literature: that is the fault
of the minister of the interior.

(Letter, from occupied Berlin, to
Archchancellor Cambacérès, 21
November 1806)

1307 Wisdom and policy dictates
that we must do as destiny demands and keep pace with the
irresistible march of events.

(To Alexander I of Russia, 2
February 1808)

1308 My principle is: France
before everything.

(Letter to Eugène Beauharnais,
23 August 1810)

1309 It is the sun of Austerlitz.

(To his officers, as the sun broke
through the morning-mist at
Borodino, 7 September 1812)

1310 The frost, which had
begun on 7 November, suddenly
became more intense, and from
November 14th to 15th and 16th,
the temperature fell to 16°C and
18°C below freezing … Those
men whom Nature had not hardened against all chances of fate
and fortune seemed shaken; they
lost their cheerfulness and good
humour and saw ahead of them
nothing but disaster and catastrophe. Those on whom she had
bestowed superior powers kept
up their spirits and normal disposition, seeing in the various or-
deals a challenge to win glory …
His Majesty's health has never
been better.

(From 29th Bulletin of the Grand
Army, dictated at Molodechno, 3
December 1812)

1311 There is only one step
from the sublime to the ridiculous.

(To Caulaincourt, December
1812, while returning by sledge
to Paris after the failure of his
Russian Campaign)

1312 France has more need of
me than I have need of France.

(Speech to Corps Législatif,
Paris, 31 December 1813)

1313 Soldiers! Come and form
your ranks beneath the flags of
your leader! He has no existence
apart from your existence …
Victory will march at a quick
pace. The eagle and the tricolour
will fly from steeple to steeple
until it reaches the towers of
Notre Dame. Then may you
show your scars without dishonour … In old age, honoured by
your fellow citizens who will
gather respectfully around you,
you shall proudly say, 'Yes, I too
was one of the Grand Army
which twice marched into Vienna,
and entered Rome, Berlin,
Madrid and Moscow, and redeemed Paris from the shame of
treason …'

(Proclamation on returning from
Elba, 1 March 1815)

1314 Like Themistocles, I come
to settle myself at the hearth of
the British people. I put myself
under the protection of their laws
– a protection which I claim from
Your Royal Highness as the
strongest, stubbornest and most
generous of my foes …

(Appeal to the Prince Regent, 13
July 1815)

1315 [At Waterloo] Everything

failed me just at the moment when everything had succeeded.

(To Comte de las Cases, St Helena, 18 June 1816)

1316 The memory I leave behind is of facts which mere words can never destroy.

(Conversation on St Helena, 21 October 1816, noted by Las Cases)

1317 The most terrible of all my battles was the one fought in front of Moscow: the French showed themselves worthy of victory and the Russians of being invincible.

(Comment on the Battle of Borodino made in conversation at St Helena, 1817)

1318 I wish my ashes to repose on the banks of the Seine, in the midst of the French people I have loved so well.

(Codicil to his Will, St Helena, 16 April 1821)

1319 An army marches on its stomach.

(*Remark traditionally attributed to Napoleon on St Helena)

1320 England is a nation of shopkeepers.

(*Attributed remark on St Helena)

NAPOLEON III (1808–73): Emperor of the French [see also, 317, 1026, 1766, 1842]

1321 The cause of which my name is the symbol – that is to say, France regenerated by the Revolution and organised by the Emperor.

(Proclamation to the French people and army during his *coup d'état*, 2 December 1851)

1322 For too long Society has resembled a pyramid which has been turned upside down and made to rest on its summit. I have replaced it on its base.

(Speech as Prince-President opening the Legislative Assembly, 29 March 1852)

1323 There is a fear expressed which I must answer. In a mood of defiance certain people are saying, 'The Empire means War'. Personally I say, 'The Empire means Peace' [*Moi, je dis: L'Empire c'est la paix*].

(Speech at Bordeaux as Prince-President of the Second Republic, seven weeks before the establishment of the Second Empire, 15 October 1852)

1324 Sovereignty over Constantinople means sovereignty over the Mediterranean.

(Speech to the French assemblies, 2 March 1854)

1325 The army is the true nobility of our country.

(Speech at a review of the
Imperial Guard, 20 March 1855)

1326 [of the leading figures in
the Second Empire] The Empress is Legitimist, my cousin is
Republican, Morny is Orleanist, I
am a socialist; the only Bonapartist is Persigny, and he is mad.

(*Alleged conversational remark
in the late 1850s)

1327 I regret that our relations
with your government are not as
good as in the past, but I beg you
to assure the Emperor that my
personal sentiments towards him
have not changed.

(Remark to Austrian ambassador,
at diplomatic reception in Paris, 1
January 1859)

1328 We must not seek to
fashion events, but let them
happen of their own accord.

(To Bismarck at Biarritz, 4
October 1865)

1329 Sire, we have been under
fire together.

(To Tsar Alexander II after a
Polish exile had fired a shot at
him as the two emperors were
returning from a review in the
Bois de Boulogne, 6 June 1867)

Jawaharlal NEHRU (1889–
1964): first Indian Prime Minister

1330 I draw strength from seeing
them and they seem to get
strength from seeing me.

(*Alleged remark about the
crowds who attended his election
meetings in the late 1950s)

1331 Stalin ... that great lover
of peace, a man of giant stature
who moulded, as few other men
have done, the destinies of his age
... The occasion is not merely
the passing away of a great figure
but perhaps the ending of an
historic era.

(Obituary tribute, Indian
Parliament, 9 March 1953)

Horatio (Viscount) NELSON
(1758–1805): English Admiral
[see also 1718]

1332 Firstly you must always im-
plicitly obey orders, without attempting to form any opinion of
your own respecting their propriety. Secondly, you must consider
every man your enemy who
speaks ill of your king; and thirdly
you must hate a Frenchman as
you hate the devil.

To a midshipman under his
command in HMS *Agamemnon*,
western Mediterranean, 1793)

1333 My character and good
name are in my own keeping, Life
with disgrace is dreadful. A glorious death is to be envied.

(Journal, 10 March 1795)

1334 Before this time tomorrow I shall have gained a peerage, or Westminster Abbey.

(To his officers on the eve of the Battle of the Nile, 31 July 1798)

1335 I had the happiness to command a band of brothers.

(Letter to Admiral Lord Howe after the Battle of the Nile, August 1798)

1336 I have only one eye: I have a right to be blind sometimes: I really do not see the signal.

(At Copenhagen, 2 April 1801)

1337 It is warm work, and this day may be the last to any of us at a moment. But, mark you! I would not be elsewhere for thousands.

(Ibid.)

1338 I am anxious to join the fleet, for it would add to my grief if any other man was to give them the Nelson touch, which WE say is warranted never to fail.

(Letter to Lady Hamilton, from off Lisbon, 25 September 1805)

1339 In case signals can neither be seen nor perfectly understood, no captain can do very wrong if he places his ship alongside that of an enemy.

(Tactical memorandum for flag officers and captains before Trafalgar, 9 October 1805)

1340 May the Great God, whom I worship, grant to my Country, and for the benefit of Europe in general, a great and glorious Victory; and may no misconduct in anyone tarnish it; and may humanity after Victory be the predominant feature in the British fleet . . .

(Prayer written on the morning of Trafalgar, 21 October 1805)

1341 I wish to say Nelson confides that every man will do his duty.

(To John Pasco, officer in charge of flag-signals HMS *Victory*, 21 October 1805: signal amended to 'England expects . . .')

1342 This is too warm work, Hardy, to last long.

(To Captain Hardy on HMS *Victory* shortly before being fatally wounded at Trafalgar, 21 October 1805)

1343 And take care of my dear Lady Hamilton, Hardy, take care of poor Lady Hamilton. Kiss me, Hardy.

. . .

Remember that I leave Lady Hamilton and my daughter Horatia as a legacy to my country – and never forget Horatia.

(Surgeon Beatty's account of Nelson's death, 21 October 1805)

Allan NEVINS (b. 1890): American historian

1344 The former allies had blundered in the past by offering Germany too little, and offering even that too late, until finally Nazi Germany had become a menace to all mankind.

(Article in *Current History*, May 1935)

John Henry NEWMAN (1801–90): Anglican priest and (later) Roman Catholic cardinal [see also 1234]

1345 Our present scope is merely to show that while our Prayer Book is acknowledged on all hands to be of Catholic origin, our [Thirty-Nine] Articles also ... are ... to say the least, not un-Catholic, and may be subscribed by those who aim at being Catholic in heart and doctrine.

(*Tract XC*, written while still vicar of St Mary's, Oxford, 1841)

1346 It would be a gain to the country were it vastly more superstitious, more bigoted, more gloomy, more fierce in its religion than at present it shows itself to be.

(*Apologia pro Vita Sua*, 1864)

1347 True religion is slow in growth and, when once planted, is difficult of dislodgement; but its intellectual counterfeit has no root in itself; it springs up suddenly, it suddenly withers.

(*The Idea of a University*, 1873)

NICHOLAS I (1796–1855): Tsar of Russia

1348 Every time I come near him, I pray God to preserve me from the Devil.

(Of Metternich, in a letter to his wife from the Münchengrätz Conference, September 1833)

1349 Gentlemen, saddle your horses! France is a Republic.

(Announcement at a palace ball in St Petersburg on hearing news of the fall of Louis Philippe, February 1848)

1350 The symptoms of a general plot against everything sacred, and especially against Russia, are clearly visible in the Hungarian rebellion. At the head of the rebellion, and acting as the principal instruments of it, are our eternal foes, the Poles.

(Letter to his Viceroy of Poland, Marshal Paskievič, 7 May 1849)

1351 Turkey seems to be falling to pieces, the fall will be a great misfortune. It is very important that England and Russia should

come to a good understanding . . .
We have a sick man on our hands,
a man gravely ill, it will be a great
misfortune if one of these days he
slips through our hands, especially
before the necessary arrange-
ments are made.

(In conversation with the British
ambassador, Seymour, 9 January
1853)

1352 The bear [Turkey] is dying
. . . You may give him musk, but
even musk will not keep him alive.

(To the British ambassador, as
reported by Seymour to the
Foreign Office, 21 February
1853)

NICHOLAS II (1868–1918):
Tsar of Russia
[See also 29, 31, 1940, 1943, 1944]

1353 There are . . . senseless
dreams of the participation of
zemstvo local government representatives in the affairs of internal
administration . . . I shall maintain
the principle of autocracy just as
firmly and unflinchingly as it was
upheld by my own ever to be
remembered dead father.

(Declaration to representatives of
the Zemstvo of Tver, 17 January
1896)

1354 I greatly miss my half-an-
hour game of patience every evening. I shall take up dominoes again
in my spare time.

(Letter to his wife, 23 February/8
March 1917, a week before the
Russian Revolution forced him to
abdicate)

1355 In these decisive days in
the life of Russia, we have
thought it a duty of conscience
. . . to abdicate the Crown of the
Russian State and to lay down the
supreme Power.

(Abdication Manifesto, Pskov,
2/15 March 1917)

**Friedrich Wilhelm NIETZ-
SCHE** (1844–1900): German
philosopher

1356 I teach you the Superman.
Man is something to be surpassed.

(*Also sprach Zarathustra*, Prologue
to Ch. 3, written 1882–3)

Florence NIGHTINGALE
(1820–1910): English hospital
reformer

1357 Knight of the Crimean
Burial Grounds, I suppose?

(Comment on the KCB
awarded, 1856, to Dr John Hall,
the incompetent British Chief of
Medical Staff in the Crimea)

1358 Do you think I should have
succeeded in doing anything if I
had kicked and resisted and re-
sented? Is it our Master's command? Is it even common sense? I

have been shut out of hospitals into which I had been ordered to go by the Commander-in-Chief – obliged to stand outside the door in the snow till night – have been refused rations for as much as 10 days at a time for the nurses I had brought by superior command. And I have been as good friends the day after with the officials who did these things – have resolutely ignored these things *for the sake of the work* . . . Who am I that should not choose to bear what my Master chooses to bear?

(Letter to a dissident nurse, 22 April 1869)

Robert NIVELLE (1856–1924): French General

1359 They shall not pass [*Ils ne passeront pas*].

(To General de Castelnau at Verdun, 23 January 1916: often attributed to Pétain)

Richard M. NIXON (b. 1913): thirty-seventh President of the USA

1360 For the first time in history we showed independence of Anglo-French policies towards Asia and Africa which seemed to us to reflect the colonial tradition. That declaration of independence has had an electrifying effect throughout the world.

(Campaign Speech, as Vice-President, after the Suez Crisis, 2 November 1956)

1361 You won't have Nixon to kick around any more.

(To newspaper correspondents after failing to be elected Governor of California, 7 November 1962)

1362 We cannot learn from one another until we stop shouting at one another, until we speak quietly enough so that our words can be heard as well as our voices. For its part, Government will listen. We will strive to listen in new ways – to the voices of quiet anguish, to voices that speak without words, the voices of the heart, to the injured voices, and the anxious voices, and the voices that have despaired of being heard.

(Inaugural address, 20 January 1969)

1363 This is the greatest week in the history of the world since the creation.

(Remark on USS *Hornet*, 24 July 1969, four days after the first moon-landing)

1364 Those who scoff at 'balance of power diplomacy' on the world scene should recognise that the only alternative to a balance of power is an imbalance of power –

and history shows us that nothing so drastically escalates the danger of war as such an imbalance.

(Press conference, 25 June 1972)

1365 These very pragmatic men [the communist leaders] ... respect strength – not belligerence, but strength ... You get something only when you have something they want to get from you. The only way we're going to get our prisoners-of-war back is by doing something to them, and that means hitting military targets in North Vietnam, retaining a residual force in South Vietnam, and continuing the mining of the harbours of North Vietnam.

(Televised press conference in which he emphasized the 'excellence' of his Administration's record on Vietnam, 29 June 1972)

1366 There will be no whitewash in the White House.

(Statement on the Watergate affair, 17 April 1973)

1367 Something else I'd like you to tell your young people. You know they look at Government, it's a sort of rugged life. They see the mistakes that are made, they get the impression that everybody is here for the purpose of feathering his nest ... Not in this Administration: not one single man or woman. And I say this to them.

There are many fine careers. The country needs good farmers, good businessmen, good plumbers, good carpenters.

(Farewell speech to his Cabinet and White House staff after resigning over the Watergate scandal, 9 August 1974)

Frederick, Lord NORTH (1732–79): British Tory Prime Minister
[see also 995, 1923]

1368 I do not know whether our Generals will frighten the enemy, but I know they frighten me whenever I think of them.

(*Alleged comment, 1776/7)

1369 Lord North cannot conceive what can induce His Majesty after so many proofs of Lord North's unfitness for his situation to determine at all events to keep him at the head of the Administration, though the almost certain consequences of His Majesty's resolution will be the ruin of his affairs.

(Letter to George III, March 1778)

1370 Your Majesty is well apprized that, in this country, the Prince on the Throne cannot, with prudence, oppose the deliberate resolution of the House of Commons ... Your Majesty's goodness encourages me ... to submit whether it will not be for Your Majesty's welfare, and even glory, to sacrifice, at this moment, former opinions, displeasures and apprehensions (though never so well-founded) to ... the public safety.

(Letter to George III vainly urging him to accept the general desire in the House of Commons for an end to the war in America, 18 March 1782)

Alfred Harmsworth, Lord NORTHCLIFFE (1865–1922): English newspaper magnate [see also 117]

1371 That matter [trouble between England and Ireland] will be settled. There may be some difficulties; there may be some delays, but there will be peace and contentment, surely, before long.

(To newspaper reporters, New York, 1921)

1372 I know Palestine. It's rather a poor country. There's a lot of unemployment there now. The danger is you may get too many people down there to fit the conditions.

(To prominent Zionists in New York, 1921)

Sir Stafford NORTHCOTE (1818–87): English Conservative politician

1373 Argue as you please, you are nowhere if that grand old man, the Prime Minister [Gladstone] insists on the other thing.

(Speech, Liverpool, 12 April 1882)

Caroline NORTON (1808–77): campaigner for married women's rights and writer

1374 I do not ask for my rights. I have no rights; I have only wrongs.

(Said in court, August 1853, after verdict upholding her husband's refusal to maintain her)

NOVGOROD Chronicle

1375 And there was a great battle with the Germans and Estonians, with the clash of shattering spears and the crash of swords so that the frozen sea began to move; and the ice could not be seen, for everywhere was covered in blood.

(A near-contemporary record of the victory of Alexander Nevsky at Pskov, 1242)

NURSERY RHYMES

1376 Please to remember
The Fifth of November,
Gunpowder, treason and plot;
We know no reason

Why gunpowder treason
Should ever be forgot.

(Traditional since the
seventeenth century, printed in
1826)

1377 The lion and the unicorn
       Were fighting for the
       crown;
       The lion beat the unicorn
       All around the town.

(Traditional since late
seventeenth century, in printed
form 1708)

1378 The brave old Duke of York
       He had ten thousand men
       He marched them up to a
       great high hill,
       Then marched them down
       again.

(Derisive verses about the
unsuccessful campaign of
Frederick, Duke of York, in the
Low Countries in 1793–4)

John NYREN (1764–1837): English cricket chronicler

1379 Oh! it was a heart-stirring
sight to witness the multitude
forming a complete and dense
circle round that noble green.
Half the county would be present,
and all their hearts with us –
Little Hambledon, pitted against
All England, was a proud thought
for the Hampshire men. Defeat
was glory in such a struggle –
Victory, indeed, made us only 'a

little lower than angels'. How
those fine brawn-faced fellows of
farmers would drink to our success! And then what stuff they
had to drink! … Punch that
would make a cat speak! … Ale
that would flare like turpentine!
… How strongly are all those
scenes, of fifty years by-gone,
painted in my memory! And the
smell of that ale comes upon me
as freshly as the new May flowers.

(Of cricket in the village of
Hambledon, Hampshire, during
the 1780s, *The Cricketers of my
Time*, 1833)

J.   Bronterre   O'BRIEN
(1805–64): Chartist and socialist

1380 Whatever God has made
belongs equally to all; it is the
common property of all God's
creatures.

(Letter replying to the moderate
Chartist, Robert Gammage,
Northern Star, 27 March 1841)

Daniel O'CONNELL (1775–
1847): Irish nationalist leader
[see also 1710]

1381 Let us never tolerate the
slightest inroad on the discipline
of our ancient, our holy Church.
Let us never consent that she
should be made the hireling of
the Ministry. Our forefathers
would have died – nay, they per-
ished in hopeless slavery – rather
than consent to such degradation.

(Speech, Dublin, 23 February 1814)

John L. O'SULLIVAN (1813–95): American editor

1382 [Other nations have tried to check] ... the fulfilment of our manifest destiny to overspread the continent allotted by Providence for the free development of our yearly multiplying millions.

(Editorial, *US Magazine & Democratic Review*, Vol. 17, July 1845)

Emile OLLIVIER (1825–1913): French Prime Minister

1383 At no time has the maintenance of peace seemed better assured than today.

(Speech, Legislative Chamber, 30 June 1870: the Franco–Prussian War began on 19 July)

1384 One is never weaker than when one appears to be supported by everybody.

(Comment, 1870)

Charlotte Elizabeth ('Liselotte'), Duchess of ORLEANS (1652–1722): sister-in-law to Louis XIV

1385 You ask whether it is true that the King [Louis XIV] has married Madame de Maintenon. I really cannot tell you. Most people think so ... To judge from what marriages are usually like in this country, their love for each other would not be so strong as it is if they were married.

(Letter to her Aunt Sophia, later Electress of Hanover, 13 May 1687)

1386 [of James II of England] Our dear King James is good and honest, but the most incompetent man I have ever seen in my life. A child of seven years would not make such silly mistakes as he does.

(Letter to the Electress Sophia, 6 June 1692)

1387 The English have always been a wicked race, but since their King William they have become worse and fallen into very vicious ways. It has been noticed that islanders are always more treacherous and wicked than the inhabitants of the terra firma.

(Letter to her stepsister Louisa, 13 January 1718)

1388 I have often seen the King [Louis XIV] consume four plates of different soups, a whole pheasant, a partridge, a large plate of salad, two big slices of ham, a dish of mutton in garlic sauce, a plateful of pastries followed by fruit and hard-boiled eggs. The King and Monsieur [his brother] greatly like hard-boiled eggs.

(Letter to Louisa, ?1682)

James OTIS (1725–83): lawyer and American patriot

1389 Taxation without representation is tyranny.

(*A legendary phrase allegedly used by Otis in the Superior Court of Massachusetts, Boston, February 1761, but surviving only as a note among the papers of John Adams)

OTTO III (980–1002): Holy Roman Emperor

1390 Are you not my own Romans? For you I have abandoned my father and denied the Saxons and all the Germans; I have made the name of Rome feared and honoured to the ends of the earth which your own ancestors never reached ... I bear you in my heart and shall not cease to love you.

(Speech during rebellion of Rome, 1000)

OTTO, Bishop of Freising (?1110–58): German chronicler

1391 [The Bishop of Gabala] was also telling us how, not many years before, one John, King and Priest, who dwells in the extreme Orient beyond Persia and Arme-

nia ... is said to be of the ancient race of those Magi who are mentioned in the Gospel.

(*Chronica* – under the events of 1145 (this is the first mention of the legendary Prester John))

Richard OVERTON (*flor.* 1642–63): English radical printer

1392 Whatever our forefathers were, or whatever they did or suffered, or were enforced to yield unto; we are the men of the present age; and ought to be absolutely free from all kinds of exorbitancies, molestations, or Arbitrary Power.

(*Remonstrance of Many Thousand Citizens and Other free-born People of England to the House of Commons*, 1646)

Robert OWEN (1771–1858): English pioneer socialist

1393 Providence now evidently designs to effect the destruction of ignorance and misery, and firmly to establish the reign of reason, intelligence and happiness.

(*A New View of Society*, 1813)

Axel OXENSTIERNA (1583–1654): Swedish statesman

1394 It seems to me that it is essential that Your Majesty should above all things labour to create a powerful fleet at sea; a fleet of good ships, and most especially a fleet very numerous, so that you may be master of every nook and cranny of the Baltic.

(Letter to Gustavus Adolphus, 8 January 1631)

Vance PACKARD (b. 1914): American author

1395 The Hidden Persuaders.

(Title of book published in 1955 criticizing the spread in Western society of advertising techniques)

Thomas PAINE (1737–1809): English radical writer

1396 Government, even in its best state, is but a necessary evil; in its worst state, an intolerable one. Government, like dress, is the badge of lost innocence; the palaces of Kings are built upon the ruins of the bowers of Paradise.

(*Common Sense*, 1776)

1397 A French bastard landing with an armed banditti and establishing himself King of England against the consent of the natives is, in plain terms, a very paltry rascally original ... The plain truth is that the antiquity of English monarchy will not bear looking into.

(Ibid.)

1398 These are the times that try men's souls.

(*The Crisis*, December 1776)

1399 Man is not the enemy of Man, but through the medium of a false system of government.

(*The Rights of Man*, Pt I, 1791)

1400 [of Burke's 'Reflections on the Revolution in France'] He pities the plumage but forgets the dying bird.

(Ibid.)

1401 If the succession runs in the line of the Conqueror, the Nation runs in the line of being conquered, and ought to rescue itself from this reproach.

(Ibid.)

1402 To establish any mode to abolish war, however advantageous it might be to Nations, would be to take from such Government the most lucrative of its branches.

(*The Rights of Man*, Pt II, 1792)

1403 My country is the world, and my religion is to do good.

(Ibid.)

1404 [of Burke] The final event to himself has been, that as he rose like a rocket, he fell like the stick.

(*Letter to the Addressers on the late Proclamation*, 1792)

Thomas PAKENHAM (1757–1836): British naval captain

1405 The able seamen of the fleet ... are the only description of men now serving His Majesty whose situation by common exercise of their trade could be bettered fourfold if they were released from the service of their country.

(Letter to the First Lord of the Admiralty, 11 December 1796)

Frantisek PALACKY (1798–1876): Czech historian and patriotic leader

1406 If the Austrian Empire had not long been in existence, in the interest of Europe – indeed, in the interest of Humanity – one would make haste to create it.

(Letter to the Frankfurt Parliament, 11 April 1848, opposing the inclusion of the Czech provinces in a 'Greater Germany')

John PALMER (*flor*. 1530s and 1540s): Sheriff of Surrey and Sussex

1407 Do ye not know that the King's Grace hath put down all houses of monks, friars and nuns? Therefore now is the time come

that we gentlemen will pull down the houses of such poor knaves as ye be.

(In answer to a petition for the return of peasants' holdings which he had appropriated at Ecclesden, West Angmering, early 1540s)

Henry Temple (Lord) PALMERSTON (1784–1865): British Liberal Foreign Secretary and Prime Minister
[see also 1657, 1783]

1408 Half the wrong conclusions at which mankind arrive are reached by the abuse of metaphors, and by mistaking general resemblance or imaginary similarity for real identity ... Therefore all that we hear every day of the week about the decay of the Turkish empire, and its being a dead body or a sapless trunk, and so forth, is pure and unadulterated nonsense.

(Letter to Henry Bulwer, 1 September 1839)

1409 It seems pretty clear that, sooner or later, the Cossack and the Sepoy, the man from the Baltic and he from the British Islands will meet in the centre of Asia. It should be our business to take care that the meeting should take place as far off from our Indian possessions as may be convenient and advantageous to us. But the meeting will not be avoided by our staying at home to receive the visit.

(Letter to John Cam Hobhouse, 14 July 1840)

1410 We have no eternal allies, and we have no perpetual enemies. Our interests are eternal, and those interests it is our duty to follow.

(Speech, H of C, 1 March 1848)

1411 Large republics seem to be essentially and inherently aggressive.

(Letter to Lord Normanby, British ambassador in Paris, 5 March 1848)

1412 As the Roman, in days of old, held himself free from indignity when he could say *Civis Romanus sum*, so also a British subject in whatever land he may be, shall feel confident that the watchful eye and the strong arm of England will protect him against injustice and wrong.

(Speech in Don Pacifico debate, H of C, 26 June 1850)

1413 You may call it coalition, you may call it the accidental and fortuitous concurrence of atoms ... but I say that when Gentlemen are in the habit of finding themselves in the same lobby, it is not unnatural to suppose that they may, under certain circumstances, be ready to unite themselves together for forming an Administration and become responsible for the opinions which they severally entertain.

(Speech, dealing with the rumours of a projected Palmerston–Disraeli coalition, 5 March 1857)

1414 England is one of the greatest powers of the world, no event or series of events bearing on the balance of power, or on probabilities of peace or war can be matters of indifference to her, and her right to have and to express opinions on matters thus bearing on her interests is unquestionable.

(Letter to Queen Victoria, 23 August 1859)

1415 There are only three men who have ever understood it: one was Prince Albert, who is dead; the second was a German professor, who became mad. I am the third – and I have forgotten all about it.

(*Alleged remark over the Schleswig-Holstein question, summer of 1863)

Christabel PANKHURST (1880–1958): British champion of women's rights

1416 So greatly did she care for freedom that she died for it. So dearly did she love women that she offered her life as their ransom. That is the verdict given at the great Inquest of the Nation on the death of Emily Wilding Davison.

(*The Suffragette*, 13 June 1913, a fortnight after Emily Davison had thrown herself under the King's horse during the Derby as a protest at the gaoling of suffragettes)

Mrs Emmeline PANKHURST (1858–1928): leader of the militant British suffragettes

1417 There is something that Governments care for far more than human life, and that is the security of property, and so it is through property that we shall strike the enemy . . . Be militant each in your own way . . . I incite this meeting to rebellion.

(Speech, Albert Hall, London, 17 October 1912)

1418 What is the use of fighting for a vote if we have not got a country to vote in? With that patriotism which has nerved women to endure torture in prison for the national good, we ardently desire that our country shall be victorious.

(Statement announcing truce in militant suffragette actions during the War, 10 August 1914)

Matthew PARIS (*flor*. 1235–50): monastic chronicler at St Albans Abbey

1419 A certain versifier, a false one, said, 'Just as England has been filthy with the defiler John, so now the filth of Hell is fouled by his foul presence'; but it is dangerous to write against a man who can easily do you wrong [*in eum inscribere qui de facili potest proscribere*].

(*Chronica Maiora*, 1216, after the death of King John on 18 October 1216)

Sir Henry PARKES (1815–96): Australian political leader

1420 With our splendid harbour, our beautifully situated city, our vast territories, all our varied and inexhaustible natural wealth, if we don't convert our colony [New South Wales] into a great and prosperous nation, it will be a miracle of error for which we shall have to answer as for a gigantic sin.

(Speech, Melbourne, 16 March 1867)

1421 Why should not the name of an Australian be equal to that of a Briton? . . . Why should not the name of an Australian citizen be equal to that of a citizen of the proudest country under the sun? . . . Make yourselves a united people, appear before the world as one, and the dream of going 'home' will die away.

(Speech to the Australian Federation Conference, Melbourne, February 1890)

Charles Stewart PARNELL (1846–91): champion of Irish Home Rule and MP

1422 When a man takes a farm from which another has been evicted, you must show him on the roadside when you meet him, you must show him in the streets of the town, you must show him at the shop counter, you must show him in the fair and the market place, and even in the house of worship, by leaving him severely alone, by putting him into a moral Coventry, by isolating him from his kind as if he were a leper of old – you must show him your detestation of the crimes he has committed.

(Speech, originating the practice of 'boycotting', Ennis, 19 September 1880)

1423 If I am arrested, Captain Moonlight will take my place.

(Remark to friends, at Wexford, 9 October 1881)

1424 No man has a right to fix the boundary of the march of a nation: no man has a right to say to his country – thus far shalt thou go and no further.

(Speech, Cork, 21 January 1885)

Paul KARADJORDJEVIĆ (1893–1976): Prince-Regent, Yugoslavia

1425 You big nations are hard; you talk of our honour – but you are far away.

(In conversation with the American Minister when under German diplomatic pressure, 20 March 1941)

Sir Robert PEEL (1788–1850): British Conservative Prime Minister [see also 539, 542]

1426 I may be a Tory, I may be an illiberal, but ... Tory as I am, I have the further satisfaction of knowing that there is not a single law connected with my name which has not had as its object some mitigation of the severity of the criminal law.

(Speech, on resigning after four years as Home Secretary, H of C, 1 May 1827)

1427 I am very far from being prepared to admit that the improvement of the situation of a common police constable by the giving him more money would increase the efficiency of the establishment ... No doubt three shillings a day will not give me all the virtues under heaven, but I do not want them. Angels would be far above my work.

(Letter to John Croker, 10 October 1829)

1428 If the spirit of the Reform Bill implies merely a careful review of institutions, civil and ecclesiastical, undertaken in a friendly temper, combining, with the firm maintenance of established rights the correction of private abuses and the redress of real grievances – in that case I can for myself and my colleagues undertake to act in such a spirit and with such intentions.

(*Tamworth Manifesto*, 1834)

1429 My earnest wish has been, during my tenure of power, to impress the people of this country with a belief that the Legislature was animated by a sincere desire to frame its legislation upon the principles of equity and justice ... Deprive me of power tomorrow, you can never deprive me of the consciousness that I have exercised the powers committed to me from no corrupt or interested motives, from no desire to gratify ambition, or attain any personal object.

(Speech on repeal of the Corn Laws, H of C, 15 May 1846)

William PENN (1644–1718): English Quaker leader

1430 I have led the greatest colony into America that ever any man did upon a private credit, and the most prosperous beginnings that were ever in it are to be found among us.

(Report on foundation of Pennsylvania, 1684)

1431 It is a reproach to religion and government to suffer so much poverty and excess.

(*Reflections and Maxims*, 1693)

Samuel PEPYS (1633–1703): English diarist and Admiralty official

1432 Here out of the window it was a most pleasant sight to see the City from one end to the other with a glory about it, so high was the light of the bonfires, and so thick round the City, and the bells rang everywhere.

(Diary, end of the Commonwealth, 21 February 1660)

1433 I went out to Charing Cross, to see Major-General Harrison hanged, drawn and quartered; which was done there, he looking as cheerful as any man could do in that condition.

(Diary, 13 October 1660)

1434 While we were talking I saw several poor creatures carried by, by constables, for being at a conventicle . . . I would to God they would either conform, or be more wise, and not be catched.

(Diary, 7 August 1664)

1435 [of Nell Gwynne, Charles II's mistress] To a play at the Duke's [of York] . . . All the pleasure of the play was, the King and my Lady Castlemaine were there; and pretty witty Nell at the King's house . . . which pleased me mightily.

(Diary, 3 April 1665)

1436 Thence I walked to the Tower; but Lord! how empty the streets are and how melancholy, so many poor sick people in the streets full of sores . . . in Westminster, there is never a physician and but one apothecary left, all being dead.

(Diary during the Plague, 16 September 1665)

1437 The King commanded me to go to my Lord Mayor from him, and command him to spare no houses, but to pull down before the fire every way. At last met my Lord Mayor in Canning-street, like a man spent, with a handkercher about his neck. To the King's message he cried, like a fainting woman, 'Lord, what can I do? I am spent: people will not obey me. I have been pulling down houses; but the fire overtakes us faster than we can do it.'

(Diary, first day of Fire of London, 2 September 1665)

1438 . . . by water to Paul's Wharfe. Walked thence and saw all the towne burned, and a miserable sight of Paul's church, with all the roofs fallen, and the body of the quire fallen into St Fayth's; Paul's school also, Ludgate and Fleet-street, my father's house and the church, and a good part of the Temple the like.

(Diary, day after Fire stopped, 7 September 1666)

1439 With Mr Slingsby of the Tower [Royal Mint] who did inform me mightily in several things – among others, that the heightening or lowering of money is only a cheat, and do good to some particular men, which if I can but remember how, I am now by him fully convinced of.

(Diary, 2 October 1666)

1440 I thank God we have not half the throng of those of the bastard breed pressing for employments which we heretofore used to be troubled with, they being conscious of their inability to pass this examination.

(Letter, after the establishment of an examination and qualification system for naval officers, 29 March 1678)

1441 It was the Rebellion and

necessity that made seamen of the King and Duke [i.e. Charles II and James II].

(Naval Minutes, 1680–1)

1442 The life of a virtuous Officer in the Navy is a continual war defensive, viz. against the Ministers of State, and in particular the Lord Treasurers, in time of peace, and all prejudiced inquisitors and malcontents with the Navy management in time of war.

(Naval Minutes, 1692)

John Joseph PERSHING (1860–1948): American General

1443 I hope that here on the soil of France and in the school of French heroes, our American soldiers may learn to battle and vanquish for the liberty of the world.

(Address at Lafayette's tomb, Paris, soon after taking command of the American Expeditionary Force on the Western Front, 4 July 1917)

Philippe PÉTAIN (1856–1951): Marshal of France

1444 I was with you in the days of glory. At the head of the Government, I shall remain with you during the days of darkness. Stay by my side . . .

(Broadcast, as Prime Minister, announcing that France was seeking an Armistice, 20 June 1940)

1445 *Nous, Philippe Pétain, Maréchal de France* . . . [We, Philip Pétain, Marshal of France . . .].

(Opening words of the French Constitutional Law appointing Pétain as Head of State, 10 July 1940)

PETER I, 'the Great' (1672–1725): Tsar of Russia [see also 631, 768]

1446 It is your military genius that has inspired my sword, and the noble emulation of your exploits has aroused in my heart the first thoughts I ever had of enlarging my Empire.

(To King William III at their first meeting, Utrecht, 11 September 1697)

1447 Now indeed with God's help the final stone has been laid in the foundation of St Petersburg.

(Postscript of letter to Admiral Apraksin reporting his victory over the Swedes at Poltava, 27 June 1709)

1448 I have not spared and I do not spare my life for my fatherland and my people . . . Two things are necessary in government, namely order and defence.

(Letter to his son, Alexis, 11 October 1715)

Hugh PETERS (1598–1660): English 'Independent' preacher

1449 Methinks all Protestant Europe seems to get new colour in her cheeks.

(Sermon to Parliament and Assembly of Divines, preached after his return from New England, 2 April 1646)

1450 I have lived in a country where in seven years I never saw beggar, nor heard an oath, nor looked upon a drunkard: why should there be beggars in your Israel where there is so much work to do?

(Ibid.)

Francesco PETRARCH (1304–74): Italian poet

1451 Everywhere was dismal abandonment, grief, destruction, weedy, untilled fields, ruined deserted houses, except for those protected by the walls of cities and strongholds. Everywhere appeared the melancholy vestiges of the English passage, the recent horrible wounds of their devastation. Nay, more, Paris itself, the capital, was surrounded, up to its gates, with a burned and wasted land. It seemed to tremble with horror at its adversity, and even the Seine that penetrates its walls seemed to mourn in terror at the city's fate.

(Letter, not sent, describing the effects of Edward III's campaign in northern France, addressed to Pierre Berguere, 27 February 1361)

PHILIP II Augustus (1165–1223): King of France
[see also 918, 1583]

1452 I have two huge lions tearing at my flanks, the so-called Emperor Otto and John, King of England. Both try with all their might to upset the Kingdom of France. I cannot leave the country myself or do without my son here.

(To Pope Innocent III, who had asked him for the last time to crusade against the Albigensian heretics, 1209)

PHILIP, Prince (b. 1921): Duke of Edinburgh

1453 We are suffering a national defeat comparable to any lost military campaign, and what is more it is self-inflicted . . . I think it is about time we pulled our fingers out . . . The rest of the world most certainly does not owe us a living.

(Speech to over a hundred leading British industrialists at

the Industrial Co-Partnership Association luncheon, London, 17 October 1961)

1454 The monarchy is part of the fabric of the country. And, as the fabric alters, so the monarchy and its people's relations to it alters.

(Interviewed on Tyne-Tees television, 20 March 1968)

Wendell PHILLIPS (1811–84): American anti-slavery lawyer and orator

1455 One on God's side is a majority.

(Speech, Brooklyn, 1 November 1859)

PHILOTHEUS (Filofei) (*flor*. early 16th century): Russian monk and scholar of Pskov

1456 To the Orthodox Christian Tsar ... who reigns over ... the Holy Ecumenical Catholic Apostolic Church ... which now shines instead of Rome and Constantinople. For the church of old Rome fell because of its heresy; the gates of the second Rome were broken down by the axes of the Mohammedan infidels; but now the church ... of your mighty realm, the third Rome, shines brighter than the sun to the ends of the earth ... Perceive, God-fearing Tsar, how all Christian empires have come

together into yours alone. Two Romes have fallen but the Third stands fast, and the Fourth there shall not be.

(To Basil III, *c*. 1510/11)

William PITT (the elder), Earl of Chatham (1708–78): British Tory Prime Minister [see also 306, 1862]

1457 The atrocious crime of being a young man, which the honourable gentleman [Walpole] has, with such spirit and decency, charged upon me, I shall neither attempt to palliate nor deny; but content myself with wishing that I may be one of those whose follies cease with their youth, and not of those who continue ignorant in spite of age and experience.

(Speech, H of C, 6 March 1741)

1458 It is now apparent that this great, this powerful, this formidable Kingdom is considered only as a province of a despicable Electorate.

(Speech, H of C, 10 December 1742)

1459 I know that I can save this country and that no one else can.

(November 1756)

1460 I was called by my Sovereign and by the Voice of the People to assist the State when others had abdicated the service of it. That being so no one can be surprised that I will go on no longer since my advice is not taken. Being responsible I *will* direct and will be responsible for nothing that I do not direct.

(Resignation speech to his Cabinet, 3 October 1761)

1461 America was conquered in Germany.

(*Attributed remark, praising the effects of the Anglo-Prussian alliance, 1762)

1462 The ministers seem to have lost sight of the great fundamental principle that France is chiefly if not solely to be dreaded by us in the light of a maritime and commercial power, and therefore by restoring to her all the valuable West India islands, and by our concessions in the Newfoundland fishing, we have given her the means of recovering her prodigious losses and becoming once more formidable to us at sea.

(Speech attacking the Preliminaries of Peace, H of C, 9 December 1762)

1463 The poorest man may in his cottage bid defiance to all the forces of the Crown. It may be frail – its roof may shake – the wind may blow through it – the storm may enter – the rain may enter – but the King of England cannot enter – all his force dares not cross the threshold of the ruined tenement!

(Parliamentary speech delivered, according to Brougham, over an Excise Bill; probably Bute's cider tax, March 1763)

1464 As to the present gentlemen, I cannot give them my confidence. Pardon me, gentlemen, confidence is a plant of slow growth in an aged bosom. Youth is the season of credulity.

(Speech attacking the Rockingham Ministry, H of C, 14 January 1766)

1465 I rejoice that America has resisted. Three millions of people, so dead to all the feelings of liberty, as voluntarily to submit to be slaves, would have been fit instruments to make slaves of the rest.

(Ibid.)

1466 Where law ends, there tyranny begins.

(Speech, H of L, 9 January 1770)

1467 Unlimited power is apt to corrupt the minds of those who possess it.

(Ibid.)

1468 There is something behind the throne greater than the King himself.

(Speech, H of L, 2 March 1770)

1469 We have a Calvinistic creed, a Popish liturgy, and an Arminian clergy.

(Speech, H of L, 19 May 1772)

1470 The spirit which now resists your taxation in America is the same which formerly opposed loans, benevolences and ship-money in England; the same spirit which called all England on its legs, and by the Bill of Rights vindicated the English constitution; the same spirit which established the great fundamental, essential maxim of your liberties – that no subject of England shall be taxed but by his own consent. This glorious spirit of Whiggism animates three millions in America, who prefer poverty with liberty to gilded chains and sordid affluence; and who will die in defence of their rights as men, as freemen.

(Speech, H of L, 20 January 1775)

1471 As an American, I would recognize to England her supreme right of regulating commerce and navigation; as an Englishman by birth and principle, I recognize to the Americans their supreme unalienable right to their property – a right which they are justified in the defence of to the last extremity. To maintain this principle is the common

cause of the Whigs on the other side of the Atlantic and on this ... In this great cause they are immovably allied; it is the alliance of God and nature – immutable, eternal, fixed as the firmament of heaven.

(Ibid.)

1472 If I were an American, as I am an Englishman, while a foreign troop was landed in my country, I never would lay down my arms – never – never – never!

(Speech, H of L, 18 November 1777)

1473 You cannot conquer America.

(Ibid.)

1474 I invoke the genius of the Constitution.

(Ibid.)

William PITT (the younger) (1759–1806): British Tory Prime Minister
[see also 236, 276]

1475 Necessity is the plea for every infringement of human freedom. It is the argument of tyrants; it is the creed of slaves.

(Speech on the India Bill, H of C, 18 November 1783)

1476 Unquestionably there never was a time in the history of this country when, from the situation of Europe, we might more reasonably expect fifteen years of peace, than we may at this present moment.

(Speech, H of C, 17 February 1792)

1477 They [the French] have stated that they would organize every country by a disorganizing principle; and afterwards they tell you all this is done by the will of the people. And then comes this plain question, what is the will of the people? It is the power of the French . . . This has given a more fatal blow to the liberties of mankind than any they have suffered, even from the boldest attempts of the most aspiring monarch.

(Speech, H of C, 1 February 1793)

1478 If France is really desirous of maintaining friendship and peace with England, she must show herself disposed to renounce her views of aggression and aggrandisement, and to confine herself within her own territory without insulting other governments, without disturbing their tranquillity, without violating their rights. And unless she consents to these terms, whatever may be our wishes for peace, the final issue must be war.

(Ibid.)

1479 It has pleased inscrutable Providence that this power of France should triumph over everything that has been opposed to it. But let us not therefore fall without making any efforts to resist it. Let us not sink without measuring its strength.

(Speech, H of C, 30 December 1794)

1480 There is one great resource which I trust will never abandon us. It has shone forth in the English character, by which we have preserved our existence and fame as a nation, which I trust we shall be determined never to abandon under any extremity, but shall join hand and heart in the solemn pledge that is proposed to us, and declare to His Majesty that we know great exertions are wanting, that we are prepared to make them and at all events determined to stand and fall by the laws, liberties and religion of our country.

(Speech, H of C, 10 November 1797)

1481 [France under the Directory] A system of tyranny, the most galling, the most horrible, the most undisguised in all its parts and attributes that has stained the page of history or disgraced the annals of the world.

(Ibid.)

1482 Let us do justice to ourselves. We have been enabled to stand forth the saviours of mankind ... We have presented a phenomenon in the character of nations.

(Speech, H of C, 3 December 1798)

1483 We will not leave the monster to prowl the world unopposed. He must cease to annoy the abode of peaceful men. If he retire into the cell, whether of solitude or repentance, thither we will not pursue him; but we cannot leave him on the throne of power.

(Speech, H of C, 7 June 1799)

1484 We must recollect ... what it is we have at stake, what it is we have to contend for. It is for our property, it is for our liberty, it is for our independence, nay, for our existence as a nation; it is for our character, it is for our very name as Englishmen, it is for everything dear and valuable to man on this side of the grave.

(Speech, H of C, 22 July 1803)

1485 Amid the wreck and the misery of nations it is our just exaltation that we have continued superior to all that ambition or that despotism could effect; and our still higher exaltation ought to be that we provide not only for our own safety but hold out a prospect for nations now bending under the iron yoke of tyranny of what the exertions of a free people can effect.

(Speech, H of C, 25 April 1804)

1486 [discussion of Allied war aims] In order to render [postwar] security as complete as possible it seems necessary, at the period of a general pacification, to form a Treaty to which all the principal powers of Europe should be Parties, by which their respective rights and possessions ... shall be fixed and recognized, and they should all bind themselves mutually to protect and support each other, against any attempt to infringe them. It should re-establish a general and comprehensive system of Public Law in Europe.

(Letter to Novosiltsov for communication to Tsar Alexander I, 19 January 1805)

1487 Europe is not to be saved by any single man. England has saved herself by her exertions, and will, as I trust, save Europe by her example.

(Speech, Guildhall, London, 9 November 1805)

1488 Roll up that map; it will not be wanted these ten years.

(On map of Europe, after hearing news of Austerlitz, December 1805)

1489 My country! Oh, my country!

(Last words, as recorded in the diary of his parliamentary colleague, George Rose, on the day of his death, 23 January 1806 [the classic biography of Pitt by Lord Stanhope gives his last words as 'Oh, my country! How I love my country' in the four-volume edition of 1861–2, and as 'Oh my country! How I leave my country' in the three-volume edition of 1879; see also 1490)

1490 I think I could eat one of Bellamy's veal pies.

(*Attributed last words, 23 January 1806)

PIUS IX (1792–1878): Pope [see also 872]

1491 O Lord God, bless Italy [*Benedite, Gran Dio, l'Italia*].

(Allocution 'Motu Proprio', 10 February 1848)

Viacheslav Konstantinovich PLEHVE (1846–1904): Russian Minister of the Interior

1492 Russia has been made by bayonets, not by diplomacy; and we must decide the questions at issue with China and Japan through bayonets and not through the pens of diplomats ... Russia [needs] ... a nice little victorious war.

(Remarks at Russian Imperial Council on Far Eastern Affairs, 7 May 1903)

Konstantin POBEDONOST-SEV (1827–1907): Russian jurist and Procurator of the Holy Synod

1493 Parliaments are the great lie of our time.

(*Moskovskii Sbornik*, 1896)

POLITICAL SLOGANS

1494 When Adam delved and Eve span,
    Who was then a gentleman?

(Slogan used in the Peasant Rebellion of 1381, taken as a text for a sermon [by John Ball?] to Tyler's men at Blackheath: June 1381)

1495 The Cat, the Rat and Lovell our dog,
    Rulen all England under an Hog.

(Comment on Richard III and his officials of state, written originally on the door of St Paul's, London, allegedly by William Collyngbourne: June 1484)

1496 Wilkes and Liberty.

(Slogan of London mob, 1764)

1497 *Liberté, Egalité, Fraternité* [Liberty, Equality, Fraternity].

(Words voted as the motto of the French Revolutionaries in the

POLITICAL SLOGANS

Cordelier Club, Paris, 30 June 1793, but in popular usage earlier)

1498 No Popery.

(Slogan used by supporters of the Duke of Portland's Government which was opposed to Catholic Emancipation in 1807, also commonly used in Charles II's reign)

1499 Tippecanoe and Tyler too.

(Republican slogan in the American election of 1840: Tippecanoe refers to the Presidential candidate, General Harrison, who had defeated Indians at Tippecanoe Creek in 1811; Tyler was the Vice-Presidential candidate)

1500 Fifty-four forty or fight!

(Slogan of American expansionists seeking a northwards extension of the Oregon frontier, election of 1844: phrase coined by Senator William Allen)

1501 Free soil, free men, free speech, Fré-mont.

(Republican slogan, 1856: the soldier and explorer John Frémont was the unsuccessful Republican Presidential nominee)

1502 Three acres and a cow.

POLITICAL SLOGANS

(Phrase in land-reform propaganda, 1885) (cf. 1246)

1503 Remember the 'Maine'!

(Slogan in the American press used by supporters of a war against Spain after the blowing up of the USS *Maine* in Havana, February 1898)

1504 Votes for Women.

(Suffragette slogan, England, 1906–14)

1505 The New Freedom.

(Campaign slogan used by Woodrow Wilson in his successful Presidential campaign in 1912)

1506 Ulster will fight and Ulster is right.

(Used by the Ulster Volunteers, opposing Irish Home Rule, 1913–14) (cf. 362)

1507 Your country needs YOU.

(Recruiting poster, showing Kitchener's pointing hand, Britain, 1914)

1508 Peace, Bread and Land.

(Slogan on workers' banners in Petrograd, February/March 1917)

1509 All Power to the Soviets!

(Petrograd workers, October/
November 1917)

1510 Keep cool with Coolidge.

(Republican campaign, US
Presidential election of 1924:
won easily by Coolidge)

1511 Not a minute on the day,
not a penny off the pay.

(Slogan coined by the miners'
leader, A. J. Cook, in April 1926
when the British coal-owners
sought reduced wages and
longer hours for the workers; the
slogan continued to be used
during the British General Strike,
4–12 May 1926)

1512 Safety First.

(Conservative Party election
slogan, 1929 (the poster using the
phrase depicted Baldwin smoking
a pipe, but the slogan was the idea
of the Party Chairman, J. C. C.
Davidson, who was blamed for the
subsequent Conservative defeat))

1513 Mussolini is always right
[*Mussolini a sempre ragione*].

(Italian Fascist decalogue, 1934)

1514 One Realm, One People,
One Leader [*Ein Reich, Ein Volk,
Ein Führer*].

(Nazi Party slogan in Germany,
first used at the Nuremberg
Rally, September 1934)

1515 *Travail,   Famille,   Patrie*
[Work, Family, Fatherland].

(Slogan of 'Vichy' France,
1940–4)

1516 I like Ike.

(Republican campaign slogan in
support of Eisenhower, 1952)

1517 *Algérie Française* [Algeria is
French].

(Slogan of the right-wing
opponents of the Fourth French
Republic, May 1958)

1518 All the way with L.B.J.

(Democratic Party's campaign
slogan, 1964)

1519 If you want a Nigger for a
neighbour, vote Labour.

(Slogan used by some
Conservatives [against the official
Conservative Party policy] during
the General Election campaign in
Smethwick constituency, October
1964. The seat was won by the
Conservatives from Labour)

James K. POLK (1705–1849):
eleventh President of the USA

1520 The people of this continent alone have the right to decide
their own destiny.

(Message to Congress, 2
December 1845)

Marco POLO (1254–1324): Venetian ambassador and explorer

1521 I shall tell you of the great and wonderful magnificence of the Great Kaan now reigning, by name Cublay Kaan ... all men know for a certain truth that he is the most potent man, as regards forces and lands and treasure that existeth in the world.

(Of his life in Cathay, 1275–92, *The Book of Marco Polo*, 1298/9)

1522 The whole city is arrayed in squares just like a chess-board, and disposed in a manner so perfect and masterly that it is impossible to give a description that should do it justice.

(Of Kublai Khan's capital, Cambaluc, later Peking, Ibid.)

1523 Chipargu [Japan] is an Island towards the east in the high seas, 1500 miles distant from the Continent; and a very great Island it is. The people are white, civilized and well-favoured.

(Ibid.)

Jeanne, Marquise de POMPADOUR (1721–64): mistress of Louis XV

1524 *Après nous le déluge* [After us, the flood].

(Remark ascribed to her towards the end of her life)

Alexander POPE (1688–1744): English poet

1525 I find myself ... hoping a total end of all the unhappy divisions of mankind by party-spirit, which at best is but the madness of many for the gain of a few.

(Letter to E. Blount, 27 August 1714)

1526 [of Isaac Newton]
Nature and Nature's laws lay hid in night:
God said, *Let Newton be!* and all was light.

(Epitaph, intended for Sir Isaac Newton, in Westminster Abbey, 1730)

1527 For forms of government let fools contest;
Whate'er is best administered is best.

(*An Essay on Man*, 8 May 1733)

POST: German newspaper, published in Berlin

1528 *Ist der Krieg in Sicht* [Is War in Sight]?

(Headline to article on French rearmament, which precipitated a diplomatic crisis, 8 April 1875)

Henry Codman POTTER (1835–1908): American Bishop

1529 We have exchanged the Washingtonian dignity for the

Jeffersonian simplicity, which in due time came to be only another name for the Jacksonian vulgarity.

(Address on the Centennial of Washington DC, 30 April 1889)

1530 If there be no nobility of descent in a nation, all the more indispensable is it that there should be nobility of ascent – a character in them that bear rule, so fine and high and pure, that as men come within the circle of its influence, they involuntarily pay homage to that which is the one pre-eminent distinction, the Royalty of Virtue.

(Ibid.)

J. Enoch POWELL (b. 1912): British independent Conservative politician

1531 I was born a Tory, am a Tory and shall die a Tory. I never yet heard it was any part of the faith of a Tory to take the institutions and liberties, the laws and customs which his country has evolved over centuries and merge them with those of eight other nations into a new made artificial state and, what is more, to do so without the willing approbation and consent of the nation.

(Speech against the 'Common Market' during the General Election campaign, Shipley, Yorkshire, 25 February 1974)

1532 Who is in Beirut and who governs Beirut is a matter of the utmost indifference to the United Kingdom.

(Speech during the Lebanon crisis, 16 September 1983)

John PRESTON (1587–1628): English Puritan divine

1533 When the enemy is assaulting the Churches afar off, he is even then striking at the roote of this Church and Commonwealle . . . It is certaine that evil is intended against us, and will come upon us, except something bee done to prevent it. For there is a Covenant between God and us, and breach of covenant causeth a quarrel; the quarrel of God shall not go unrevenged . . . At this time are not present enemies not only stirred up but united together, and we disjoined to resist them?

(Sermon preached before Charles I at Whitehall, October 1627)

Daniel PRICE (1581–1631): Anglican clergyman, royal chaplain

1534 The Virginian desireth it, the Spaniard envieth us; and yet our own lazy, drowsy, yet barking countrymen traduce it, who should honour it, if it was but for the memory of that Virgin Queen of eternal memory, who was the first Godmother of that land and nation.

(Sermon in support of Virginia expedition of 1609)

John Boynton PRIESTLEY (1894–1984): British writer

1535 These 'Brighton Belles' and 'Brighton Queens' left that innocent foolish world of theirs – to sail into the inferno, to defy bombs, shells, magnetic mines, torpedoes, machine-gun fire – to rescue our soldiers ... Our great-grandchildren, when they learn how we began this War by snatching glory out of defeat, and then swept on to victory, may also learn how the little holiday steamers made an excursion to hell and came back glorious.

(BBC radio *Postscript*, broadcast on 5 June 1940, the day after completion of the Dunkirk evacuation)

Pierre-Joseph PROUDHON (1809–65): French socialist

1536 Property is theft [*La propriété c'est le vol*].

(*Qu'est-ce que la Propriété?*, 1840)

William PRYNNE (1600–69): English Puritan pamphleteer

1537 A woman with cut hair is a filthy spectacle, and much like a monster ... it being natural and

comely to women to nourish their hair, which even God and nature have given them for a covering, a token of subjection, and a natural badge to distinguish them from men.

(*Histriomastix*, 1632)

1538 It hath evermore been the notorious badge of prostituted strumpets and the lewdest Harlots, to ramble abroad to plays and to playhouses; whither no honest, chaste or sober girls or women, but only branded Whores and infamous Adulteresses, did usually resort in ancient times.

(Ibid.)

1539 Popular stage-plays are sinful, heathenish, lewd, ungodly Spectacles and most pernicious Corruptions, condemned in all ages as intolerable Mischiefs to Churches, to Republics, to the manners, minds and souls of men.

(Ibid.)

PTOLEMY of Lucca (?1250–?1310): Italian political theorist

1540 Certain regions are servile by nature, and such should be governed by despotical government ... Those, however, who are virile in mind, bold of heart, and confident in their intelligence, such men cannot be ruled except by a republic ... This kind of government flourishes best in Italy.

(*On the Rule of Princes*, begun by Thomas Aquinas, *c.* 1305)

PUNCH: English humorous weekly periodical (est. 1841)

1541 One good turn deserves another.

(Caption to cartoon celebrating Disraeli's elevation to the peerage a few months after Queen Victoria became Empress of India: 16 August 1876)

1542 Oh, I say! By-the-bye! What's the French for 'Compromise'?

(Caption to a Tenniel cartoon of Disraeli addressing Bismarck with his hand on the door of the conference room for the Berlin Congress, 22 June 1878)

1543 Dropping the Pilot.

(On the resignation of Bismarck, 29 March 1890)

1544 Bravo, Belgium.

(Caption to a cartoon of a Belgian peasant-boy defying a German intruder, 12 August 1914)

Samuel PURCHAS (1575–1626): English chronicler of overseas enterprise

1545 [of Tsar Ivan the Terrible]

Bloodiness is a slippery foundation of Greatness.

(Introduction to Horsey's narrative of his visit to Moscow 1573, *Purchas, his Pilgrims*, Pt 2, 1625)

Israel PUTNAM (1718–90): American Revolutionary soldier

1546 Men, you are all marksmen: don't one of you fire until you see the whites of their eyes.

(At Battle of Bunker Hill, 17 June 1775: the remark is sometimes attributed to Putnam's superior, Colonel William Prescott)

John PYM (1584–1643): English Parliamentarian leader

1547 Shall it be treason to embase the King's coin, though but a piece of twelvepence or sixpence – and must it not needs be the effect of a greater treason to embase the spirits of his subjects, and to set a stamp and character of servitude upon them?

(Speech at Strafford's trial, 12 April 1640)

1548 A Parliament is that to the Commonwealth which the soul is to the body ... It behoves us therefore to keep the facility of that soul from distemper.

(Speech, H of C, 17 April 1640)

François QUESNAY (1694–1774): political economist, founder of the French Physiocrats

1549 *Laissez-faire* [Let it do – i.e. do not interfere].

(*Le Droit naturel*, 1765)

Josiah QUINCY (1772–1864): American Federalist

1550 As it will be the right of all, so it will be the duty of some, definitely to prepare for a separation, amicably if they can, violently if they must.

(Speech in debate on State rights, US House of Representatives, 14 January 1811)

Fitzroy Somerset, Lord RAGLAN (1788–1855): British General

1551 Lord Raglan wishes the cavalry to advance rapidly to the front and try to prevent enemy carrying away the guns. Troop of Horse Artillery may accompany. French cavalry is on your left. Immediate.

(Written order to Lieutenant-General Lord Lucan prompting the charge of the Light Brigade at Balaclava, 25 October 1854)

Thomas RAINBOROWE (?–1648): English radical soldier

1552 I think that the poorest He that is in England hath a life to live as well as the greatest He, and therefore truly, sirs, I think that every man that is to live under a government ought first, by his own consent, to put himself under that government.

(To Cromwell and Ireton in the 'Army debates' at Putney, 29 October 1647)

Sir Walter RALEIGH (?1552–1618): English explorer and writer
[see also 218, 864, 1762]

1553 Who would therefore repose trust in such a nation of ravenous strangers, and especially in those Spaniards which more greedily thirst after English blood, than after the lives of any other people in Europe, for the many overthrows and dishonours they have received at our hands, whose weakness we have discovered to the world?

(Report of the last fight of the *Revenge*, written and printed in 1591)

1554 Guiana is a country that hath yet her maidenhead, never sacked, turned, nor wrought, the face of the earth hath not been torn, nor the virtue and salt of the soil spent by manurance, the graves have not been opened for gold, the mines not broken with sledges, nor their images pulled down out of their temples.

(Account of his discovery of
Guiana, 1595)

1555 Instead of a Lady whom
Time had surprised, we had an
active King who would be present
at his own business.

(Speech in his own defence at his
trial for treason [referring to
James I's succeeding Elizabeth I],
Winchester, 20 November 1603)

1556 It were an horrible dishonour to be over reached by any of
these dry and subtil headed
Spaniards.

(Discourse on the marriage of
Prince Henry, written 1611)

RALPH, Abbot of Coggeshall
(?–1216): English monastic
chronicler

1557 [of King John's journey
through the fenland] Besides, a
very great grief troubled him
[King John], for he had lost his
chapel with his relics and some of
his packhorses with different
kinds of household effects at the
Wellstream, during the course of
that journey. Many of his household, also, were drowned in the
waters of the sea and sucked into
the quicksand there.

(*Chronicon Anglicanum* for
October 1216)

Jacques RANDON (1795–
1871): Marshal of France and
Minister of War

1558 It is France that has been
defeated at Sadowa.

(Comment on the significance of
the Prussian victory over Austria
at Sadowa/Königgrätz on 3 July
1866)

Ronald REAGAN (b. 1911):
fortieth President of the USA.

1559 [President Carter's foreign
policy] . . . is like the sorry tap-
ping of Neville Chamberlain's
umbrella on the cobblestones of
Munich.

(Comment early in 1980, after
Russian invasion of Afghanistan)

1560 Recession is when your
neighbour loses his job. Depression is when you lose yours. And
recovery is when Jimmy Carter
loses his.

(Presidential campaign speech,
Jersey City, NJ, 1 September
1980)

1561 Never before in our history has America been called
upon to face three grave threats
to our very existence, any one of
which could destroy us. We face
a distressing economy, a
weakened defence and an energy
policy based on the sharing of
scarcity.

(Acceptance speech after Presidential nomination by the Republican Party Convention, Detroit, 17 July 1980)

1562 All of us need to be reminded that the federal government did not create the states – the states created the federal government.

(Inaugural address, 20 January 1981)

John REDMOND (1856–1918): Irish politician

1563 What you have done for Frenchmen in Quebec, what you have done for Dutchmen in the Transvaal, you should now do for Irishmen in Ireland.

(Speech, in favour of Irish Home Rule, H of C, 30 March 1908)

1564 I say to the Government that they may tomorrow withdraw every one of their troops from Ireland. Ireland will be defended by her armed sons from foreign invasion, and for that purpose the armed Catholics in the South will be only too glad to join arms with the armed Protestant Ulstermen. Is it too much to hope that out of this situation a result may spring which will be good not merely for the Empire but for the future welfare and integrity of the Irish nation?

(Speech, H of C, 3 August 1914)

RED STAR: official journal of the Soviet Ministry of Defence

1565 The Iron Lady of British politics is seeking to revive the cold war.

(Comment on speech by Mrs Thatcher at Kensington in the previous week: 23 January 1976; earliest use of the appellation)

John REED (1887–1920): American left-wing journalist

1566 Ten Days that Shook the World.

(Title of his eyewitness account of the Bolshevik seizure of power in Petrograd, November 1917; the book was published in 1919)

Erich Maria REMARQUE (E.P. Remark) (1898–1970): German novelist

1567 All Quiet on the Western Front.

(Title of his translated novel *Im Westen nichts Neues* (1929): the title is intended as an ironical commentary on war communiqués)

Ernest RENAN (1823–92): French scholar and historian

1568 War is, in a sense, one condition of progress, the whip cut preventing a country from going to sleep and forcing satisfied mediocrity to shake off its apathy.

(*La Réforme Intellectuale et Morale*, 1871)

Jean Paul de Gondi, Cardinal de RETZ (1614–79): French political intriguer

1569 I decided to do evil deliberately, the worst offence before God and the wisest course before man ... I resolved that I would fulfil scrupulously every duty of my profession and that I would be as zealous for the welfare of others as I would be wicked for myself.

(On appointment as Co-adjutor to his uncle, the Archbishop of Paris, 1644; *Mémoires*, 1717)

1570 Richelieu leaned to the good whenever his interests did not draw him towards evil.

(Ibid.)

REVOLUTIONARY SONGS

1571 With spades and hoes and
    ploughs, stand up now,
    stand up now,
    With spades and hoes and
    ploughs, stand up now,
    Your freedom to uphold,
    seeing Cavaliers are
    bold,
    To kill you if they could,
    and rights from you to
    hold,

Stand up now, Diggers all.

('The Diggers' Song', 1649, probably composed by Winstanley, q.v.)

1572 *Ça Ira!* [That will go!]

(Revolutionary song: primarily a folk-dance first popular in Paris in early July 1791)

1573 *Allons enfants de la patrie,*
    Le jour de gloire est arrivé
    [Come children of the
      fatherland,
    The day of glory has arrived]

(Opening lines of 'La Marsellaise', written by Rouget de Lisle, 1760–1836, on 25 April 1792 as 'Chant de guerre pour l'armée du Rhin', but particularly associated with the march of the Marseilles Revolutionaries to Paris three months later)

1574 Then raise the scarlet standard
    high!
    Beneath its shade we'll live
    and die!
    Though cowards flinch,
    and traitors jeer,
    We'll keep the Red Flag
    flying here!

('The Red Flag', words attributed to James Connell, 1852–1929)

1575 Arise, ye starvelings from your
    slumbers,
    Arise, ye prisoners of want!

For reason in revolt now thunders
And at last ends the age of cant.
Now away with all your superstition;
Servile masses, arise, arise!
We'll change forthwith the old condition
And spurn the dust to win the prize.
Then, comrades, come rally,
And the last fight let us face,
L'Internationale unites the human race.

(English version of the international anthem of socialist workers, written in French by the Communard Eugène Pottier, in 1871)

Cecil RHODES (1853–1902): South African statesman

1576 The unctuous rectitude of my [English] countrymen.

(Speech, Port Elizabeth, 24 December 1896)

1577 So little done, so much to do.

(*Alleged last words, 1902)

David RICARDO (1772–1823): English political economist

1578 The interest of the landlord is always opposed to the interests of every other class in the community.

(*Principles of Political Economy and Taxation*, 1817)

1579 The natural price of labour is that price which is necessary to enable the labourers, one with another, to subsist and perpetuate their race, without either increase or diminution.

(Ibid.)

Sir Stephen RICE (1637–1715): Chief Baron of the Irish Exchequer

1580 I will drive a coach and horses through the Act of Settlement [i.e. The Irish Act of Settlement of 1661].

(*Alleged remark, 1686)

RICHARD I (1157–99): King of England
[see also 1655]

1581 Dear Lord, I pray Thee to suffer me not to see Thy Holy City, since I cannot deliver it from the hands of Thy enemies.

(*In sight of Jerusalem, but realizing that he could not take the city, 1192: story current in the thirteenth century)

1582 *Dieu et mon droit* [God and my right].

(Battle-words chosen at Gisors, September 1198, to assert that the rulers of Normandy owed no vassalage to the Kings of France; subsequently the phrase became the motto of the royal arms of England)

1583 By God's throat, even if that castle were all built of butter and not of iron and stone, I have no doubt it would defend me against him [King of France] and all his forces.

(Of his new castle, Gaillard, 1198/9)

RICHARD II (1365–99): King of England

1584 Do not dispute any more or grieve for the death of this lewd traitor. I myself will be your King, I will be your captain and leader. Follow me to the field and you shall have everything you desire.

(To the rebels at Smithfield after the death of Wat Tyler, 15 June 1381)

1585 My God! this is a wonderful land and a faithless one; for she has exiled, slain, destroyed and ruined so many Kings, so many rulers, so many great men, and she is always diseased and suffering from differences, quarrels and hatred between her people.

(In the Tower of London, 21 September 1399)

RICHARD III (1452–85): King of England
[see also 1048]

1586 On this day will I end all battles or else here finish my life.

(*Alleged response to offer of a horse to flee from Bosworth Field, 22 August 1485: cf. Buck, no. 213)

Armand Jean Duplessis, Cardinal de RICHELIEU (1585–1642): French statesman, chief minister to King Louis XIII
[see also 1570]

1587 Courage, Father Joseph, Breisach is ours.

(To his *alter ego*, the Capuchin Joseph du Tremblay, who was dying, 17 December 1638. Breisach was regarded as the key fortress on the middle Rhine and had been besieged for four months)

1588 When Your Majesty decided to give me a place in your councils . . . I promised to employ all my energy and all the authority it pleased you to give me in order to ruin the Huguenot party, to bring down the pride of the Nobles, to reduce your subjects to their duties, and to raise your name among foreign nations to the place which it ought to hold.

(To Louis XIII, Prefatory essay in the *Testament Politique*, written ?1641)

1589 To know how to dissimulate is the knowledge of kings.

(Maxims in *Testament Politique*, 1641)

1590 To make a law, yet not see that it is enforced, is to authorise what you have yourself forbidden.

(Ibid.)

1591 Not least among the qualities in a great King is a capacity to permit his ministers to serve him.

(Ibid.)

1592 It is essential to banish pity in judging crimes against the State.

(Ibid.)

1593 Secrecy is the first essential in affairs of the State.

(Ibid.)

1594 When the people are too comfortable it is not possible to restrain them within the bounds of their duty ... They may be compared to mules who, being accustomed to burdens, are spoilt rather by rest than by labour.

(Ibid.)

1595 It is unnecessary for a man

to attend to public affairs without any interruption: such concentration is, indeed, more liable to render him useless than any other behaviour.

(Ibid.)

1596 Wounds inflicted by the sword heal more easily than those inflicted by the tongue.

(Ibid.)

Castel dos RIOS (*flor.* late 17th century): Spanish ambassador to France

1597 The Pyrenees no longer exist [*Il n'y a plus de Pyrénées*].

(To Louis XIV, who had announced his grandson's acceptance of the Spanish throne, 16 November 1700: wrongly attributed by Voltaire to Louis XIV)

Maximilien ROBESPIERRE (1758–94): French Revolutionary [see also 286]

1598 Citizens, do you want a revolution without Revolution?

(Speech to the Convention, 5 November 1792)

1599 Citizens, we are talking of a republic, and yet Louis lives! We are talking of a republic, and the person of the King still stands between us and liberty ... Because the country must live, Louis must die.

(Speech, Convention, 3 December 1792)

Duc de la ROCHEFOU-CAULD-LIANCOURT (1747–1827): French courtier

1600 No, Sire, it is a revolution [*Non, Sire, c'est une révolution*].

(Replying to Louis XVI's query, '*C'est une révolte?*' on hearing, at Versailles, the news of the fall of the Bastille: morning of 15 July 1789)

John Wilmot, Earl of ROCHESTER (1647–80): English courtier and satirist [see also 250]

1601 Here lies a great and mighty King
Whose promise none relied on;
He never said a foolish thing,
Nor ever did a wise one.

(Mock epitaph on Charles II, ?1670)

1602 [of Charles II] A merry monarch, scandalous and poor.

(*A Satire on King Charles II*, for which he was banished from Court, ?1676)

Mme Marie Jeanne ROLAND (1754–93): French Revolutionary

1603 Liberty, oh Liberty, what crimes are committed in thy name.

(Apostrophizing a Statue of Liberty, Paris, before her execution, 8 November 1793)

John ROLFE (?1585–1622): colonialist

1604 For the good of the Plantation, the honour of our Country, for the glory of God, for mine own salvation, and for the converting ... an unbelieving creature, namely Pocahontas.

(Explanation of his marriage to Pocahontas in April 1614, in letter to Sir Thomas Dale, Marshal of Virginia, pub. 1615)

1605 Whereupon a peace was concluded, which still continues so firm, that our people yearly plant, and reap quietly, and travel in the woods afowling and ahunting as freely and secure from fear of danger or treachery as in England.

(On 'Peace of Pocahontas' between Indians and colonists in Virginia, 1614: *True Relation of State of Virginia*, 1616)

Franklin Delano ROOSEVELT (1882–1945): thirty-second President of the USA

1606 I pledge you – I pledge myself – to a new deal for the American people.

(Speech accepting nomination, Democratic Convention, Chicago, 2 July 1932)

1607 Let me assert my firm belief that the only thing we have to fear is fear itself.

(First Inaugural Address, 4 March 1933)

1608 In the field of world policy; I would dedicate this nation to the policy of the good neighbour.

(Ibid.)

1609 Governments can err. Presidents do make mistakes, but the immortal Dante tells us that divine justice weighs the sins of the cold-blooded and the sins of the warm-hearted in different scales. Better the occasional faults of a Government that lives in a spirit of charity than the consistent omissions of a Government frozen in the ice of its own indifference.

(Speech, accepting renomination, Philadelphia, 27 June 1936)

1610 I see one-third of a nation ill-housed, ill-clad, ill-nourished.

(Second Inaugural Address, 20 January 1937)

1611 When peace has been broken anywhere, the peace of all countries everywhere is in danger.

('Fireside Chat' broadcast, 3 September 1939)

1612 A conservative is a man with two perfectly good legs who, however, has never learned to walk forwards . . . A reactionary is a somnambulist walking backwards . . . A radical is a man with both feet firmly planted – in the air.

('Fireside Chat' broadcast, 26 October 1939)

1613 On this tenth day of June 1940, the hand that held the dagger has struck it into the back of its neighbour . . . Neither those who sprang from that ancient stock nor those who have come hither in later years can be indifferent to the destruction of freedom in their ancestral lands across the seas.

(Speech, Charlottesville, Virginia, 10 June 1940, the day Mussolini declared war on France and Britain)

1614 We must be the great arsenal of democracy.

('Fireside Chat' broadcast, 29 December 1940)

1615 In the future days, which we seek to make secure, we look forward to a world founded upon four essential freedoms.

The first is freedom of speech and expression – everywhere in the world.

The second is freedom of every person to worship God in his own way – everywhere in the world.

The third is freedom from want
. . .

The fourth is freedom from fear.

(Third Inaugural Address, 6 January 1941)

1616 Yesterday, December 7, 1941 – a date that shall live in infamy – the United States of America was suddenly and deliberately attacked by naval and air forces of the Empire of Japan.

(War message to Congress, referring to the attack on Pearl Harbor, 8 December 1941)

1617 It is fun to be in the same decade with you.

(Cable to Churchill in response to sixtieth birthday greetings, 30 January 1942)

1618 [The American and British Governments] . . . are determined to accept nothing less than the unconditional surrender of Germany, Italy and Japan . . .

(Statement delivered informally to the Press by the President after the Casablanca Conference, 24 January 1943)

Theodore **ROOSEVELT** (1858–1919): twenty-sixth President of the USA
[see also 810]

1619 I feel as strong as a bull moose.

(In letter to Henry Cabot Lodge, dated 29 October 1895: the simile was often used by Roosevelt before it became the nickname of his independent Progressive Party in the summer of 1912)

1620 I wish to preach, not the doctrine of ignoble ease, but the doctrine of the strenuous life.

(Speech, Chicago, 10 April 1899)

1621 Let me make as vigorous a plea as I know how in favour of saying nothing that we do not mean, and of acting without hesitation up to whatever we say. A good many of you are probably acquainted with the old proverb, 'Speak softly and carry a big stick – you will go far' . . . This is the attitude we should take as regards the Monroe Doctrine.

(Speech, Minnesota State Fair, 2 September 1901)

1622 A man who is good enough to shed his blood for the country is good enough to be given a square deal afterwards. More than that no man is entitled to, and less than that no man shall have.

(Speech, Springfield, Illinois, 4 June 1903)

1623 In the Western hemisphere the adherence of the United States to the Monroe Doctrine may force the United States, however reluctantly, in flagrant cases of wrongdoing or impotence, to the exercise of an international police power.

(Message to Congress, 6 December 1904)

1624 The men with the muck-rakes are often indispensable to the well-being of society; but only if they know when to stop raking the muck.

(Speech, at laying of Corner-Stone of office building of House of Representatives, Washington DC, 14 April 1906)

1625 Malefactors of great wealth . . .

(Speech, Provincetown, Massachusetts, 20 August 1907)

1626 I stand for the square deal . . . I mean not merely that I stand for fair play under the present rules of the game, but that I stand for having those rules changed so as to work for a more substantial equality of opportunity and of reward for equally good service.

(Speech, Osawatomie, 31 August 1910)

1627 Do not hit at all if it can be avoided, but never hit softly.

(*Autobiography*, 1913)

1628 Practical efficiency is common, and lofty idealism not uncommon; it is the combination which is necessary, and the combination is rare.

(Ibid.)

1629 We have room in this country for but one flag, the Stars and Stripes . . . We have room for but one loyalty, loyalty to the United States . . . We have room for but one language, the English language.

(Final message to the American Defense Society, 3 January 1919: Roosevelt died two days later)

Archibald Philip Primrose, Lord ROSEBERY (1847–1929): British Liberal Prime Minister

1630 I perceive . . . one very formidable rival . . . who . . . is encroaching on us as the sea encroaches on the weak parts of the coast – I mean Germany.

(Speech, Epsom, 24 July 1896)

1631 It is beginning to be hinted that we are a nation of amateurs.

(Rectorial Address, Glasgow University, 16 November 1900)

1632 [of the British Empire] How marvellous it all is! Built not by saints and angels, but the work of men's hands; cemented with men's honest blood and with a world of tears, welded by the best brains of centuries past; not without the taint and reproach incidental to all human work, but constructed on the whole with pure and splendid purpose. Human, and yet not wholly human – for the most heedless and the most cynical must see the finger of the Divine.

(Ibid).

Jean-Jacques ROUSSEAU (1712–78): French political theorist [see also 982]

1633 Man is born free; and everywhere he is in chains.

(Opening words of *Contrat Social*, 1762)

1634 The English people imagine themselves to be free, but they are wrong: it is only during the election of members of parliament that they are so.

(Ibid.)

1635 [of Corsica] I have a presentiment that one day this small island will astonish Europe.

(Ibid.)

1636 Take from before my eyes this wounding sword, O Frederick! Look into your heart! Are you able to reconcile yourself to death before you become the greatest of men? Let me see Frederick, formidable and just, fill his realm with happy people whose father he should be, and Jean-Jacques Rousseau, enemy of kings, will come to die with joy upon the steps of his throne.

(Letter to Frederick II of Prussia, 30 October 1762)

Agnes Maude ROYDEN (1887–1967): British Congregationalist Minister

1637 The Church [of England] should be no longer satisfied to represent only the Conservative Party at prayer.

(Address, Life and Liberty Movement, Queen's Hall, London, 16 July 1917)

RUDOLF I (1218–91): Holy Roman Emperor

1638 By God, let any man who will come to me! I have not become King to live hidden in a wardrobe.

([?] After coronation at Aix, Aachen, 1273)

Robert Alexander RUNCIE (b. 1924): Archbishop of Canterbury

1639 Royalty puts a human face on the operations of government.

(Sermon at celebration of the Queen Mother's Eightieth Birthday, St Paul's Cathedral, 15 July 1980)

1640 I rejoice that the successors of Gregory and Augustine stand here today in this great church. But our unity is not in the past only, but also in the future.

(Welcoming Pope John Paul II to Canterbury Cathedral, 29 May 1982)

1641 Those who dare to interpret God's will must never claim Him as an asset for one nation or group rather than another. War springs from the love and loyalty which should be offered to God being applied to some God substitute, one of the most dangerous being nationalism.

(Sermon at the Falkland Islands Thanksgiving Service, St Paul's Cathedral, 26 July 1982)

John RUSHWORTH (?1612–90): Clerk to House of Commons

1642 His Majesty entered the House, and as he passed up towards the Chair, he cast his eye on the right hand near the Bar of the House where Mr Pym used to sit; but His Majesty not seeing him there (knowing him well) went up to the Chair and said 'By your leave (Mr Speaker) I must borrow your chair a little'.

(From *Historical Collections*, on Charles I's attempt to arrest the five MPs, 4 January 1642; cf. 336, 1068)

John RUSKIN (1819–1900): English writer and critic

1643 Along the iron veins that traverse the frame of our country, beat and flow the fiery pulses of its exertion, hotter and faster every hour. All vitality is concentrated through those throbbing arteries into the central cities; the country is passed over like a green sea by narrow bridges, and we are thrown back in continually closer crowds on the city gates.

(*Seven Lamps of Architecture*, 1849)

1644 Men don't and can't live by exchanging articles, but by producing them. They don't live by trade, but by work. Give up that foolish and vain title of Trades Unions; and take that of Labourers' Unions.

(Open letter to the Trades Unions of England, 31 August 1880, *Fors Clavigera*, Vol. VIII, dated 29 September 1880)

Bertrand RUSSELL, Earl Russell (1872–1970): British

philosopher and champion of nuclear disarmament

1645 This idea of weapons of mass extermination is utterly horrible and is something which no one with one spark of humanity can tolerate. I will not pretend to obey a government which is organising a mass massacre of mankind.

(Speech encouraging civil disobedience in support of nuclear disarmament, Birmingham, 15 April 1961)

Lord John RUSSELL (1792–1878): British Liberal Prime Minister [see also 523]

1646 If peace cannot be maintained with honour, it is no longer peace.

(Speech, Greenock, 19 September 1853)

Sir William Howard RUSSELL (1820–1907): British journalist

1647 Gathering speed at every stride, they dash on towards that thin red streak topped with a line of steel.

(Reporting Russian cavalry charge on 93rd Highlanders at Balaclava, 25 October 1854, printed in *The Times*, 15 November: the phrase later corrupted into 'thin red line')

1648 Such scandalous behaviour on the part of soldiers I should have considered impossible as with some experience of camps and armies I have never even in alarm among camp followers seen the like of it.

('The Bull Run Despatch', reporting on the Union army after the Battle of First Bull Run, 21 July 1861, printed in *The Times*, 6 August)

1649 ... The three terrible Fates, before whose eyes the power of Imperial France was being broken to atoms.

(Description of the King of Prussia, Moltke and Bismarck at the Battle of Sedan, 1 September 1870: *My Diary during the last Great War*, 1874)

Mohammed Anwar el-SADAT (1918–81): President of the Arab Republic of Egypt

1650 I know the risks I take among my Arab brothers, who do not understand my purposes. They may be fatal risks – but that is of no consequence. Remember what is at stake.

(In conversation with US Secretary of State, Alexander Haig, Cairo, April 1981, five months before Sadat's assassination)

Antoine Louis Léon de SAINT JUST (1767–94): French Revolutionary

1651 The forms of our procedure [for the trial of Louis XVI] are found, not in civil law, but in the law of nations ... How, indeed, may we judge a king as a citizen? For judging means applying the law. But law implies a common foundation of justice. And what common foundation of justice is there between humanity and kings? ... It is impossible to reign innocently ... Every citizen possesses the same right over a king that Brutus had over Caesar.

(Maiden speech in the Convention, Paris, 18 November 1792)

John Jervis, Earl ST VINCENT (1735–1823): British Admiral

1652 I do not say the French cannot come, I only say they cannot come by sea.

(Comment, as First Lord of the Admiralty, to Addington's Cabinet, discussing the possibility of invasion, summer 1803)

SALADIN (1137–93): Saracen General, Sultan of Damascus and Cairo

1653 When God has given into my hands the rest of the Christian towns, I shall divide my State among my children; I shall leave them my last instructions and

then, bidding them farewell, I shall embark on that sea to go and subdue the isles and the countries of the West. I do not want to lay down my arms until there is no longer a single infidel on earth.

(To Beha-ed-Din, at Ascalon, December 1188/January 1189)

1654 I do not want them to get used to shedding blood so young; at their age they do not know what it means to be a Moslem or an infidel, and they will grow accustomed to trifling with the lives of others.

(To Beha-ed-Din, when Saladin's children asked if they might kill a prisoner, ?1191)

1655 I have long since been aware that your king [Richard I] is a man of the greatest honour and bravery, but he is imprudent ... and shows too great recklessness of his own life ... I would rather have abundance of wealth, with wisdom and moderation, than display immoderate valour and rashness.

(To Bishop of Salisbury, near Jerusalem, after truce of 2 September 1192)

Robert Arthur Talbot Gascoyne Cecil, Marquis of SALISBURY (1830–1903): British Conservative Prime Minister [see also 319, 557, 561]

1656 Peace without honour is not only a disgrace, but, except as a temporary respite, it is a chimera.

('Foreign Politics', *Quarterly Review*, April 1864)

1657 Under a more heroic minister and in a less self-seeking age, it is probable that England would have preferred the risk, whatever its extent, to the infamy of betraying an ally whom she had enticed into peril. But our Ministry is not heroic; and our generation, though not indifferent to glory, prefers it when it is safe and cheap.

(Article attacking Palmerston's failure to support Denmark against Prussia, *Quarterly Review*, July 1864)

1658 English policy is to float lazily downstream, occasionally putting out a diplomatic boat-hook to avoid collisions.

(Comment quoted by his daughter, Gwendolen, in the biography of her father. The remark appears to have been made in 1877)

1659 I cannot go very far with those who dread the Russians. Except the size of the patch they occupy on the map, there is nothing about their history or their actual condition to explain the abject terror which deprives so many Anglo-Indians and so many of our military party here of their natural sleep . . . Their people are unwarlike, their officials corrupt, their rulers only competent when borrowed from Germany.

(Letter to Viceroy of India, Lytton, 27 April 1877)

1660 The commonest error in politics is sticking to the carcasses of old policies.

(Speech, Hatfield, 25 May 1877)

1661 Our national fault is that too much softness has crept into our councils; we imagine that great national dangers can be conjured away by a plentiful administration of platitudes and rose-water.

(Speech, National Conservative Club, London, 7 March 1887)

1662 We are part of the community of Europe and we must do our duty as such.

(Speech, Caernarvon, 10 April 1888)

1663 No country whose borders adjoin Turkey can look at the problem of the Armenians . . . with the same emotional and philanthropic spirit with which you, in your splendid isolation, are able to examine all the circumstances . . . No fleet in the world can get over the mountains of Taurus to protect the Armenians.

(Speech, Guildhall, London, 9 November 1896)

1664 Our first duty is towards the people of this country, to maintain their interests and their rights; our second duty is to all humanity.

(Ibid.)

1665 It is a superstition of an antiquated diplomacy that there is any necessary antagonism between Russia and Great Britain.

(Ibid.)

1666 We know that we shall maintain against all comers that which we possess, and we know, in spite of the jargon about isolation, that we are amply competent to do so.

(Speech, Albert Hall, London, 4 May 1898)

1667 You may roughly divide the nations of the world as the living and the dying ... The weak States are becoming weaker and the strong States are becoming stronger ... For one reason or another – from the necessities of politics or under the pretence of philanthropy – the living nations will gradually encroach on the territory of the dying, and the seeds and causes of conflict among civilized nations will speedily appear ...

(Ibid.)

1668 The German ambassador ... speaks of our 'isolation' as constituting serious danger for us. Have we ever felt that danger practically? If we had succumbed in the revolutionary war, our fall would not have been due to our isolation ... It is impossible for us to judge whether the 'isolation' under which we are supposed to suffer, does or does not contain in it any elements of peril. It would hardly be wise to incur novel and most onerous obligations, in order to guard against a danger in whose existence we have no historical reason for believing ...

(Memorandum written as Prime Minister for the Foreign Secretary, Lansdowne, opposing a German proposal that Britain should join the Triple Alliance, 29 May 1901)

William SANCROFT (1617–93): Dean of St Paul's, later Archbishop of Canterbury

1669 What you whispered in my Ear at your last coming hither is now come to pass. Our work at the West-end of St Paul's is fallen about our Ears ... Therefore ... we most earnestly desire your Presence and Assistance with all possible speed.

(Letter to Christopher Wren, after unsuccessful attempts to repair Old St Paul's following the Fire of London, 25 April 1668)

John Montagu, Earl of SAND-WICH (1718–92): English Whig politician

1670 I'll be at your Board, when at leisure from cricket.

(Message to the First Lord of the Admiralty after his appointment as a Lord Commissioner of the Admiralty, June 1745)

George   SANTAYANA (1863–1952): American philosopher and novelist

1671 Those who cannot remember the past are condemned to repeat it.

(*The Life of Reason*, Vol. 1 (1905))

Friedrich   von   SCHILLER (1759–1805): German poet and historian

1672 The history of the World is the World's court of justice [*Die Weltgeschichte ist das Weltgericht*].

(Inaugural Lecture as History Professor at Jena, 26 May 1789)

Sir John SEELEY (1834–95): British historian

1673 We [the English] seem, as it were, to have conquered and peopled half the world in a fit of absence of mind.

(*The Expansion of England*, 1883)

1674 If there is pauperism in

Wiltshire and Dorsetshire, this is but complementary to unowned wealth in Australia. On the one side there are men without property; on the other there is property waiting for men.

(Ibid.)

1675 History is past politics, and politics present history.

(*Growth of British Policy*, 1895)

John   SELDEN   (1584–1654): English antiquarian and jurist

1676 Ignorance of the law excuses no man: not that all men know the law, but because 'tis an excuse every man will plead, and no man can tell how to refute him.

(*Table-talk*, 1689, reports of remarks in the last twenty years of his life)

1677 [of Exorcism] Casting out devils is mere juggling: they never cast out any but what they first cast in.

(Ibid.)

1678 Old friends are best. King James used to call for his old shoes, for they were best for his feet.

(Ibid.)

1679 They that govern most make least noise.

(Ibid.)

W. Nassau SENIOR (1790–1864): English Professor of Political Economy

1680 This barbarous feeling of nationality . . . has become the curse of Europe.

(Diary, 20 May 1850, *Journals in France and Italy*, Vol. 1)

William Henry SEWARD (1801–72): US Senator

1681 There is a higher law than the Constitution.

(Speech attacking Fugitive Slave Law, Senate, 11 March 1850)

1682 Shall I tell you what this collision means? They who think it is accidental, unnecessary, the work of interested or fanatical agitators, and therefore ephemeral, mistake the case altogether. It is an irrepressible conflict between opposing and enduring forces, and it means that the United States must and will, sooner or later, become either entirely a slave-holding nation, or entirely a free-labour nation.

(Speech, Rochester, NY, 25 October 1858)

G. Bernard SHAW (1856–1950): dramatist and socialist

1683 Democracy substitutes election by the incompetent many for appointment by the corrupt few.

(*Maxims for Revolutionists*, ?1903)

1684 Those who minister to poverty and disease are accomplices in the two worst of all crimes.

(Ibid.)

1685 Liberty means responsibility. That is why most men dread it.

(Ibid.)

1686 Assassination is the extreme form of censorship.

(*The Rejected Statement*, 1916)

1687 Idiots are always in favor of inequality of income (their only chance of eminence), and the really great in favor of equality.

(*The Intelligent Woman's Guide to Socialism and Capitalism*, 1928)

George SHELL (1821–39): Welsh Chartist

1688 I shall this night be engaged in a glorious struggle for freedom, and should it please God to spare my life I shall see you soon; but if not, grieve not for me, I shall have fallen in a noble cause.

(Letter to his parents a few hours before being killed in the Newport Rising, 3 November 1839)

Percy BYSSHE SHELLEY (1792–1822): English poet

1689 I met Murder in the way – He had a mask like Castlereagh.

(*The Mask of Anarchy*, 1819)

1690 [of George III] An old, mad, blind, despised and dying King.

(Sonnet: *England in 1819*)

Philip SHERIDAN (1831–88): American General

1691 If I owned Texas and Hell, I would rent out Texas and live in Hell.

(*Alleged remark as a junior officer, Fort Clark, Texas, 1855)

1692 The only good Indian I ever saw is a dead Indian.

(On learning that a 'good Indian' Chief was to be presented to him; Fort Cobb, January 1869)

William Tecumseh SHERMAN (1820–91): American General

1693 There is many a boy here to-day who looks on war as all glory, but, boys, it is all hell. You can bear this warning voice to generations yet to come. I look upon war with horror.

(Speech, Columbus, Ohio, 11 August 1880)

Sir Philip SIDNEY (1554–86): English poet and soldier

1694 Certain it is that in our plainest homeliness, yet never was the Albion nation without poetry ... Poetry is the companion of camps.

(*Apologie for Poetry*, 1580)

1695 Thy necessity is yet greater than mine.

(On giving his water-bottle to a dying soldier at the Battle of Zutphen, 22 September 1586)

(Abbé) Emmanuel Joseph SIEYÈS (1748–1836): French Revolutionary

1696 Who will dare deny that the Third Estate contains within itself all that is needed to constitute a nation? ... What would the Third Estate be without the privileged classes? It would be a whole in itself, and a prosperous one. Nothing can be done without it, and everything would be done far better without the others.

(Pamphlet, *Qu'est-ce que le Tiers État?*, circulated in Paris in January 1789)

1697 I survived [*J'ai vécu*].

(On being asked, in old age, what he had done during the Terror epoch of the French Revolution)

Aeneas SILVIUS (1405–64): Bishop of Trieste, later Pope Pius II

1698 Of the two lights of Christendom, one has been extinguished.

(On learning of the fall of Constantinople, 1453)

1699 We look upon Pope and Emperor only as names in a story or as heads in a picture. Every city has its own sovereign; there are as many princes as there are houses; how then will you persuade this multitude of rulers to take up arms?

(At the Congress of Regensburg, convened to consider a crusade to recapture Constantinople from the Turks, 1454)

Sir John SIMON (1873–1954): British Foreign Secretary and Chancellor of the Exchequer

1700 If Joan of Arc had been born in Austria and worn a moustache, she might have conveyed much the same impression.

(Letter to George V, after meeting Hitler for the first time, 27 March 1935, quoted by K. Rose, *King George V*)

1701 To tax and to please is no more given to man than to love and be wise.

(Speech introducing his budget, H of C, 25 April 1938)

George Castrioti SKANDER-BEG (1405–68): Albanian patriotic hero

1702 Come what may, I am the friend of virtue and not of fortune.

(Letter to Ferdinand of Naples, 1460)

Samuel SMILES (1812–1904): English Liberal reformer

1703 The healthy spirit of self-help created amongst working people would more than any other measure serve to raise them as a class, and this, not by pulling down others, but by levelling them up to a higher and still advancing standard of religion, intelligence and virtue.

(*Self-help*, 1859)

Adam SMITH (1723–90): Scottish economist

1704 To found a great empire for the sole purpose of raising up a people of customers, may at first sight appear a project fit only for a nation of shopkeepers. It is, however, a project altogether unfit for a nation of shopkeepers; but extremely fit for a nation that is governed by shopkeepers.

(*Wealth of Nations*, Bk IV, 1775)

1705 It is only under the shelter of the civil magistrates that the owner of that valuable property, acquired by the labour of many years, or perhaps many successive generations, can sleep a single night in security.

(Ibid., Bk V)

John SMITH (1580–1631): adventurer, writer

1706 As Geography without History seemeth a carcase without motion; so History without Geography, wandereth as a vagrant without a certain habitation.

(*General History of Virginia*, Bk 5, 1624)

1707 History is the memory of time, the life of the dead, and the happiness of the living.

(*Advertisements for the unexperienced Planters of New England, or anywhere*, 1631)

1708 Why should the brave Spanish soldiers brag: The sun never sets in the Spanish dominion, but ever shineth on one part or other we have conquered for our King.

(Ibid.)

Sydney SMITH (1771–1845): English writer, Canon of St Paul's Cathedral

1709 The moment the very name of Ireland is mentioned, the English seem to bid adieu to common feeling, common pru-

dence and common sense, and to act with the barbarity of tyrants, and the fatuity of idiots.

(*Peter Plymley Letters*, 1807)

1710 [of O'Connell] The only way to deal with such a man as O'Connell is to hang him up and erect a statue to him under the gallows.

(*Table-talk*, no date)

1711 [of Macaulay] He has occasional flashes of silence, that make his conversation perfectly delightful.

(Ibid.)

1712 [of Daniel Webster] Daniel Webster struck me much like a steam-engine in trousers.

(Ibid.)

Jan Christiaan SMUTS (1870–1950): Field Marshal and Prime Minister of South Africa

1713 Perhaps it is God's will to lead the people of South Africa through defeat and humiliation to a better future and a brighter day.

(Speech to Boer delegates at Vereeniging peace talks, 31 May 1902)

1714 Europe is being liquidated and the League of Nations must be the heir to this great estate. The peoples left behind by the decomposition of Russia, Austria and Turkey are mostly untrained politically; many of them are either incapable of or deficient in power of self-government; they are mostly destitute and will require much nursing towards economic and political independence.

(*The League of Nations: a Practical Suggestion*, 16 December 1918)

1715 What was everybody's business in the end proved to be nobody's business. Each one looked to the other to take the lead, and the aggressors got away with it.

(Speech, explaining failure of League of Nations, to Empire Parliamentary Association, London, 25 November 1943)

Edward Seymour, Duke of SOMERSET (1506–52): Protector of the Kingdom
[see also 590]

1716 This is to make an end of all wars, to conclude an eternal and perpetual peace.

(Open letter to the people of Scotland justifying the English invasion of their country, January 1548)

John Babsone Lane SOULE (1815–91): American journalist

1717 Go West, young man, go West.

(Editorial, *Terre Haute Express*, Indiana, 1851)

Robert SOUTHEY (1774–1843): English poet and writer

1718 The death of Nelson was felt in England as something more than a public calamity; men started at the intelligence and turned pale, as if they had heard of the loss of a dear friend.

(*The Life of Nelson*, 1813)

Herbert SPENCER (1820–1903): British pioneer sociologist

1719 No one can be perfectly free till all are free; no one can be perfectly moral till all are moral; no one can be perfectly happy till all are happy.

(*Social Statics*, Pt IV, 1851)

1720 This survival of the fittest, which I have here sought to express in mechanical terms, is that which Mr Darwin has called 'natural selection, or the preservation of favoured races in the struggle for life'.

(*The Principles of Biology*, III, 1867)

1721 The liberty the citizen enjoys is to be measured not by the governmental machinery he lives under, whether representative or other, but by the paucity of restraints it imposes on him.

(*Man versus the State*, written 1883–4)

1722 The Republican form of Government is the highest form of government; but because of this it requires the highest type of human nature – a type nowhere at present existing.

(Essay on *The Americas*, 1891)

Joseph   Vissarionivitch STALIN (1897–1953): Soviet Marshal and dictator
[see also 1331]

1723 In departing from us, Comrade Lenin ordained that we should hold high and keep pure the dignity of party members: we vow to thee, Comrade Lenin, that we shall with honour fulfil this thy commandment. In leaving us, Comrade Lenin ordained that we should guard the unity of our Party as the apple of our eye: we vow to thee, Comrade Lenin, that we shall with honour fulfil this thy commandment ... We vow to thee, Comrade Lenin, that we shall not spare our lives in seeking to strengthen and broaden the alliance of the workers of the whole world.

(Funeral oration for Lenin, Moscow, 26 January 1924)

1724 Socialism in one country ...

(Basic thesis of *Problems of Leninism*, published in the autumn of 1924 to counter Trotsky's theory of permanent revolution)

1725 Dizziness with Success.

(Title of article in *Pravda*, 2 March 1930, urging 'comrades' not to collectivize the countryside recklessly)

1726 [of Cromwell] In the name of the constitution, he took up arms, executed the king, dissolved Parliament, imprisoned some and beheaded others.

(In conversation with H. G. Wells, Moscow, 1934)

1727 The Pope! How many divisions has *he* got?

(To Laval, 13 May 1935, after the French Foreign Minister had asked that Russia should do something to encourage the Catholics in order to please the Pope: see Churchill, *Second World War*, I, p. 105)

1728 To attempt to export revolution is nonsense.

(To Roy Howard, American newspaper magnate, 1 March 1936)

1729 Let manly images of our great ancestors – Alexander Nevsky, Dimitry Donskoi, Kusma Minin, Dimitry Pozharsky, Alexander Suvorov, Mikhail Kutuzov – inspire you in this war. May the victorious banner of the great Lenin uphold you.

(Speech to the Red Army, Moscow, 7 November 1941)

1730 Communism fits Germany as a saddle fits a cow.

(In conversation with the Polish leader, Mikolajczyk, August 1944)

1731 I will shake my little finger – and there will be no more Tito. He will fall.

(In conversation with Khrushchev, spring 1948, according to Khrushchev, 20 February 1956)

Sir Henry Morton STANLEY (1841–1904): Central African explorer

1732 Dr Livingstone, I presume?

(On finding David Livingstone, of whom no news had been heard for five years, at Ujiji on Lake Tanganyika, October 1871: *How I found Livingstone*, 1872)

Charles E. STANTON (1859–1933): American Colonel

1733 Lafayette, we are here.

(With members of US Expeditionary Force at Lafayette's tomb, Paris, 4 July 1917)

Edwin McMasters STANTON (1814–69): US Secretary of War

1734 Now he belongs to the ages.

(*Alleged remark on hearing of Abraham Lincoln's death, 15 April 1865)

Adlai E. STEVENSON (1900–65): American Democratic politician and Governor of Illinois

1735 There is no evil in the atom – only in men's souls.

(Speech, Hartford, Connecticut, 18 September 1952)

1736 We can chart our future clearly and wisely only when we know the path which has led to the present.

(Speech, Richmond, Virginia, 20 September 1952)

1737 When political ammunition runs low, inevitably the rusty artillery of abuse is always wheeled into action.

(Speech, New York, 22 September 1952 [Stevenson, the Democratic candidate in the Presidential Election, was being derided as a 'leftist egghead' by the Republican Press])

Robert Louis STEVENSON (1850–94): Scottish author

1738 Politics is perhaps the only profession for which no preparation is thought necessary.

(*Familiar Studies of Men and Books*, 1882)

John STRACHEY (1901–63): British Labour politician

1739 [of Ramsay Macdonald] Mr Macdonald has become ... that type of actor which the cruel French call a '*M'as tu vu?*' 'Have you seen me as the Prime Minister? My greatest role I assure you', Mr Macdonald is anxiously asking the nation. Yes, we have seen him.

(*The Coming Struggle for Power*, Pt V, 1932)

Thomas Wentworth, Earl of STRAFFORD (1593–1641): English statesman, chief minister to King Charles I

1740 Divide not between Protestant and Papist ... divide not nationally, betwixt English and Irish. The King makes no distinction betwixt you.

(To Irish Parliament, as Lord Deputy of Ireland, 15 July 1634)

1741 Nevertheless I do conceive we might raise here some three or four thousand Men, whereof as many as may be to be English. For howbeit the Irish might do very good Service, being a People

removed from the Scottish, as well in Affections as Religion; yet it is not safe to train them up more than needs must in the military Way.

(To King Charles I, from Ireland, 28 July 1638)

1742 You have an army in Ireland you may employ here to reduce this kingdom.

(At Council meeting, according to Sir Harry Vane's notes, 5 May 1640)

1743 If words spoken to friends, in familiar discourse, spoken in one's chamber, spoken at one's table, spoken in one's sick-bed ... if these things shall be brought against a man as treason ... it will be a silent world ... and no man shall dare to impart his solitary thoughts or opinions to his friend and neighbour.

(At his trial, 5 April 1641)

1744 [I] wish that every man would lay his hand on his heart, and consider seriously whether the beginnings of the people's happiness should be written in letters of blood.

(At his execution, 12 May 1641)

Stratford Canning, Lord STRATFORD DE REDCLIFFE (1786–1880): British diplomat

1745 I wish ... as a matter of humanity ... that the Greeks were put in possession of their whole patrimony and that the Sultan were driven, bag and baggage, into the heart of Asia.

(Letter to George Canning, 29 September 1821)

Philip STUBBES (*flor.* 1580s–91): English Puritan pamphleteer

1746 Footeball ... causeth fighting, brawling, contention, quarrel picking, murder, homicide and great effusion of bloode, as daily experience teacheth.

(*Anatomie of Abuses*, 1583)

1747 [of going to plays on Sundays] Where is the master that hath had a conscience to restrain his servants ... or the servant that hath ... accepted ... restraint being made unto him, and which hath not rather burst out into ungodly and disobedient speeches, murmuring that because he hath wrought all the week, therefore he should have liberty to do what he list on the Sabbath?

(Ibid.)

Charles Brandon, Duke of SUFFOLK (?1484–1545): brother-in-law to Henry VIII

1748 It was never merry in England whilst we had Cardinals among us.

(On Cardinal Campeggio's reference back to Rome of Henry's plea to annul his marriage, July 1528)

SUGER, Abbot of St Denis (1081–1152): French monk and diplomat

1749 Since it is neither right nor natural for Frenchmen to be subject to Englishmen, but rather for Englishmen to be subject to Frenchmen, the outcome of the event mocked his vile expectation.

(Of William II's campaigns against France, 1097/8, *Life of Louis VI*)

Maximilien de Bethune, Duc de SULLY (1559–1641): French statesman, chief minister to King Henry IV

1750 The English amuse themselves sadly according to the custom of their country.

(*Mémoires, c.* 1630; possibly refers originally to his visit to England in June 1603)

SUN Yat-sen (1867–1925): Chinese revolutionary leader

1751 The foundation of the government of a nation must be built upon the rights of the people, but the administration must be entrusted to experts. We must not look upon these experts as stately and grand presidents and ministers, but simply as our chauffeurs, as guards at the gate, as cooks, physicians, carpenters or tailors.

(*The Three Principles of the People*, definitive version of 1924)

Eduard, Count von TAAFFE (1833–95): Austrian Prime Minister

1752 As a minister it is my policy to keep all the nationalities within the [Habsburg] Monarchy in a balanced state of well-modulated dis-satisfaction.

(Informal comment explaining the nationalities policy of his Government, 1879–93; probable date, 1881)

Charles-Maurice de TALLEYRAND (1754–1838): French statesman and diplomat [see also 356, 704, 1120, 1238, 1932]

1753 Nobody who did not live in the years around 1780 can have known the pleasure of living.

(Remark to Guizot and quoted by him in his *Mémoires*)

1754 They have learnt nothing and forgotten nothing.

(*Alleged comment on the attitude of the exiled émigrés in 1796)

1755 Too frightened to fight each other: too stupid to agree.

(Comment on the attitude of the Allies at the Congress of Vienna in November 1814)

1756 Now, Sire, the coalition is dissolved and forever. France is no longer isolated in Europe ... So great and fortunate a change may only be attributed to that Protection of Providence, so plainly visible in the restoration of Your Majesty.

(Letter to Louis XVIII informing him of a secret treaty concluded at Vienna between Austria, France and Britain, 3 January 1815)

1757 One must do M. Fouché the justice to recognize that he has left out none of his friends.

(Comment on perusing the list submitted by Fouché to Louis XVIII of public figures who had compromised themselves by supporting Napoleon on his return during the Hundred Days, 1815)

1758 Above all, do not become too excited over your work [*Et surtout pas trop de zèle*].

(*Alleged advice to a young diplomat, *c.* 1820)

1759 It is no longer an event, it is only an item of news.

(Comment on learning of the death of Napoleon, 1821)

1760 I am perhaps the only man of distinguished birth . . . who has not for a single week of his life known the joy of staying under his parental roof.

(*Mémoires*, Vol. 1, written *c.* 1821)

1761 Sire, Your Majesty forgets the post-chaise.

(Reply to Charles X, who had remarked 'Once a King is threatened there is no choice for him but the throne or the scaffold', December 1829)

Richard TARLTON (?–1588): comic actor, jester

1762 See, the Knave commands the Queen.

(Reported remark [on Sir Walter Raleigh] that lost him Elizabeth I's favour)

R. H. TAWNEY (1880–1962): English economic historian, socialist theorist

1763 The instinct of mankind warns it against accepting at their face value spiritual demands which cannot justify themselves by practical achievements. And the road along which the organized workers, like any other class, must climb to power, starts from the provision of a more effective economic service than their masters, as their grip upon industry becomes increasingly vacillating and uncertain, are able to supply.

(*The Acquisitive Society*, 1921)

1764 As long as men are men, a poor society cannot be too poor to find a right order of life, nor a rich society too rich to have need to seek it.

(Ibid.)

A. J. P. TAYLOR (b. 1906): English historian

1765 Human blunders usually do more to shape history than human wickedness.

(*The Origins of the Second World War*, Ch. 10, 1961)

1766 [Of Napoleon III] Like most of those who study history, he learned from the mistakes of the past how to make new ones.

(Broadcast, 6 June 1963)

Norman TEBBIT (b. 1931): English Conservative politician

1767 I grew up in the 1930s with unemployment. My father did not riot: he got on his bike and looked for work.

(First major speech as Employment Secretary, Party Conference, Blackpool, 15 October 1981)

Wilhelm von TEGETTHOFF (1827–71): Austrian Admiral

1768 Armoured vessels will charge the enemy and sink him.

(Signal before engaging Italian fleet at Battle of Lissa, 20 July 1866)

Alfred, Lord TENNYSON (1809–92): English Poet Laureate

1769 Bury the Great Duke
    With an empire's lamentation . . .
    The last great Englishman is low . . .
    For this is England's greatest son,
    He that gained a hundred fights
    Nor ever lost an English gun . . .
    Not once or twice in our rough island-story
    The path of duty was the way to glory . . .

(*Ode on Death of the Duke of Wellington*, 1852)

1770 [for the wedding of Princess Alexandra to the Prince of Wales, later Edward VII]
    Sea-King's daughter from over the sea, Alexandra!

Saxon and Norman and Dane are we,
But all of us Danes in welcome of thee, Alexandra!

(*A Welcome to Alexandra*, March 1863)

Margaret Hilda THATCHER (b. 1925): British Conservative Prime Minister
[see also 1565]

1771 We want a society where people are free to make choice, to make mistakes, to be generous and compassionate. This is what we mean by a moral society – not a society where the state is responsible for everything and no one is responsible for the state.

(Speech, Zurich University, 14 March 1977)

1772 Where there is discord, may we bring harmony. Where there is error, may we bring truth. Where there is doubt, may we bring faith. Where there is despair, may we bring hope.

(Misquotation of St Francis of Assisi, made on entering 10 Downing Street for the first time as Prime Minister, 4 May 1979)

1773 We shall not be diverted from our course. To those waiting with bated breath for that favourite media catch-phrase, the U-turn, I have only this to say:

'You turn if you want; the lady's not for turning'.

(Address, Party Conference, Brighton, 10 October 1980)

1774 There is no alternative.

(Phrase used on several occasions, 1979–80)

William Makepiece THAYER (?1820–98): American writer

1775 From Log Cabin to White House.

(Title of biography of the twentieth President of the USA, James Garfield, 1831–81)

Adolphe THIERS (1797–1877): first President of the Third French Republic [see also 1206]

1776 The Republic will be conservative, or it will not exist [*La République sera conservatrice ou elle ne sera pas*].

(Presidential message to the French National Assembly, November 1872)

1777 There is only one throne, and three people cannot sit on it.

(Final speech as President, 24 May 1873)

Roy THOMSON, Lord Thomson of Fleet (1894–1976): Canadian-born English newspaper proprietor

1778 A licence to print money.

(Retrospective comment on the financial rewards coming from the authority, which the government gave him, to establish commercial television in Scotland, 1955)

THE TIMES: English newspaper

1779 [reporting a French government's plan to build thirty-four new warships] Good news this for old England! It saves us the trouble and expense of building them ourselves, for they are sure to find their way into our ports.

(26 November 1798)

1780 On Monday morning a duel took place between General Thornton and Mr Theodore Hook. After exchanging one shot each, the affair was amicably settled. It originated in a silly dispute on the subject of the dance called the *Waltz*, the General having praised it in high terms, and the Author having bitterly reprobated it as leading to the most licentious consequences.

(Wednesday, 22 July 1812)

1781 In speaking of the successes of the Russians, we are obliged to abate the excess of our joy, not from doubt of their magnitude or reality, for upon these our countrymen may rely; but from mere apprehension lest the vicissitude of human affairs, which does not usually suffer mankind to exult beyond measure upon any occasion whatever, should, by we know not what unexpected reverse, abate somewhat of the transcendent felicity which is promised the World by the overthrow and disgrace of its most detested and detestable tyrant.

(17 December 1812)

1782 It is a great evil of the present day, that such is the poverty of the more humble classes of the community – such being also the state of the Press with reference to taxation – that if they do read, or know anything of public affairs, it must be in the cheapest forms; and hence they become the dupes, to a certain extent, of the basest and most profligate of men.

(3 January 1817)

1783 Perhaps Lord Palmerston, if the subject is not too coarse or too trivial to occupy the polite attention of so fine a gentleman, will order some inquiry to be made respecting certain irregularities in the transmission of mercantile correspondence from Lisbon ... A hint may be necessary, if not in the case of the Lisbon ambassador, yet to some others of our noble functionaries,

whose minds being dedicated to sublimer affairs, have forgot or never learned that Great Britain is actually a commercial kingdom and does really derive some of its wealth and importance from trade and manufactures.

(Leading article criticizing the allegedly high-handed attitude of the foreign service under Palmerston, 7 May 1832)

1784 Nothing has yet happened to mitigate those apprehensions, which within the last fortnight we have from day to day expressed, of evil likely to befall the new reign if the probable causes of it should not be well examined and prepared against it. The very depth and fulness of his loyal attachment to his QUEEN ought to make a virtuous Englishman so much the more solicitous to protect her from perils of which it is scarcely in the nature of things that she should of herself be conscious.

(On accession of Queen Victoria, 21 June 1837)

1785 There was yesterday witnessed a sight the like of which has never happened before, and which in the nature of things can never be repeated. They who were so fortunate as to see it, hardly knew what most to admire, or in what form to clothe the sense of wonder, and even of mystery, which struggled within them.

(On opening of the Great Exhibition, 2 May 1851)

1786 The Duke of Wellington had exhausted nature and exhausted glory. His career was one unclouded longest day.

(On the death of Wellington, 16 September 1852)

1787 The nation has just sustained the greatest loss that could possibly have fallen upon it. Prince Albert . . . the very centre of our social system, the pillar of our State, is suddenly snatched from us, without even warning sufficient to prepare us for a blow so abrupt and so terrible.

(On the death of the Prince Consort, 16 December 1861)

1788 To employ women and children unduly is simply to run into debt with Nature.

(4 March 1867)

1789 [of Zola's open letter concerning Dreyfus (cf. 2001)] The accuser Zola is a man who has gained for himself a very prominent place in French literature as a writer of fiction of a peculiar kind, but has not hitherto shown, so far as we are aware, any very special care for public justice or any special interest in the fate of the oppressed.

(14 January 1898)

1790 The French . . . are not the sort of people who consume their own smoke. When not on good terms with themselves, they are apt to be troublesome to other nations.

(16 November 1898: a comment on the dangerous international repercussions of the Dreyfus agitation)

1791 We shall not pretend that there is nothing in his long career which those who respect and admire him would wish otherwise.

(On the accession of Edward VII, 23 January 1901)

1792 We are all Home Rulers today.

(26 March 1919)

1793 The Constitution is to be amended in order that she [Mrs Simpson] may carry in solitary prominence the brand of unfitness for the Queen's Throne.

(8 December 1936: an attack upon the suggestion that Edward VIII should contract a morganatic marriage with Mrs Simpson)

1794 *Omnium consensu capax Imperii nisi imperasset* – the well-worn quotation from Tacitus is irresistible. It can hardly have been a better verdict upon the

Emperor Galba than it is upon King Edward that all men would have judged him worthy of the Throne if he had never ascended it.

(Leading article on the abdication of Edward VIII, 11 December 1936)

1795 It might be worthwhile for the Czechoslovak Government to consider whether they should exclude altogether the project, which has found favour in some quarters, of making Czechoslovakia a more homogeneous state by the cession of that fringe of alien populations who are so contiguous to the nation to which they are united by race.

(7 September 1938)

1796 No conqueror returning from a victory on the battlefield has come home adorned with nobler laurels than Mr Chamberlain from Munich yesterday.

(1 October 1938)

1797 [of the Conservative Party Election manifesto, 1955] Thirty-two pages, price 6d, liberally peppered with platitudes, high-sounding phrases, and cautious qualifications, it provides a maximum of rhetoric and a minimum of a programme.

(30 April 1955)

1798 The modern world has suffered many acts, like Hitler's march into the Rhineland or the Stalinist overthrow of freedom in Czechoslovakia, which were claimed to be assertions of domestic sovereignty. They were, in fact, hinges of history. Nasser's seizure of the Suez Canal Company is another such turning point. Quibbling over whether or not he was 'legally entitled' to make the grab will delight the finicky and comfort the faint-hearted, but entirely misses the real issues ... There can be no stability and confidence in the world so long as agreements can be scrapped with impunity.

(1 August 1956)

1799 We may be a good people grown careless; we are not a bad people grown hardened.

(Leading article on British reactions to Egypt's nationalization of the Suez Canal, 27 August 1956)

1800 Nations live by the vigorous defence of their interests ... Doubtless it is good to have a flourishing tourist trade, to win Test matches and to be regaled by photographs of Miss Diana Dors being pushed into a swimming pool. But nations do not live by circuses alone. The people, in their silent way, know this better than the critics. They still want Britain great.

(Ibid.)

1801 Eleven years of Conservative rule have brought the nation psychologically and spiritually to a low ebb.

(After the Profumo Affair, 11 June 1963)

TIMUR (Tamburlaine) (1335?–1405): Tartar Emir

1802 The whole area of the inhabitable world is not worth having two monarchs.

(*Attributed saying)

1803 It is better to be at the right place with ten men than absent with ten thousand.

(*Attributed saying)

Alfred von TIRPITZ (1849–1930): German Admiral

1804 To me the Navy never seemed an end in itself, but rather a function of our maritime interests. Without sea-power the position of Germany in the World was that of a mollusc without a shell.

(*Erinnerungen*, 1919)

Joseph Broz TITO (1892–1980): Marshal and President of Yugoslavia
[see also 1731]

1805 'Our teaching is no dogma, but leadership for action' . . . thus Lenin spoke and taught And now

they want us to confine ourselves to a few narrow formulae in building Socialism.

(Speech, 5th Party Congress at Topčider, Belgrade, 21 July 1948)

Silius TITUS (1623–1703): English soldier and politician

1806 To trust expedients with such a [Roman Catholic] king on the throne would be just as wise as if there were a lion in the lobby, and we should vote to let him in and chain him, instead of fastening the door to keep him out.

(Speech, H of C, 7 January 1680, opposing a compromise over the Exclusion Bill)

Alexis de TOCQUEVILLE (1805–59): French political observer and historian

1807 I sought the image of democracy, in order to learn what we have to fear and to hope from its progress.

(Of his travels in USA during the 1820s, *Democracy in America*, 1835)

Arnold TOYNBEE (1852–83): pioneer English economic historian and social reformer

1808 The Industrial Revolution.

(Phrase first used as a title of lectures delivered at Oxford 1880–1 and published posthumously, 1884)

Heinrich von TREITSCHKE (1834–96): German historian and politician

1809 It was the railways which first dragged the [German] nation from economic stagnation ... With such force did they break in upon all the old habits of life that already in the eighteen-forties the outward appearance of Germany was completely changed.

(*Deutsche Geschichte*, IV, 1889)

1810 The English think Soap is Civilization.

(*Alleged comment in a Berlin lecture, no date, but between 1875 and 1895)

George Macaulay TREVEL-YAN (1876–1962): British historian

1811 The poetry of history lies in the quasi-miraculous fact that once, on this familiar spot of ground, walked other men and women, as actual as we are today, thinking their own thoughts, swayed by their own passion, but now all gone, one generation vanishing after another, gone as utterly as we ourselves shall shortly be gone like ghosts at cock-crow.

(*Clio*, 1904, revised 1913)

1812 [The historian] will give the best interpretation who, having discovered and weighed all the important evidence available, has the largest grasp of intellect, the warmest human sympathy, the highest imaginative powers.

(Ibid.)

1813 Disinterested intellectual curiosity is the life blood of real civilisation.

(Preface to *English Social History*, 1942)

1814 Truth is the criterion of historical study; but its impelling motive is poetic.

(Ibid.)

1815 If the French noblesse had been capable of playing cricket with their peasants, their chateaux would never have been burnt.

(Ibid. Ch. XIII)

1816 Education ... has produced a vast population able to read but unable to distinguish what is worth reading.

(Ibid., Ch. XVIII)

1817 It is still too early to form a final judgement on the French Revolution.

(Address, National Book League, London, 30 May 1945)

Lev TROTSKY (1879–1940): Russian communist and revolutionary theorist
[see also 372]

1818 In a country economically backward, the proletariat can take power earlier than in countries where capitalism is advanced.

(*Permanent Revolution*, written 1928, based on pamphlet written 1906)

1819 Marxism is above all a method of analysis.

(Ibid.)

1820 A liberal senator was looking at the motionless trams ... some with broken windows, some tipped over on the tracks, and was recalling the July days of 1914 on the eve of war: 'It seemed that the old attempt was being renewed.' The senator's eyes did not deceive him; the continuity is clear. History was picking up the ends of the revolutionary threads broken by the war, and tying them in a knot.

(Events in Petrograd 24/5 February 1917 (O.S.); *History of the Russian Revolution*, written 1929–30)

1821 Can it be that a mere tram-car, run-down, dirty, dilatory,

draped with clusters of people, leads from St Petersburg in its death-agony into the workers' quarters so passionately and tensely alive with a new hope? The blue-and-gold cupola of Smolny Convent announces from afar the headquarters of the insurrection. It is at the edge of the city, where the tram-line ends.

('The Conquest of the Capital', October/November 1917; ibid.)

1822 Revolutions are always verbose.

(Ibid.)

Harry S. TRUMAN (1884–1972): thirty-third President of the USA

1823 Every segment of our population, and every individual, has a right to expect from his government a Fair Deal.

(Speech to Congress, 6 September 1945)

1824 The buck stops here.

(Notice on his Presidential desk)

1825 A politician is a man who understands government, and it takes a politician to run a government. A statesman is a politician who's been dead ten or fifteen years.

(Interview reported in *New York World Telegram*, 12 April 1958)

1826 [of Eisenhower] He's a good man. The only trouble was, he had a lot of damn fool Republicans around him.

(Comment, December 1963)

Barbara TUCHMAN (b. 1912): American historian

1827 No more distressing moment can ever face a British government than that which requires it to come to a hard and fast and specific decision.

(*August 1914*, Ch. 9: 1962)

Owen TUDOR (*c.* 1399–1461): husband of Henry V's widow, Catherine

1828 That head shall lie on the stock which was wont to lie on Queen Catherine's lap.

(Before his execution at Hereford, February 1461)

Anne-Robert-Jacques TURGOT (1727–81): French statesman, Finance Minister under King Louis XVI

1829 This people [the American] is the hope of the human race. It may become the model.

(Letter to Dr Richard Price, 1778)

UNITED NATIONS CHARTER: Preamble (drafted in part by Field-Marshal Smuts and by John Foster Dulles, among others)

1830 We the Peoples of the United Nations, determined to save succeeding generations from the scourge of war, which twice in our lifetime has brought untold sorrow to mankind, and to reaffirm faith in fundamental human rights, in the dignity and worth of the human person, in the equal rights of men and women and of nations large and small, and to establish conditions under which justice and respect for the obligations arising from treaties and other sources of international law can be maintained, and to promote social progress and better standards of life in larger freedom, and for these ends, to practice tolerance and live together in peace with one another as good neighbours, and to unite our strength to maintain international peace and security, and to ensure by the acceptance of principles and the institution of methods, that armed force shall not be used, save in the common interest, and to employ international machinery for the promotion of the economic and social advancement of all peoples, have resolved to combine our efforts to accomplish these aims . . .

(Signed at San Francisco, 26 June 1945)

UNESCO CONSTITUTION:
Preamble

1831 Since wars begin in the minds of men, it is in the minds of men that the defences of peace must be constructed.

(1946)

Count S. S. UVAROV
(1786–1855): adviser to Tsar Nicholas I of Russia on internal affairs

1832 Our general duty consists of this: that the education of the people be conducted in conformity with the supreme intention of our august monarch and in the united spirit of Orthodoxy, Autocracy and Nationality.

(Memorandum on becoming Minister of Education, 2 April 1833)

William H. VANDERBILT
(1821–85): American railway financier and director

1833 The public be damned! I'm working for my stockholders.

(Reply to a newspaper reporter who asked him if the proposed withdrawal of an unprofitable express train was against the public interest: Chicago, 1883)

VENETIAN AMBASSADOR
to England (*flor.* 1500)

1834 [The English] do not believe that there are any other people than themselves, or any other world than England: and whenever they see some handsome foreigner, they say 'he looks like an Englishman' and 'What a pity he is not English'.

(First Relation to the Venetian Senate, ?1502: probably written by the Secretary of Francesco Capello, first Venetian ambassador to England)

Charles Gravier VERGENNES
(1717–87): French Foreign Minister

1835 It is the right of France, placed as she is in the centre of Europe, to exercise an influence in all matters of importance. Her king, like a supreme arbiter, can consider his throne a tribunal instituted by Providence to ensure respect for the rights and possessions of other rulers.

(Memorandum for Louis XVI, 12 April 1777)

Pierre VERGNIAUD (1753–93): French Revolutionary

1836 There has been reason to fear that the Revolution may, like Saturn, devour each of her children one by one.

(Remark attributed to him at his trial by Lamartine, November 1793)

Sir Edmund VERNEY
(1590–1642): English Cavalier
soldier

1837 I have eaten his [i.e. the
king's] bread, and served him
near thirty years, and will not do
so base a thing as to forsake him,
and choose rather to lose my life
(which I am sure I shall do) to
preserve and defend those things
which are against my conscience
to preserve and defend; for I will
deal freely with you, I have no
reverence for the bishops.

(On setting up of King's standard
at Nottingham, August 1642)

VICTORIA (1819–1901):
Queen of England
[see also 461, 726, 1784, 1943]

1838 I will be good.

(To Baroness Lehzen, 11 March
1830, as recalled by Lehzen in a
letter to the Queen, 2 December
1867)

1839 I was awoke at 6 o'clock by
Mamma, who told me that the
Archbishop of Canterbury and
Lord Conyngham were here, and
wished to see me. I got out of bed
and went into my sitting-room
(only in my dressing-gown) and
alone, and saw them. Lord Conyngham (the Lord Chamberlain)
then acquainted me that my poor
Uncle, the King, was no more,
and had expired at 12 minutes

past 2 this morning, and consequently that I am *Queen*.

(Journal entry, Kensington
Palace, 20 June 1837)

1840 Dear Uncle is given to believe that he must rule the roast
everywhere. However, that is not
a necessity.

(Letter to Prince Albert about
King Leopold I of Belgium, 8
December 1839)

1841 You forget, my dearest
Love, that I am the Sovereign and
that business can stop and wait
for nothing.

(Letter to Prince Albert, who had
proposed a honeymoon of more
than two or three days, 21
January 1840)

1842 There I stood, at the arm
of Napoleon III his nephew,
before the coffin of our bitterest
foe, I, the granddaughter of that
King who hated him most and
who most vigorously opposed
him, and this very nephew, who
bears his name, being my nearest
and dearest ally!

(Visit to Napoleon I's tomb, Paris,
Journal, 24 August 1855)

1843 Today dear Papa has gone
to Oxford to see how Bertie [later
Edward VII] is getting on in that
old monkish place which I have a
horror of.

(Letter to her eldest daughter, Princess Victoria of Prussia, 31 October 1859)

1844 This mad, wicked folly of 'Women's Rights' with all its attendant horrors, on which her [the Queen's] poor sex is bent, forgetting every sense of womanly feeling and propriety. Lady Amberley ought to get a *good whipping.*

(Letter to Sir Theodore Martin, 29 March, 1870. Lady Amberley [Bertrand Russell's mother] had recently expressed advanced views)

1845 Oh, if the Queen were a man, she would like to go and give those Russians, whose word one cannot believe, such a beating! We shall never be friends again till we have it out.

(Letter to Lord Beaconsfield, 10 January 1878)

1846 Please understand that there is no one depressed in this house; we are not interested in the possibilities of defeat; they do not exist.

(To A. J. Balfour during the 'Black Week' of the Boer War, December 1899)

1847 [of Gladstone] He speaks to Me as if I was a public meeting.

(*Remark ascribed to her by G. W. E. Russell)

1848 We are not amused.

(*Alleged rebuke, which appears to have been first made in 1889)

Alfred de VIGNY (1797–1863): French novelist and poet

1849 The army is a nation within the nation; it is a vice of our time.

(*Servitude et grandeur militaires*, 1835, Ch. 1)

François Marie Arouet, VOLTAIRE (1694–1778): French philosopher
[see also 306, 675, 982]

1850 The English nation is the only one on earth which has successfully regulated the power of its kings by resisting them; and which, after repeated efforts, has established that beneficial government under which the Prince, all powerful for good, is restrained from doing ill.

(*Lettres philosophiques*, published 1734, probably written 1730)

1851 This body, which called itself and still calls itself the Holy Roman Empire, was neither Holy, nor Roman, nor an Empire.

(*Essai sur les Moeurs*, original text 1756, definitive version 1769)

1852 In this country [England] it is thought well to kill an Admiral from time to time in order to encourage the others.

(*Candide*, written 1757–9: refers to Admiral Byng's execution, 14 March 1757)

1853 [of Claud-Arien Helvetius and his book *De L'Esprit*, which was publicly burnt in 1758] I liked the author ... but I never approved either the errors of his book, or the trivial truths he so vigorously laid down. I have, however, stoutly taken his side when absurd men have condemned him for these same truths.

('Homme': *Dictionnaire Philosophique Portatif*, 1764: this remark is probably the origin of 'I disapprove of what you say, but I will defend to the death your right to say it.' This attributed principle is not found earlier than the twentieth century, and then only in English)

1854 [of the French] Your nation is divided into two species: one is of idle monkeys mocking at everything; the other is of tigers who tear.

(Letter to Madame du Deffand, 21 November 1766)

1855 The Catholic princes have not the courage to declare that the Church must be subject solely to the laws of the sovereign. Only your illustrious sovereign [Catherine II] follows the correct course: she pays the priests; she opens and shuts their mouths;

they are under her orders and everything remains undisturbed.

(Letter to Count Shuvalov, 3 December 1768)

1856 They say that God is always on the side of the big battalions.

(Letter to Le Riche, 6 February 1770)

Augusta of Saxe-Gotha, Princess of WALES (1719–72): mother of King George III

1857 George, be a King.

(*Alleged injunction to her son, attempting to strengthen his character, 1761)

Lech WALESA (b. 1943): Polish Trade Unionist

1858 He who once became aware of the power of Solidarity and who breathed the air of freedom will not be crushed.

(Nobel Peace Prize lecture, read for him, at Oslo, 11 December 1983)

Henry WALLACE (1888–1965): US Vice-President

1859 The century on which we are entering can be and must be the century of the common man.

(Address: 'The Price of Free World Victory', New York, 8 May 1942)

Sir William WALLACE (?1272–1305): Scottish General and patriotic leader

1860 I have brought you to the ring, hop gif ye kun.

(To Scottish infantry at Battle of Falkirk, 22 July 1298)

Edmund WALLER (1606–87): English poet and diplomat

1861 Under the tropic is our
          language spoke,
          And part of Flanders hath
          received our yoke.

(*Upon the Death of the Lord Protector*, 1658)

Horace WALPOLE, fourth Earl of Orford (1717–97): English political spectator and writer

1862 I write . . . to congratulate you on the lustre you have thrown on this country. Sir, do not take this for flattery: there is nothing in your power to give that I would accept; nay there is nothing I could envy, but what I believe you would scarce offer me – your glory.

(Letter to the elder Pitt in the 'year of victories', October 1759)

1863 Everybody talks of the constitution, but all sides forget that the constitution is extremely well, and would do very well, if they would but let it alone.

(Letter to Sir Horace Mann, 18/19 January 1770)

1864 By the waters of Babylon we sit down and weep, when we think of thee, O America!

(Letter to Mason, 12 June 1775)

1865 All the sensible Tories I ever knew were either Jacobites or became Whigs; those that remained Tories remained fools.

(*Memoirs of the Reign of George III*, Vol. 1)

1866 [of C.J. Fox, *c*. 1782–3] His bristly, black person and shagged breast, quite open and rarely purified by any ablutions, was wrapped in a foul night-gown, and his bushy hair dishevelled. In these Cynic weeds and with Epicurean good humour, did he dictate his politics, and in this school did the heir to the throne attend his lessons and imbibe them.

(*Last Journals*, Volume II)

Sir Robert WALPOLE, first Earl of Orford (1676–1745): English Whig Prime Minister

1867 Madam, there are fifty thousand men slain this year in Europe, and not one Englishman.

(To Queen Caroline, 1734)

1868 I took the right sow by the ear.

(Replying to a friend's question of why he cultivated the friendship of Queen Caroline of Anspach rather than George II's mistresses: remark probably made in 1734)

1869 They may ring their bells now; before long they will be wringing their hands.

(Remark on hearing church bells welcoming a declaration of war against Spain, 19 October 1739)

1870 I have lived long enough in the world to know that the safety of a minister lies in his having the approbation of this House. Former ministers, Sir, neglected this and therefore they fell; I have always made it my first study to obtain it, and therefore I hope to stand.

(Speech, H of C, 21 November 1739)

1871 A patriot, Sir! Why patriots spring up like mushrooms! I could raise fifty of them within the four and twenty hours. I have raised many of them in one night. It is but refusing to gratify an unmeasurable or insolent demand, and up starts a patriot.

(Speech, H of C, 13 February 1741)

1872 My Lord Bath, you and I are now two as insignificant men as any in England.

(To Pulteney, on their promotion to H of L as Earl of Bath and Earl of Orford, February 1742)

1873 Oh, do not read history, for that I know must be false.

(*Alleged remark, as he lay ill in bed, to his secretary, ?1744–5)

Thomas of WALSINGHAM (?–1419): monastic chronicler at St Albans Abbey

1874 In this year King Edward of England made Lord Edward, his son and heir, Prince of Wales and Count of Chester. When the Welsh heard this, they were overjoyed, thinking him their lawful master, as he was born in their lands.

(*Historia Anglicana* for 1300–1. Edward, later King Edward II, was born at Caernarfon in 1284 and created Prince of Wales in February 1301)

George   WASHINGTON (1732–99): General and first President of the USA [see also 1063]

1875 [on being accused as a child of cherry tree vandalism] Father I cannot tell a lie. I did it with my little hatchet.

(*A tale apparently invented by his earliest popular biographer, Mason Weems, in 1800)

1876 You will therefore send me none but natives.

(Orders for recruiting of his bodyguard, after an attempt had been made to poison him, 30 April 1777)

1877 Put none but Americans on guard tonight.

(*Apparently a legendary version of the preceding entry, 30 April 1777)

1878 I can answer but for three things, a firm belief in the justice of our Cause, close attention in the prosecution of it, and the strictest integrity.

(After being elected to command army, 19 June 1775)

1879 It is our true policy to steer clear of permanent alliance with any portion of the foreign world.

(Farewell address to People of United States, 17 September 1796)

William WATSON (?1559–1603): English jurist

1880 You go against that general maxim in the laws which is '*Fiat justitia et ruant coeli*' ['Let justice be done even though the skies fall'].

('Seventh Question' in *Ten Quodlibettical Questions concerning Religion and State*, 1601)

Beatrice WEBB (1858–1943): English socialist

1881 It was a strange London on Sunday ... We sauntered through the crowd to Trafalgar Square where Labour, socialist, pacifist demonstrators – with a few trade union flags – were gesticulating from the steps of the monuments to a mixed crowd of admirers, hooligan warmongers and merely curious holidaymakers. It was an undignified and futile exhibition, this singing of the Red Flag and passing of well-worn radical resolutions in favour of universal peace.

(*Diary*, Tuesday, 4 August 1914)

Sidney WEBB (1859–1947): English socialist

1882 The economic side of the democratic ideal is ... socialism itself.

(*Fabian Essays*, 1889)

1883 No philosopher now looks for anything but the gradual evolution of the new order from the old . . . History shows us no example of the sudden substitutions of Utopian and revolutionary romance.

(Ibid.)

1884 How anyone can fear that the British electorate, whatever mistakes it can make or may condone, can ever go too far or too fast is incomprehensible to me . . . The Labour Party, when in due course it comes to be entrusted with power, will naturally not want to do everything at once . . . Once we face the necessity of putting our principles . . . into execution from one end of the kingdom to the other . . . the inevitability of gradualness cannot fail to be appreciated.

(Chairman's address, Labour Party Conference, London, 26 June 1923)

Daniel WEBSTER (1782–1852): US Senator
[see also 1712]

1885 The gentleman has not seen how to reply to this otherwise than by supposing me to have advanced the doctrine that a national debt is a national blessing.

(Speech, Senate, 26 January 1830)

1886 It is, Sir, the people's Constitution, the people's government, made for the people, made by the people, and answerable to the people.

(Ibid.)

1887 When my eyes shall be turned to behold for the last time the sun in heaven . . . let their last feeble and lingering glance . . . behold the gorgeous ensign of the republic . . . bearing for its motto . . . in characters of living light, blazing on all its ample folds, as they float over the sea and over the land, and in every wind under the whole heavens, that other sentiment, dear to every true American heart, 'Liberty *and* Union, now and forever, one and inseparable!'

(Peroration, ibid.)

1888 [of Alexander Hamilton] He smote the rock of the national resources, and abundant streams of revenue gushed forth. He touched the dead corpse of the Public Credit, and it sprang upon its feet.

(Speech, New York, 10 March 1831)

1889 On this question of principle . . . they [the Colonies] raised their flag against a power . . . which has dotted over the surface of the whole globe with her possessions and military posts, whose morning drum-beat, following the sun, and keeping company with the hours, circles the earth with one continuous and unbroken strain of the martial airs of England.

(Speech, US Senate, 7 May 1834)

1890 I was born an American; I will live an American; I shall die an American.

(Speech, US Senate, on 'the Compromise Bill', 17 July 1850)

Arthur Wellesley, Duke of WELLINGTON (1769–1852): British Field-Marshal and Tory Prime Minister
[see also 172, 259, 459, 722, 1769, 1786]

1891 Being born in a stable does not make a man a horse.

(On learning he was described as an Irishman because he was born in Dublin, *c.* 1807)

1892 I don't know what effect these men will have upon the enemy, but, by God, they terrify me.

(*Comment on a draft of troops sent to him in Spain, 1809)

1893 We have in the service the scum of the earth as common soldiers.

(Despatch from Vitoria to Lord Bathurst, War Minister, 2 July 1813)

1894 I have got an infamous army, very weak and ill-equipped, and a very inexperienced staff.

(Letter to Lord Stewart at the start of the Waterloo campaign, 8 May 1815)

1895 [on being asked if he expected desertions from the French army] Not upon a man from the colonel to the private in a regiment – both inclusive. We may pick up a marshal or two, perhaps; but not worth a damn.

(To Creevey, May/early June 1815)

1896 Up Guards and at them again.

(At Waterloo, 18 June 1815, as reported in a letter of Ensign Batty of the Foot Guards four days later)

1897 Hard pounding this, gentlemen; try who can pound the longest.

(Waterloo, 18 June 1815)

1898 It has been a damned serious business – Blücher and I have lost 30,000 men. It has been a damned nice thing – the nearest run thing you ever saw in your life ... By God! I don't think it would have done if I had not been there.

(To Creevey, 19 June 1815)

1899 The finger of Providence

was upon me, and I escaped unhurt.

(Letter to Lady Frances Webster, after Waterloo, 19 June 1815)

1900 I really believe I owe my spirit of enterprise to the tricks I used to play in the garden.

(When revisiting the House in which he had been a pupil at Eton, 22 January 1818)

1901 The Battle of Waterloo was won on the playing-fields of Eton.

(*Apocryphal epigram, posthumously coined [cf. 1900 above; and see the discussion in Elizabeth Longford's *Wellington, The Years of the Sword*, pp. 16–17])

1902 There is nothing worse than a battle won except a battle lost.

(To Philip von Neumann, 11 January 1821)

1903 Publish and be damned.

(*Alleged reply to a blackmailing publisher, December 1824)

1904 There never was such a humbug as the Greek affair altogether. However, thank God it has never cost us a shilling, and never shall.

(Comment, as Prime Minister, on the Greek War of Independence, February 1828)

1905 Beginning reform is beginning revolution.

(To Mrs Arbuthnot, 7 November 1830)

1906 If you believe that, you'll believe anything.

(Retort to a government official who had mistaken him for the Secretary of the Royal Academy and greeted him as 'Mr Jones, I believe', *c.* 1830)

1907 [of Napoleon] I used to say of him that his presence on the field made the difference of forty thousand men.

(To Lord Stanhope, 2 November 1831)

1908 I never saw so many bad hats in my life.

(On seeing first Reformed Parliament, 1832)

1909 Buonaparte's whole life, civil, political and military, was a fraud. There was not a transaction, great or small, in which lying and fraud were not introduced.

(Letter to Croker, 29 December 1835)

1910 There is no such thing as *a little War* for a great Nation.

(Speech, H of L, 16 January 1838)

1911. What is the best to be done

for the country? How can the Government be carried on?

(Conversation with Stanhope, 18 May 1839: possible origin of 'The Queen's government must be carried on')

1912 Try sparrow-hawks, Ma'am.

(On being asked by Queen Victoria how to free the new 'Crystal Palace' from hundreds of birds, April 1851)

1913 All the business of war, and indeed all the business of life, is to endeavour to find out what you don't know by what you do; that's what I called 'guessing what was at the other side of the hill'.

(To Mrs Croker at Folkestone, 3 September 1852)

Herbert George WELLS (1866–1946): English writer

1914 The Victorian epoch ... was ... a gigantic experiment of the most slovenly and wasteful kind ... Will anyone, a hundred years from now, consent to live in the houses the Victorians built, travel by their roads or railways, value the furnishings they made to live among or esteem, except for curious or historical reasons, their prevalent art and the clipped and limited literature that satisfied their souls?

(*The New Machiavelli*, 1911)

1915 The War that will end War.

(Title of book, 1914)

1916 Human history becomes more and more a race between education and catastrophe.

(*The Outline of History*, 1920)

Peter WENTWORTH (1530–96): English MP and champion of parliamentary rights in Queen Elizabeth I's reign

1917 In this House, which is termed a place of free speech, there is nothing so necessary for the preservation of the prince and State as free speech; and without this it is a scorn and mockery to call it a Parliament House, for in truth it is none but a very school of flattery and dissimulation, and so a fit place to serve the devil and his angels in, and not to glorify God and benefit the Common-wealth.

(Speech, H of C, 8 February 1576)

[Thomas WENTWORTH, *see* **STRAFFORD]**

John WESLEY (1703–91): English preacher and founder of Methodist movement [see also 993]

1918 I look upon all the world as my parish.

(Journal, 11 June 1739)

1919 I want to know one thing – the way to heaven; how to land safe on that happy shore. God Himself has condescended to teach the way; for this very end he came from heaven. He hath written it down in a book. O give me that book!

(Preface to *Sermons*, written in 1747)

Maxime WEYGAND (1867–1965): French General

1920 I believe the French army to be of greater intrinsic value than ever before in its history; its armaments are of the first quality, its fortifications of the highest order, its morale excellent and its leadership outstanding.

(Speech, 4 July 1939)

Samuel   WHITBREAD (1758–1815): Radical Whig politician

1921 Sir, in a political point of view, nothing can possibly afford greater stability to a popular government than the education of your people.

(Speech, H of C, 19 February 1807)

John WILKES (1727–97): English radical politician
[see also 1496]

1922 In vain will such a minister, or the foul dregs of his power, the tools of despotism and corruption, preach up 'the spirit of concord . . .' They have sent the spirit of discord through the land and I will prophesy it will never be distinguished but by the extinction of their power.

(From article attacking the King's Speech and Grenville, the minister who had drafted it, in No. 45 of the *North Briton*, 23 April 1763)

1923 The nation, Sir, suspects that the regular ministerial majorities in parliament are bought and that the Crown has made a purchase of the House with the money of the people. Hence the ready, tame and servile compliance to every royal verdict issued by the minister [Lord North] . . . It is almost universally believed, sir, that this debt has been contracted in corrupting the representatives of the people.

(Speech attacking increased Civil List, H of C, 16 April 1777)

WILLIAM I (1027–87): King of England
[see also 1397, 1975]

1924 It is not with temerity nor unjustly but after deliberation and in defence of right that I have crossed the sea into this country . . . Moreover . . . I do not think it right that either my men or his

[Harold's] should perish in conflict over a quarrel that is none of their making. I am therefore ready to risk my life against his in single combat to decide whether the kingdom of England should by right be his or mine.

(At Hastings before the battle, October 1066)

1925 I have not consented to pay fealty, nor will I now, because I never promised it, nor do I find that my predecessors ever paid it to your predecessors.

(Letter to Pope Gregory VII, ?1075)

WILLIAM   II   (1056–1100): King of England [see also 48, 1749]

1926 By the Holy Face of Lucca neither he nor any other shall be archbishop at this time except myself.

(When Anselm was proposed as Archbishop of Canterbury, 1093)

WILLIAM   III   (1650–1702): Prince of Orange and King of England [see also 1387, 1446]

1927 There is one certain means by which I can be sure never to see my country's [Holland's] ruin: I will die in the last ditch.

(To the Duke of Buckingham who was trying to persuade him not to oppose the French, 1672)

1928 It seems to me very extraordinary that it should be impossible to have esteem and regard for a young man without it being criminal.

(Letter to Lord Portland who had reproached William for his friendship with Keppel, June 1697)

1929 People in Parliament now occupy themselves with private animosities and party quarrels and think little of the national interest. It is impossible to credit the serene indifference with which they consider events outside their own country.

(Letter to Antonius Heinsius, January 1699)

1930 The eyes of all Europe are upon this Parliament . . . if you do in good earnest wish to see England hold the balance of Europe and to be indeed at the head of the Protestant interest, it will appear by your right improving the present opportunity.

(Opening of Parliament, 31 December 1701)

1931 Every bullet has its billet.

(*Saying attributed to William III by Wesley in his journal, 6 June 1765)

WILLIAM   IV   (1765–1837): King of England

1932 [on learning of Talleyrand's appointment as ambassador in London] There are few Individuals whose Career appears to His Majesty to have been more disreputable and although the King does not question his Talents, especially for Intrigue, He does not consider the Selection of a Man of his Character . . . to be either creditable to Himself or Complimentary to His Majesty.

(Letter to Lord Aberdeen, 11 September 1830)

1933 No good when the wind's in the south-east.

(Audible comment on hearing Court chaplain pray for rain, during a drought, Brighton, 1831)

WILLIAM II (1859–1941): German Emperor
[see also 792]

1934 I express to you my sincere congratulations that you and your people, without appealing to the help of foreign powers, have succeeded, by your own energetic action against the armed bands which invaded your country as disturbers of the peace, in restoring peace and in maintaining the independence of the country against attacks from without.

(Telegram to President Kruger of the Transvaal on the repulse of the Jameson Raid, 3 January 1896)

1935 The German Empire has become a world empire. Everywhere, at the farthest points of the globe, dwell thousands of our fellow countrymen. German trade, German science, German energy sail the oceans.

(Speech, Berlin, 18 January 1896)

1936 Will you kindly accept a drawing I have sketched for you showing the Symbolizing figures of Russia and Germany as sentinels at the Yellow Sea for the proclamation of the Gospel of Truth and Light in the East. I drew the sketch in the Xmas week under the blaze of the lights of the Xmas trees.

(Letter in English to Tsar Nicholas II, 4 January 1898)

1937 Gentlemen, from this tower the world is ruled.

(To the officers of his suite, outside the Round Tower of Windsor Castle, 21 November 1899)

1938 We have fought for our place in the sun and won it. Our future is on the water.

(Speech at the Elbe regatta, June 1901)

1939 I hope that under [the Sultan's] sovereignty a free Morocco will remain open to the peaceful competition of all nations, without monopoly or annexation, on a policy of absolute equality.

(Speech at Tangier, 31 March 1905)

1940 The Tsar [Nicholas II] is not treacherous but he is weak. Weakness is not treachery, but it fulfils all its functions.

(Marginal comment on despatch from German ambassador to Russia, 16 March 1907)

1941 So the famous 'encirclement' of Germany has finally become a complete fact ... A great achievement, which arouses the admiration even of him who is to be destroyed as its result! Edward VII is stronger after his death than am I who am still alive!

(Marginal comments on a telegram from the German ambassador in St Petersburg from which William II decided that 'England, Russia and France have agreed among themselves' to 'wage a war of extermination against us', 30 July 1914)

1942 We draw the sword with a clear conscience and with clean hands.

(Speech from the throne, Berlin, 4 August 1914)

1943 To think that George and Nicky should have played me false! If my grandmother had been alive she would never have allowed it!

(In conversation with Princess Blücher during the second week of August 1914; references are to King George V, Tsar Nicholas II and Queen Victoria)

1944 I and my cousins George and Nicholas shall make peace when the proper time has come.

(To the American ambassador, early January 1916)

1945 [of Hitler] The machine is running away with *him* as it ran away with *me*.

(In exile at Doorn, to Sir Robert Bruce-Lockhart and Sir John Wheeler-Bennett, 27 August 1939)

Shirley WILLIAMS (b. 1930): British Social Democratic Party politician

1946 The British civil service ... is a beautifully designed and effective braking mechanism.

(Speech, Royal Institute of Public Administration, 11 February 1980)

Sir Harold WILSON (b. 1916): British Labour politician and Prime Minister

1947 We meet the challenge of the modern world with an effete Venetian oligarchy, a Government who themselves reflect the nation's besetting weakness of family connexions and aristocratic recruitment.

(Speech, attacking the Macmillan Government, H of C, 18 April 1961)

1948 The Britain that is to be forged in the white heat of this revolution.

(Speech, Labour Party Conference, Scarborough, 1 October 1963: generally misquoted as '. . . heat of the technological revolution')

1949 The selection has been through the machinery of an autocratic cabal. I am worried to know how a scion of an effete establishment can understand the scientific revolution. After half a century of democratic advance the whole process has ground to halt with a Fourteenth Earl.

(Speech criticizing the appointment of Lord Home as Prime Minister; Belle Vue, Manchester, 19 October 1963)

1950 The Labour Party is a moral crusade or it is nothing.

(Speech to Scottish Labour Party, Rothesay, 5 September 1964)

1951 A week is a long time in politics.

(Aphorism said on several occasions, 1965)

1952 Given a fair wind, we will negotiate our way into the Common Market, head held high, not crawl in . . . Negotiations? Yes. Unconditional acceptance of whatever terms we are offered? No.

(Speech, Bristol, 20 March 1966)

1953 A natural democratic revolt is now giving way, in the name of militancy, to pressures which are anything but democratic . . . It is difficult for us to appreciate the pressures which are being put on men I know to be realistic and reasonable not only in their executive capacity but in the highly organized strike committees in the individual ports by this tightly knit group of politically motivated men.

(Speech denouncing militancy in the National Union of Seamen, H of C, 20 June 1966)

1954 In a recent interview I was asked what, above all, I associated with socialism in this modern age: I answered if there was one word I would use to identify modern socialism, it was 'Science'.

(Speech, Daresbury, 17 June 1967)

1955 Tonight we must face the new situation. First what this means. From now on the pound abroad is worth 14% or so less in terms of other currencies. It does not mean, of course, that the pound here in Britain, in your pocket or purse or in your bank, has been devalued.

(Broadcast after announcing a devaluation of the pound, 18 November 1967)

1956 We are creating a Britain of which we can be proud. And the world knows it. The world's tourists are coming here in their millions . . . They are coming here to buy because they get better value in our shops than anywhere else in Europe. But they are coming, above all, because the new Britain is exciting . . . Yes, Britain with a Labour Government is an exciting place.

(Speech, Labour Party Conference, Brighton, 30 September 1969)

1957 The Party needs to protect itself against the activities of small groups of inflexible political persuasion, extreme so-called 'Left' and in a few cases extreme so-called 'Moderates', having in common only their arrogant dogmatism. These groups are not what this Party is all about. Infestation of this kind thrives only in minuscule local parties . . . I have no wish to lead a Party of political zombies.

(Speech, Labour Party Conference, Blackpool, 30 September 1975)

Woodrow **WILSON** (1856–1924): twenty-eighth President of the USA

1958 If it's reorganization, a new deal and a change you are seeking . . . vote for me, or not vote at all.

(Presidential campaign speech, Camden, New Jersey, 24 October 1910: the first political use of the phrase 'new deal')

1959 The nation has been deeply stirred . . . The feelings with which we face this new age of right and opportunity sweep across our heartstrings like some air out of God's own presence, where justice and mercy are reconciled and the judge and the brother are one.

(First Inaugural Address, 4 March 1913)

1960 Human rights, national integrity, and opportunity as against material interests – that . . . is the issue which we now have to face. I want to take this occasion to say that the United States will never again seek one additional foot of territory by conquest.

(Speech at Mobile, Alabama, 27 October 1913)

1961 The people of the United States are drawn from many nations, and chiefly from the nations now at war . . . Some will wish one nation, others another, to succeed in this momentous struggle . . . I venture . . . to speak a solemn word of warning . . . The United States must be neutral in fact as well as in name during these days that are to try men's souls. We must be impartial in thought as well as in action.

(Message to the Senate, 19 August 1914)

1962 There is such a thing as a man being too proud to fight.

(Address, Philadelphia, 10 May 1915)

1963 We have stood apart, studiously neutral.

(Message to Congress, 7 December 1915)

1964 America cannot be an ostrich with its head in the sand.

(Speech, Des Moines, New Mexico, 1 February 1916)

1965 I am proposing . . . that the nations should with one accord adopt the doctrine of President Monroe as the doctrine of the world . . . that every people should be left free to determine its own policy, its own way of development, unhindered, unthreatened, unafraid, the little along with the great and powerful . . . These are American principles, American policies. We could stand for no others. And they are also . . . the principles of mankind and must prevail.

(Speech to the Senate, 22 January 1917)

1966 The world must be safe for democracy. Its peace must be planted upon trusted foundations of political liberty.

(Address to Congress, 2 April 1917)

1967 It is not an army that we must train for war: it is a nation.

(Speech, Washington, 12 May 1917)

1968 What we demand in this war is nothing peculiar to ourselves. It is that the world be made fit and safe to live in . . . The programme of the world's peace, therefore, is our programme; and that programme, the only possible programme, as we see it is this: I. Open covenants of peace, openly arrived at, after which there shall be no private international understandings of any kind but diplomacy shall proceed always frankly and in the public view . . . XIV. A general association of nations must be formed under specific covenants for the purpose of affording mutual guarantees of political independence and territorial integrity to great and small states alike.

(Speech to Congress containing the 'Fourteen Points', 8 January 1918)

1969 There shall be no annexations, no contributions, no punitive damages ... Peoples and provinces must not be bartered about from sovereignty to sovereignty as if they were chattels or pawns in a game. Self-determination is not a mere phrase. It is an imperative principle which statesmen will henceforth ignore at their peril.

(Address to Congress on the Principles of Peace, 11 February 1918)

1970 Logic! Logic! I don't give a damn for logic. I am going to include pensions.

(To his advisers on reparations at the Paris Peace Conference, April 1919)

1971 Sometimes people call me an idealist. Well, that is the way I know I am an American. America is the only idealistic nation in the world.

(Address, Sioux Falls, 8 September 1919)

Sir Francis WINDEBANK (1582–1646): English politician, Secretary of State to King Charles I

1972 O the great judgments of God! That pig of a Henry VIII committed such sacrilege by profaning so many ecclesiastical benefices in order to give their goods to those who being so rewarded might stand firmly for the King in the Lower House; and now the King's greatest enemies are those who are enriched by these benefices.

(To Panzani, Papal envoy, April 1635)

William WINDHAM (1750–1810): English War Minister

1973 Those entrusted with arms ... should be persons of some substance and stake in the country.

(Speech, H of C, 22 July 1807)

Duke of WINDSOR *see* **Edward VIII**

Gerrard WINSTANLEY (1609–?61): English leader of the radical Diggers [see also 1571]

1974 Seeing the common people of England by joint consent of person and purse have cast out Charles our Norman oppressor, we have by this victory recovered ourselves from under his Norman yoke.

(To General Fairfax, 8 December 1649)

1975 Therefore England beware ... William the Conqueror's Army begins to gather into head again ... for though their chief captain Charles be gone, yet his Colonels ... his Counsellors ... and Soldiers ... all which did steal away our Land from us when they killed and murdered our Fathers in that Norman conquest.

(After the Diggers had been arrested, 1649)

1976 None ought to be lords or landlords over another, but the earth is free for every son and daughter of mankind to live free upon.

(Letter to Fairfax about the Diggers' take-over of St George's Hill in Surrey, 1649)

1977 Why may we not have our Heaven here (that is, a comfortable livelihood in the Earth) and Heaven hereafter too, as well as you, God is no respecter of Persons?

(*An Appeal to all Englishmen*, 26 March 1650)

Serge Y. WITTE (1849–1915): first Prime Minister of Russia

1978 The World is in flames today for a cause which interests Russia first and foremost, a cause which is essentially the cause of the Slavs and which is of no concern to France or to England.

(Conversation in retirement with the French ambassador, Paléologue, 10 September 1914)

James WOLFE (1727–59): English General

1979 The formidable sea and land armament, which the people of Canada now behold in the heart of their country, is intended by the King, my master, to check the insolence of France, to revenge the insults offered to the British colonies, and totally to deprive the French of their most valued settlement in North America.

(Proclamation to the people of Quebec from Wolfe's headquarters at Laurent, 28 June 1759)

1980 The General ... repeated nearly the whole of Gray's Elegy ... adding, as he concluded, that he would prefer being the author of that poem to the glory of beating the French tomorrow.

(Account by J. Robinson of Wolfe at Quebec, 12 September 1759)

1981 What, do they run already? Then I die happy.

(*Alleged last words on seeing the French retreating at Quebec, 13 September 1759)

Thomas WOLSEY (1472/3–1530): Lord Chancellor of England under King Henry VIII and Cardinal Archbishop of York

1982 I see the matter against me how it is framed. But if I had served God as diligently as I have done the King, he would not have given me over in my grey hairs.

(To Sir William Kingston, Constable of the Tower of London, while under arrest for high treason, November 1530)

1983 [of Henry VIII] He is a prince of royal courage and hath a princely heart; and rather than he will miss or want part of his appetite, he will hazard the loss of one-half of his kingdom.

(Ibid.)

Elizabeth WORDSWORTH (1840–1932): first Principal of Lady Margaret Hall, Oxford

1984 She was a gentlewoman, a scholar, and a saint, and after being married three times she took a vow of celibacy; what more could be expected of any woman?

(Suggestion that college should be named for Lady Margaret Beaufort (1443–1509), put to founding committee in 1879)

William WORDSWORTH (1770–1850): English poet

1985 Bliss was it in that dawn to be alive,
But to be young was very heaven!

(The French Revolution, as it appeared to enthusiasts in 1789, *The Prelude*, Bk xi, written 1799–1805)

1986 Once did she hold the gorgeous East in fee,
And was the safeguard of the West.
Venice, the eldest Child of Liberty.

('On the Extinction of the Venetian Republic: Once did She Hold', *National Independence and Liberty*, Pt I, 1807)

1987 Two Voices are there; one is of the sea,
One of the mountains; each a mighty Voice,
In both from age to age thou didst rejoice,
They were thy chosen music, Liberty!

('Thought of a Briton on the Subjugation of Switzerland: Two Voices are There', ibid.)

1988 Another year! – another deadly blow!
Another mighty Empire overthrown!
And we are left, or shall be left, alone.

('Another Year!', ibid.: refers to Napoleon's victories at Jena and Friedland)

Sir Christopher WREN
(1632–1723): English architect

1989 The Women, as they make here the Language and Fashions and meddle with Politicks and Philosophy, so they sway also in Architecture ... but Building certainly ought to have the Attribute of eternal, and therefore the only Thing uncapable of new Fashions.

(Letter to a friend at Oxford after Wren had seen building of Versailles, summer 1665)

1990 The Louvre for a while was my daily Object, where no less than a thousand Hands are constantly employed in the Works ... which altogether make a School of Architecture, the best probably at this Day in Europe.

(Ibid.)

1991 Bernini's design of the Louvre I would have given my Skin for, but the old reserv'd Italian gave me but a few Minutes View.

(Ibid.)

1992 ... concerning the Repair of St Paul's, some may possibly aim at too great a Magnificence, which neither the Disposition, nor Extent of this Age will probably bring to a Period. Others again may fall so low as to think of piecing up the old Fabrick ... I suppose your Lordships may think proper to take a Middle Way.

(Proposals for the repair of Old St Paul's, before the Great Fire, laid before the Commissioners, 1 May 1666)

John WYCLIFFE (?1320–84): English religious leader

1993 I believe that in the end the truth will conquer them.

(Answer to prohibition of his teaching by John of Gaunt, Duke of Lancaster, 1381)

1994 Now Herod and Pontius Pilate have become friends ... since at this earthshattering Council they have condemned Christ for a heretic ... it seems obvious they are going to make heretics of individual Christians.

(Defence after his condemnation by the Council of London [Herod and Pilate are the bishops and the monastic orders], 1382)

1995 I am always glad to explain my faith to anyone, and above all to the Bishop of Rome ... Christ during His life upon earth was of all men the poorest, casting from Him all worldly authority. I deduce from these premises, as a simple counsel of my own, that the Pope should surrender all temporal authority to the civil power and advise his clergy to do the same.

(On being ordered to appear at Papal Court, 1384)

St Francis XAVIER (1506–52): Jesuit missionary in the East

1996 The fatigues of working among intelligent people, anxious to learn in what religion they would best save their souls, bring with them immense satisfaction. The number of people who came to question and discuss was such that I can truly say that never in my life had I so much spiritual joy and consolation.

(Letter to the Fathers in Europe, of his Japanese mission, 29 January 1552)

Brigham YOUNG (1801–77): American Mormon leader

1997 It is enough. That is the right place.

(From Little Mountain, Utah, overlooking Great Salt Lake Valley at the end of the fifteen-week Mormon trek westwards, 24 July 1847)

George Malcolm YOUNG (1882–1959): British historian

1998 The greater part of what passes for diplomatic history is little more than the record of what one clerk said to another clerk.

(*Victorian England: Portrait of an Age*, 1936)

Israel ZANGWILL (1864–1926): English dramatist

1999 America is God's Crucible, the great Melting-Pot where all races of Europe are melting and reforming! . . . God is making the American.

(*The Melting Pot*, 1908)

John ŽIŽKA (1370–1424): Czech rebel and patriotic leader

2000 Defend yourselves bravely against the misdeeds which those Germans commit against you, follow the example of the Czechs of old who, their pikes firmly propped, defended not only God's cause but their own also.

(Letter to the people of Domazlice during the Hussite rebellion, 12 September 1421)

Emile ZOLA (1840–1902): French novelist
[see also 1789]

2001 *J'Accuse* ['I Accuse'].

(Banner headline over an open letter to the President of the Republic, concerning the Dreyfus Case, in Clemenceau's newspaper *L'Aurore*, 13 January 1898)

Index of Key-words

(Numbers refer to the entries and not to pages)

where there is d., may we bring hope 1772
despicable: d. Electorate 1458
despise: not d. Clemenceau . . . only take a different view 1019
despotical: regions . . . servile . . . should be governed by d.
　government 1540
despotism: d. tempered by casualness 14
　France . . . d. tempered by epigrams 284
　handed over to a ruthless d. 69
　tools of d. and corruption 1922
　unremitting d. . . . and degrading submissions 947
destined: I am d. for something 421
destiny: do as d. demands 1307
　manifest d. 1382
　people of this continent alone . . . decide . . . their d. 1520
destroyers: d., wasters and spoilers of your Fatherland 801
destruction: all is to the d. of the Church 639
detestation: show him your d. of the crimes he has committed 1422
devil: first Whig was the D. 994
　from the D. he came 137
　hate a Frenchman as you hate the d. 1332
　I pray God to preserve me from the D. 1348
　little laud to the D. 53
　surely the d. drove them on 781
　to the D. he shall return 137
devils: casting out d. is mere juggling 1677
　in their entrails they were Atheists and D. 453
　though there were as many d. as tiles on the roof 1133
devour: Revolution may . . . d. . . . her children one by one 1836
diamonds: love of d. and love of smuggling 877
Dickon: for D. thy master is bought and sold 214
dictates: way that Providence d. 884
dictators: d. ride . . . upon tigers 379
　establishment of personal contact with the d. 328
　only generals who gain successes can set up d. 1092
dictatorship: d. of the proletariat 1202, 1209
die: And shall Trelawny d. 824
　better to d. on your feet than live on your knees 914
　content to d. for God's eternal truth 207
　country must live, Louis must d. 1599
　d. in the last ditch 1927
　either be fond to live or fear to d. 606
　I resolve . . . to d. in the maintenance of it 335
　If I d., avenge me 1295
　they d. to vex me 1235
died: D., has he? 1120

great waste of people of the E. 224
I know my heart to be entirely E. 46
lustre and glory of E. liberty 472
melancholy vestiges of the E. passage 1451
moment . . . Ireland is mentioned, the E. . . . bid adieu to common feeling 1709
Spaniards which more greedily thirst after E. blood 1553
vigorous rule of an E. majority 582
you . . . cheat the French and I the E. 1226
Englishman: attachment to his Queen ought to make virtuous E. . . . protect her 1784
beggar is still . . . an E. 1285
E. is the unfittest person on earth 229
fifty thousand men slain this year . . . and not one E. 1867
if I were an American as I am an E. 1472
last great E. 1769
pity he is not an E. 870
Englishmen: all the nation, whether E., Danes or Britons 585
Americans . . . second chop E. 875
neither right nor natural for Frenchmen to be subject to E. 1749
reveal Himself . . . first to His E. 1257
we are E. 480
ensign: gorgeous e. of the republic 1887
entangle: never to e. ourselves in the broils of Europe 960
enthusiasm: e., a quality which ought never to be possessed by an Archbishop 553
environed: happy on being e. with a great ditch 483
envy: nothing I could e. but . . . your glory 1862
epigrams: despotism tempered by e. 284
epoch: heroes of an e. 835
my life has coincided with a wretched e. 1239
equal: all men are created e. 506
all men are created e. and independent 946
all were created e. by nature 108
e. and exact justice to all men 953
equality: for a more substantial e. of opportunity 1626
Liberty, E., Fraternity 1497
Liberty, E., Fraternity . . . each . . . signifies Peace 1046
To the cry of 'E.' 80
when security and e. are in conflict 130
equals: with thine e., familiar 221
equilibrium: disturbed and nearly destroyed that political e. 563
equity: frame its legislation upon principles of e. and justice 1429
equivocate: I will not e. 694
err: Governments can e. 1609

error: commonest e. in politics is   1660
    e. has never come into my mind   1243
    e. is often more earnest than truth   553
    political e. to practise deceit   669
Essex: seek not to be E.   218
established: Church of England e. by Queen Elizabeth   335
establishment: scion of an effete e.   1949
estate: fourth e. of the realm   1140
    in the Reporter's Gallery, there sat a Fourth E.   289
    Third E. contains . . . all . . . to constitute a nation   1696
estates: Three E. in Parliament   289
Estonians: there was a great battle with the Germans and E.   1375
eternal: liberty . . . is e. vigilance   489
Eton: Battle of Waterloo . . . playing-fields of E.   1901
Europe: connected as we are with . . . E.   279
    economically the soundest thing that existed in E.   150
    E. . . . for me the essence of a fatherland   1240
    E. is apart and England is not of her flesh and body 1020
    E. is being liquidated and the League . . . must be the heir   1714
    E. is our common home   192
    E. of Nations . . . E. of States   520
    eyes of all E. are upon this Parliament   1930
    France is no longer isolated in E.   1756
    general and comprehensive system of public law in E.   1486
    great New Order in E.   890
    in 1914 E. had arrived at a point   789
    lamps are going out all over E.   788
    never entangle ourselves in the broils of E.   960
    never to suffer E. to intermeddle with cis-Atlantic affairs   960
    Paris sneezes, E. catches cold   1241
    powerful States of E. have made alliances   321
    Protestant E. seems to get new colour in her cheeks   1449
    regard for the liberties of E.   199
    rights of the smaller nationalities of E.   60
    save E. by her example   1487
    Soviets . . . occupy all eastern . . . E.   763
    spectre is haunting E.   1199
    this small island will astonish E.   1635
    to create E. in time   13
    to salvage E.'s culture   12
    torch of war in E.   883
    we are part of the community of E.   1662
    western E. . . . domination of a single power   787
    whoever speaks of E. is wrong   161
    word 'E.' on the lips of politicians   159

hawkers: h. of indulgences cajole money 1130
Haydn: there is a certain H., who has some peculiar ideas 1189
hazard: h. the loss of one-half his kingdom 1983
head: bowed his comely h. 1194
    cut off his h. with the crown upon it 471
    h. of this great family 727
    that h. shall lie on the stock 1828
    we as h. and you as members are conjoined 854
healing: not heroics but h. 814
health: His Majesty's h. has never been better 1310
healthy: h. spirit of self-help 1703
hear: time will come when you will h. me 533
heard: I will be h. 694
heart: Calais lying on my h. 1213
    Catholic in h. and doctrine 1345
    h. and stomach of a king 607
    Its seat is in the h. 689
    thing which is nearest the h. of this nation 342
hearts: never care to lose the h. of any for justice's sake 934
heat: immortal garland . . . not without dust and h. 1256
heaven: as near to h. by sea as by land 754
    H. here . . . and H. hereafter too 1977
    Maid sent here by the King of H. 963
    'this house . . . nigh h. as mine own' 1281
    to be young was very h. 1985
    want to know one thing – the way to h. 1919
heavens: how to go to heaven not how the h. go 680
hedges: In England . . . living h. 1284
Hell: farmers of Kansas must raise . . . more H. 1060
    H. is fouled by his foul presence 1419
    If I owned Texas and H. . . . rent out Texas and live in H. 1691
    suck the monster to the lowest hole in H. 293
    war is all H. 1693
helm: sitting at the h. of this Imperial Majesty 510
helots: British subjects . . . in the position of h. 1252
hemisphere: compensation in another h. 281
Henry: that pig of a H. VIII 1972
here: buck stops h. 1824
    H. I am, h. I stay 1161
    H. I stand 1132
    I might have got h. on my own 391
heretic: I shall never be a h. 1131
Herod: Now H. and Pontius Pilate have become friends 1994
heroes: fit country for h. to live in 740
    h. of an epoch 835

want a Nigger for a neighbour, vote L.   1519
what [Victoria] . . . have thought of a L. Government   726
labourers: enable the l. . . . to subsist   1579
    title . . . take that of L.' Unions   1644
labouring: rights and interests of the l. man   89
labours: l. and sacrifices incurred for defending the society   1249
Lady: Iron L. of British politics   1565
lady: L. whom Time had surprised   1555
    Old L. of Threadneedle Street   746
Lady Hamilton: L. H. . . . a legacy to my country   1343
lady's: l. not for turning   1773
Lafayette: L., we are here   1733
Lambeth: L. should now be Catesby's horizon   908
lamp: I lift my l. beside the golden door   1059
lamps: l. are going out all over Europe   788
land: Lord suffered His own L. to be lost   136
    Peace, Bread and L.   1508
    steal away our L. . . . in that Norman conquest   1975
    wonderful l. and a faithless one   1585
landing: desire the l. of that Prince   629
    l. operation against her [England]   888
landlord: l. is a gentleman   734
    l. . . . opposed to the interest of every other class   1578
lands: l. of the rising peoples   1010
language: but one l., the English l.   1629
    l. which we can all understand   32
    under the tropic is our l. spoke   1861
languages: l. are the pedigree of nations   986
lap: head . . . wont to lie on Queen Catherine's l.   1828
lass: came with a l., it will pass with a l.   942
last: die in the l. ditch   1927
    dominoes . . . l. one will go over very quickly   597
    l. great Englishman   1769
    l. territorial claim which I have   886
    l. to consent to the separation   715
    this day may be the l. to any of us   1337
lasts: if only it l.   177
late: always too l. or too little   744
    offering Germany too little . . . too l.   1344
Latin: better . . . than the L. mitre   576
    scour up my old L.   608
latitude: being in the l. of 63' 8"   501
laud: little l. to the Devil   53
laugh: play with death and l. at it   1301
laurels: no conqueror . . . nobler l. than Mr Chamberlain   1796

INDEX OF KEY-WORDS

discretion rather than the rigid letter of the l. — 780
every l. is an evil — 131
every man who comes ... entitled to protection of English l. — 1180
general and comprehensive system of Public L. in Europe — 1486
higher l. than the Constitution — 1681
human l. ... accordance with right reason — 51
if we have violated any l. ... not done intentionally — 1121
ignorance of the l. excuses no man — 1676
L. ... cannot be changed but by Parliament — 434
l. of nature and of nations — 244
l. on the one side ... lawlessness upon the other — 758
Nature and l. denieth to all woman — 1038
Necessity hath no l. — 479
no one ... l. in common with another — 17
not single l. connected with my name ... not had ... mitigation — 1426
where l. ends ... tyranny begins — 1466
lawful: except by l. judgement of his peers — 1171
it shall be l. ... to leave our kingdom — 1173
lawlessness: law on the one side ... l. upon the other — 758
laws: fixed l. of his kingdom to be set aside — 853
I always had your l. on my breast — 487
L. chang'd according to the Power of the Sword — 338
nothing to do with the l. but obey them — 907
restoring a due obedience to the l. — 708
secure the repeal of bad or obnoxious l. — 775
stand and fall by the l., liberties and religion of our country — 1480
layman: l. ... ought ... to defend [abused Christianity] ... with the sword — 1102
lazily: English policy is to float l. downstream — 1658
leader: your King, I will be your captain and l. — 1584
leadership: morale excellent and its l. outstanding — 1920
League: Europe ... liquidated and the L. of Nations must be the heir — 1714
L. of Nations grows in moral courage — 1156
my devotion to this great L. of Nations — 318
organisations of the L. of Nations — 742
Our policy is ... membership of the L. — 583
purposes of this war ... attained if there is a L. of Nations — 1065
we believe in a L. system — 67
leap: one giant l. for mankind — 54
learn: we cannot l. ... until we stop shouting — 1362
learnt: forgotten nothing and l. nothing — 579
governments have l. nothing from history — 834
l. nothing and forgotten nothing — 1754

l. and the unicorn . . . fighting for the crown 1377
we, who struck the l. down 195
lions: two huge l. tearing at my flanks 1452
listen: Government will l. 1362
literature: limited l. that satisfied their souls 1914
we have no l. 1306
little: always too late or too l. 744
great empire and l. minds 230
l. man, l. man, if your father had lived 610
no . . . *l. War* for a great Nation 1910
so l. done, so much to do 1577
liturgy: we have . . . a Popish l. 1469
live: country must l., Louis must die 1599
either be fond to l. or fear to die 606
I have striven to l. worthily 33
I will l. 421
long l. the Duma 275
Rogues, would you l. for ever 672
lives: enough l. have been sacrificed 1095
living: divide the nations as . . . the l. and the dying 1667
fact of l. in society 1249
rest of the world . . . not owe us a l. 1453
scale of l. must be reduced 373
Livingstone: Dr L., I presume 1732
lobby: as if there were a lion in the l. 1806
locks: shaking her invincible l. 1259
log: From L. Cabin to White House 1775
logic: don't give a damn for l. 1970
London: City of L. remains as it is 322
country must diminish, if L. do so increase 936
deplorable fire near Fish Street in L. 626
greater than L. with the suburbs 332
key to India is L. 565
L. is a modern Babylon 543
man tired of L. is tired of life 992
walls of L. may be battered 731
Londoner: spirit of the L. 731
long: you have sat too l. 39
week is a l. time in politics 1951
longer: not fit that you should sit here any l. 425
longest: career was one unclouded l. day 1786
lords: fail very completely in the House of L. 531
House of L. . . . Mr Balfour's poodle 733
House of L. . . . Outer Mongolia for retired politicians 126
l. and commons of this realm 246

only Bonapartist . . . is m. 1326
Madam: M. I may not call you 602
Mademoiselle: M. is at the gate 1275
madness: m. of many for the gain of a few 1525
Magi: John, King and Priest . . . of the ancient race of those M. 1391
magistrates: power of . . . m. is . . . from the people 1262
   shelter of the civil m. 1705
Magna Charta: M. C. is such a fellow 436
magnanimity: m. in politics 230
magnificence: great and wonderful m. of . . . Cublay Kaan 1521
magnificent: m., but not war 184
Magyar: M. has no need to have his horses dance 1221
maid: M. sent here by the King of Heaven 963
maidenhead: Guiana . . . country that hath yet her m. 1554
'Maine': Remember the M. 1503
maintain: if . . . not m. justice, justice will not m. us 86
Maintenon: King has married Madame de M. 1385
majesty: consequences of His M.'s resolution . . . ruin 1369
majority: government of the absolute m. 265
   m. are wrong 504
   One on God's side is a m. 1455
make: m. the world safe for diversity 1014
malefactors: m. of great wealth 1625
malice: m. towards none 1094
   rancour and m. do remain 616
man: brave bad m. 404
   century of the common m. 1859
   M. belongs wherever he wants to go 191
   M. is born free, and everywhere he is in chains 1623
   M. is not the enemy of M. 1399
   M. is something to be surpassed 1356
   m. who loves to fold his legs and have out his talk 995
   most unfortunate m. in the history of parties 413
   natural, inalienable and sacred rights of m. 507
   no m. good enough to govern another m. without . . . consent 1081
   no other m. . . . demonstrated power of the spirit over . . . things 465
   regard for a young m. without it being criminal 1928
   standing with the greatest m. you had ever seen 999
   this nation should commit itself . . . to landing a m. on the Moon 1011
   Turkey . . . sick m. on our hands 1351
manifest: m. destiny 1382
mankind: crucify m. on a cross of gold 210
   determining the future destinies of m. 492
   general and fixed convictions of m. 747
   government . . . organising a mass massacre of m. 1645

m. is part of the fabric of the country 1454
National Assembly . . . will decide fate of the m. 1266
never . . . happens that . . . m. is well constituted 1160
money: heightening or lowering of m. is only a cheat 1439
let the bloodhounds of m. beware 1061
licence to print m. 1778
purchase of the House with the m. of the people 1923
money-box: the ever-recurring rattle of the m. 1042
Mongol: no subject . . . take a M. for servant 701
monkeys: idle m. mocking at everything 1854
monkish: that old m. place which I have a horror of 1843
monks: crowd of m. . . . quarrelling for a key . . . in Palestine 1031
Monroe: adherence of the United States to the M. Doctrine 1623
adopt doctrine of President M. as doctrine of the world 1965
attitude . . . as regards the M. Doctrine 1621
Monsieur: King and M. greatly like hard-boiled eggs 1388
monster: suck the m. to the lowest hole in Hell 293
we will not leave the m. to prowl the world unopposed 1483
woman with cut hair . . . much like a m. 1537
Montesquieu: I would certainly canonise M. 304
moon: just as m. receives light from sun, so . . . royal power . . .
pontifical 915
nation should commit itself . . . to landing a man on the M. 1011
moonlight: Captain M. will take my place 1423
moral: Labour party is a m. crusade 1950
m. issue . . . as old as the scriptures 1015
no one . . . m. till all are m. 1719
this is what we mean by a m. society 1771
morale: m. excellent and its leadership outstanding 1920
morality: British public in one of its periodical fits of m. 1141
morally: m. entitled to come within . . . constitution 752
More: put . . . Sir Thomas M. to death 350
morganatic: rumours of a m. marriage alliance will follow 812
Morocco: hope . . . M. will remain open to . . . all nations 1939
Mortimer: Where's M. 462
Moscow: flames of M. were the aurora of liberty 441
M. itself is great 332
M. . . . sponge that will suck him [Napoleon] dry 1041
most terrible of all my battles . . . fought in front of M. 1317
Moslem: do not know . . . a M. or an infidel 1654
mother: how naturally the m. loveth the child 1212
m. of Parliaments 201
though she will not be a m. 225
motivated: tightly knit group of politically m. men 1953
moustache: If Joan of Arc had been born in Austria and worn a m. 1700

Solidarity: he who once became aware of the power of S. 1858
solitary: no man dare impart his s. thoughts 1743
   s., poor, nasty, brutish and short 893
solitude: in the tumult of great events, s. 517
Somerset: duke's of S. arraignment of felonious treason 590
something: s. must be done 593
somnambulist: reactionary . . . s. walking backwards 1642
song: You have silenced the old s. 943
Soubise: lose it with Marshal S. 514
soul: Caroline, a happy, merry s. 294
   Parliament . . . to the Commonwealth . . . s. to the body 1548
souls: no evil in the atom – only in men's s. 1735
   times that try men's s. 1398
sound: s. mind in a s. body, is . . . happy state in this world 1098
   s. mind in a s. body . . . to serve God 1126
soup: King consumed four plates of different s. 1388
South: compact which exists between the North and the S. 696
   may be for or against the S. 751
South Africa: God's will . . . peoples of S. A. . . . defeat and
     humiliation 1713
south-east: no good when the wind's in the s. 1933
southern: so much talked of S. Continent 445
sovereign: bandy civilities with my S. 983
   I am the S. . . . business can stop and wait for nothing 1841
   Magna Charta . . . will have no s. 436
   no subjects or Commons more love . . . S. Lord 857
   obligation of subjects to the s. 896
   s. is absolute 303
   's. power' is no parliamentary word 436
   subject and a s. are clean different things 338
   s. under a constitutional monarchy . . . has three rights 95
   what . . . to be a subject and what to be a s. 606
sovereignty: brings down the pride of s. 92
   s. resides essentially in the nation 507
Soviet: there is no S. domination of Eastern Europe 643
soviets: All power to the S. 1509
sow: right s. by the ear 1868
   s. by the right ear 851
spaghetti: ticker tape ain't s. 1044
Spain: in S. . . . they never answer letters 405
   into the midst of S., into their land 653
   singeing . . . King of S.'s beard 85, 575
   supposed the King of S. had not wished to write 603
Spaniards: dry and subtil headed S. 1556
   natural gravity of the S. 168

S. . . . thirst after English blood 1553
the S. envieth us 1534
win this game and to thrash the S. 573
spaniels: delight to have a number of little s. 627
Spanish: burning issue of imperialism . . . out of the S. War 211
Love the S. 1112
S. dynasties go and come 405
spark: single s. can start a prairie fire 1181
sparrow-hawks: Try s., Ma'am 1912
speak: difficult to s. and impossible to be silent 243
he was so long beginning to s. 283
S. for England 38
Speaker: By your leave (Mr S.) I must borrow your chair 1642
speaks: s. to Me as if I was a public meeting 1847
species: nation is divided into two s. 1854
spectre: s. is haunting Europe 1199
speculations: s. of lasting tranquillity 808
speech: first is freedom of s. 1615
this House . . . a place of free s. 1917
speed: they desired . . . him . . . be gone with all s. 213
spices: East, where s. grow 263
spirit: glorious s. of Whiggism 1470
healthy s. of self-help 1703
her majesty hath pronounced . . . her 's.' 222
power of the s. over material things 465
sent the s. of discord through the land 1922
s. of the Reform Bill 1428
s. radically opposed to liberty 798
you represented . . . s. of France 592
spirits: embase the s. of his subjects 1547
spiritual: never in my life . . . so much s. joy 1996
splendid: our s. isolation 772
your s. isolation 1663
splendidly: Empire stands s. isolated 645
splendour: Coronation not symbol of . . . s. that is gone 612
our times will appear . . . s. 1220
sponge: s. that will suck him dry 1041
spring: Treasury is the s. of business 90
spurs: Let the boy win his s. 587
square: good enough to be given a s. deal 1622
I stand for the s. deal 1626
squeeze: s. her until you can hear the pips squeak 700
stabbed: German army was s. in the back 878
stability: no s. . . . so long as agreements can be scrapped 1798
stable: Being born in a s. does not make a man a horse 1891

only t. men . . . ever understood it 1415
T. acres and a cow 1502
t. shillings a day . . . not give . . . virtues under heaven 1427
throne: I grew up upon the t. 925
one t., and three people cannot sit on it 1777
she . . . was to be sat on his t. the next day 252
something behind the t. greater than the King 1468
t. a tribunal instituted by Providence 1835
T. . . . cannot . . . oppose . . . House of Commons 1370
unfitness for the Queen's T. 1793
worthy of the T. if he had never ascended it 1794
Thucydides: *The Times* . . . T. 430
ticker tape: T. ain't spaghetti 1044
tigers: paper t. 1185
t. are getting hungry 379
t. who tear 1854
tightly: t. knit group of politically motivated men 1953
tiles: as many devils as t. on the roof 1133
timber: houses are all of t. 332
time: advantage of t. and place 572
fool all the people some of the t. 1083
great lie of our t. 1493
Lady whom T. had surprised 1555
peace for our t. 327
t. is on our side 753
uncomfortable t. to preach 1055
Times: one copy of *T.* . . . Thucydides 430
weekday bible, as *T.* is sometimes called 697
times: our t. will appear . . . splendour 1220
these are the t. that try men's souls 1398
timid: entrust the care of freedom to the weak or the t. 596
Tippecanoe: T. and Tyler, too 1499
tired: man t. of London is t. of life 992
tit: little t. of 18 made all at once into a Queen 461
title-page: question . . . a t. to a great tragic volume 7
Tito: there will be no more T. 1731
today: no time . . . peace better assured than t. 1383
together: Let us go forward t. 369, 383
Sire, we have been under fire t. 1329
toil: blood, t., tears and sweat 384
tolerated: democracy . . . has t. the Right Honourable Gentleman 139
Tom Thumb: withdrew my attention, and thought about T.T. 998
tomb: t. of our own might 1127
tongue: nation . . . citizens speaking the same t. 1231
neither eye to see nor t. to speak in this place 1068

Index of Key-words in Foreign Languages